The Separable User Interface

Computers and People Series

Edited by

B. R. GAINES and A. MONK

Monographs

Communicating with Microcomputers. An introduction to the technology of man–computer communication, *Ian H. Witten* 1980
The Computer in Experimental Psychology, *R. Bird* 1981
Principles of Computer Speech, *I. H. Witten* 1982
Cognitive Psychology of Planning, *J-M. Hoc* 1988
Formal Methods for Interactive Systems, *A. Dix* 1991

Edited Works

Computing Skills and the User Interface, *M. J. Coombs and J. L. Alty (eds)* 1981
Fuzzy Reasoning and Its Applications, *E. H. Mamdani and B. R. Gaines (eds)* 1981
Intelligent Tutoring Systems, *D. Sleeman and J. S. Brown (eds)* 1982 (1986 paperback)
Designing for Human–Computer Communication, *M. E. Sime and M. J. Coombs (eds)* 1983
The Psychology of Computer Use, *T. R. G. Green, S. J. Payne and G. C. van der Veer (eds)* 1983
Fundamentals of Human–Computer Interaction, *Andrew Monk (ed)* 1984, 1985
Working with Computers: Theory versus Outcome, *G. C. van der Veer, T. R. G. Green, J-M. Hoc and D. Murray (eds)* 1988
Cognitive Engineering in Complex Dynamic Worlds, *E. Hollnagel, G. Mancini and D. D. Woods (eds)* 1988
Computers and Conversation, *P. Luff, N. Gilbert and D. Frohlich (eds)* 1990
Adaptive User Interfaces, *D. Browne, P. Totterdell and M. Norman (eds)* 1990
Human–Computer Interaction and Complex Systems, *G. R. S. Weir and J. L. Alty (eds)* 1991
Computer-supported Cooperative Work and Groupware, *Saul Greenberg (ed)* 1991
The Separable User Interface, *E.A. Edmonds (ed)* 1992

Practical Texts

Effective Color Displays: Theory and Practice, *D. Travis* 1991

EACE Publications
(Consulting Editors: *Y. WAERN and J-M. HOC*)

Cognitive Ergonomics, *P. Falzon (ed)* 1990
Psychology of Programming, *J-M. Hoc, T. R. G. Green, R. Samurcay and D. Gilmore (eds)* 1990

The Separable User Interface

Edited by

Ernest A. Edmonds
Loughborough University of Technology

ACADEMIC PRESS
Harcourt Brace Jovanovich, Publishers
London San Diego New York
Boston Sydney Tokyo Toronto

ACADEMIC PRESS LTD.
24/28 Oval Road,
London NW1 7DX

United States Edition published by
ACADEMIC PRESS INC.
San Diego, California 92101–4311

This book is printed on acid-free paper

A catalogue record for this book is available from the British Library

ISBN 0–12–232150–2

Filmset by Columns of Reading Ltd., Reading, Berks.
Printed and bound in Great Britain by
TJ Press (Padstow) Ltd, Cornwall

Contents

Acknowledgements

I would like to thank the authors of papers included in this volume, both for their agreement to reproduce their work and, even more so, for their contribution to the field and my own understanding. A number of researchers have made important contributions that, for various reasons, I have not been able to acknowledge by the inclusion of specific papers. In this category I wish to mention the particular contributions of Jim Foley, Brian Gaines, Paul ten Hagen, Tom Moran and Günther Pfaff.

A number of people have helped me in the preparation of the book: Conn Copas, Bryan Murray, Louise Williams, Linda Candy, particularly for constructing the index, and Jackie Highfield who handled the many, sometimes difficult, secretarial services. Thanks to them all. Any remaining flaws are my responsibility.

1. Introduction

The Emergence of the Separable User Interface

Ernest Edmonds

Based on a paper first published in the *ICL Technical Journal*
Volume 7, Number 1, pp 54–63, 1990

The Emergence of the Separable User Interface

ERNEST EDMONDS

1 THE USER INTERFACE

The user interface to a computer system goes under a number of names, including the human–computer interface, the computer–human interface, the front end and the man–machine interface. Whilst 'front-end' tends to be used in the restricted domain of so-called intelligent interfaces and 'man–machine interface' is sometimes used to refer to systems that do not involve computers, for the purpose of this chapter they can all be considered to be synonymous. Many papers and books on the user interface exist, including ones that give detailed advice on how to design and how to construct them. Nevertheless, there is still no universally agreed definition of the user interface. For example:

> 'The human interface with computers is the physical, sensory and intellectual space that lies between computers and ourselves.' (Bolt, 1984)

> 'The user interface is that part of a system that the user comes in contact with physically, perceptually, or conceptually.' (Moran, 1980)

> 'The functionality defines what the program can do, and the user interface defines how users tell the program what to do, and how the program tells users what it did.' (Szekely, 1988)

In fact, many authors omit a definition altogether (e.g. Shneiderman, 1987).

In English, the normal use of the word 'interface' is to name the relationship between two entities, particularly where that relationship is well defined. Increasingly, however, in computing the term 'interface' has been applied to special devices that enable one of the objects to hold the given relationship with the other. Thus, for example, one might have to buy a special 'interface' in order to enable one's computer to operate a particular printer. A similar tendency has occurred in the case of the user

THE SEPARABLE USER INTERFACE
ISBN 0–12–232150–2

interface. The study of the relationship between the user and the computer is, now, most frequently known as the study of human–computer *interaction*. The user *interface* normally refers to the hardware and software that enable the computer to play its part in the interaction. It is widely assumed that it is possible to identify this interface as part of the system and, conversely, that it is possible to identify components that perform functions that should not be seen as part of the interface. It is this assumption that is the central concern of this book.

2 EARLY WORK

Without doubt, the most important early work in this field was done by William Newman. This work built upon Sutherland (1965) in important respects but, nevertheless, represents the first significant steps towards the current concern for the object known as the user interface.

Newman (1968a) described a virtual input device that enabled the user to enter numerical data on a continuous scale with the aid of a light pen or a similar device. Newman termed his logical device a 'light handle' because it can be seen as a simulation of a handle that can be wound in order to increase or decrease the associated numerical value. The significance of this work was that it demonstrated the possibility of constructing what, today, might be known as an 'interaction object': that is, a self-contained software module that uses the physical input/output devices available in order to enable the user to provide some particular kind of input to the machine. Whilst, in modern terms, this might be seen to be a very low level of separation, it represented an important conceptual step.

The most significant early work was, however, Newman's system for interactive graphical programming (Newman, 1968b). A *network definition language* was introduced that partly defined interactive software in the form of state diagrams. A compiler for this language could generate run-time code. This system was based upon a distinction between the *reaction handler*, with its associated tables, and the *procedure component*. The network definition language was compiled into the tables that the reaction handler used, as it were, to run the user interface. The procedure component was written in a conventional language that did not deal directly with any interaction with the user. The mechanism for linking the two aspects was the insertion of program blocks into the definition of each appropriate state of the state diagram. Thus, the network definition language defined the user interface together with its links to the functional part of the system, namely, the procedure component.

Whilst Newman's Light Handle and his reaction handler both demonstrate the separation of user interface issues from functional ones, the distinction between them, in this respect, is very important. The separation offered by the Light Handle is that of an interaction object that can be evoked by the functional code but that looks after itself once active. The Reaction Handler is quite different, in that it is in control of the system and evokes functional actions as required. It is, therefore, an example of a separate user interface. The paper did not, however, address the issue of the precise scope of concern of the procedure component. Indeed, at that time, this was perhaps not a major issue but more recently, as will be discussed below, it has become a significant point of debate.

Parnas (1969) also proposed the use of transition state diagrams for the representation of dialogues, although he advocated them only for the 'top level' of user interface design and so, in his work, they did not lead directly to implementation. The links between the user interface and the functional components of the system were not associated with states, as in Newman's case, but with the arcs between states. The method was to label each arc with an input/output pair, representing the user input that would cause the arc to be traversed, and the output that would result. Only simple examples were discussed and, as with Newman, no detailed discussion of the issues of user interface/functional component separation was given.

Denert (1977), in considering the proposition described above, introduced two more innovations. Firstly, he recognized the computational limitations of state diagrams, which represent finite-state machines, and proposed the use of recursive state diagrams, which are much more powerful. Secondly, he dealt with the interconnection of the user interface and the functional component by introducing 'task nodes' into the diagrams, which call the functional code. In some respects, this is similar to Parnas' scheme but it adds the possibility of different branching depending on the outcome of the functional operation. Thus, we now have the concept of the functional code changing the course of the dialogue. It appears that, for the separation of the user interface from the functional code to be a reality for complex systems, both of Denert's innovations are required.

3 FIRST-GENERATION USER INTERFACE SYSTEMS

During the 1970s a number of research workers followed William Newman's early example and constructed user interface software systems that, in various ways, provided for a separation between the user interface and the functional code. Stalling (1974) demonstrated a system for generating dialogue code that worked somewhat after the manner of a report generator program. Florentin (1977) elaborated upon this and noted the importance of the linking of the dialogue code to the rest of the system. However, neither author added significantly to the specific discussion of separability.

Maher and Bell (1977) specifically proposed a virtual machine as the key user interface module. They illustrated their work with a user interface to a database, and discussed briefly some problems that arose with the separation of concerns. In particular, they found that it was convenient to organize the database in a particular way for the benefit of the user interface, but that this conflicted with other requirements.

Black (1977) described another system which provided a separate 'dialogue processor' which managed the user interface. A dialogue specification language was provided that compiled into a form directly usable by the dialogue processor. In this system, the dialogue processor produced a 'target file' which contained the input required by the functional component. Clearly, this was a simple view by today's standards and so, again, problematic issues of separation were not addressed.

State diagrams are popular for the specification of user interfaces, but several other formalisms are also used. Green (1985) suggested that one of the earliest examples of a grammar-based user interface system was that reported by Edmonds and Guest (1977), who showed how a grammar-based language could be used to define an interface flexibly. It was used to construct a programming tutor and so was demonstrated as a feasible system. However, it is again true that the simplicity of the separation between the user interface and the functional system was such that the issues often seen now as problems of separability were not discussed.

Ian Newman (1978) demonstrated how separation could be used to provide a variety of interfaces to a single system. Practical work was again done to prove the point but, as before, the particularly difficult issues of separability that are perceived today were not considered. Gaines and Facey (1977) extended Basic to provide explicit user interface control, and Lafuente and Gries (1978) extended Pascal in order to provide what they called 'dialogue frames', each of which could include a procedural block. Thus, the structure of this user interface was somewhat similar to Newman's (1968b). The difference was that Lafuente and Gries provided an extension of a standard programming language, whereas Newman kept his interface code quite separate from the functional code.

4 USER INTERFACE SPECIFICATION

Whilst work on the specification of user interfaces has not in general addressed the issue of separability directly, it is quite clear that the whole enterprise is founded upon the notion of separability. If it were not so, what would it be that one was specifying?

An important model for these specifications was proposed by Moran (1980), which took a view of the user interface that had a number of levels incorporated into three components: physical, communication and conceptual. A key point is that, in this view, only the conceptual component needs direct contact with the functional aspects of the system. In Moran's view the conceptual component contained two levels: the *task level*, concerned with the structuring of the task domain for the benefit of the user; and the *semantic level*, 'built around a set of objects and manipulations of those objects. To the system these are data structures and procedures; to the user they are conceptual entities and conceptual operations on those entities' (Moran, 1980). The semantic level was seen as a way of representing the system's functional capability. This particular aspect of the structure of a user interface has proved quite fruitful in attempts to clarify the separation from the functional code. This paper, and its elaboration (Moran, 1981), proposed that the user interface could be specified in a well-defined set of levels. Closely related ideas were proposed in a widely referenced paper by Foley *et al.* (1984). This work has been influential both in the study of user interface specification and, more specifically, in the study of architectures for separable user interfaces.

Mark Green (1981) reported a notation for the specification of user interfaces and presented it in the context of a traditional software development model. Whilst that model is no longer necessarily accepted (see for example, Hekmanpour and Ince (1987), or earlier questioning by Edmonds (1974)), the specification ideas are not invalidated. Green's notation includes the notion of atomic objects and operations that correspond to Moran's objects and manipulations. These represent the lowest level of the system of concern to the interface: beyond that, is the concern of the functional code. This has been the standard view of separation. In his paper, however, Green introduced an important additional property at this level: he allowed for the specification of *invariants*. These are relationships which must hold between operators and objects. Whilst he only gave a simple example of an invariant, it is clear that it is entirely unrealistic to consider objects as independent and that quite complex invariants may be required. The only question at issue is whether the invariants can and should be seen as the concern of the user interface.

Edmonds (1981) consolidated earlier work and put forward a specification notation that combined state diagrams with grammars, each having their appropriate role. This work continued the tradition begun by William Newman, in that a compiler was available for the notation. The links between the user interface and the functional code were provided partly in the manner of Parnas as described above, except that the input/output specifications on an arc could have a complex transformation relating them, so that specific inputs in the appropriate class could generate relevant outputs. The outputs were passed to the functional code at a 'task node', as in Denert's model.

Naturally, the early work in the field did not address the issue of specifying user interfaces that handle direct manipulation specifically. However, Jacob (1986) showed how the methods that employ state diagrams can accommodate direct manipulation and, in particular, event handling.

The use of propositional production systems to unify the earlier approaches has been advocated by Olson (1990). The key issue of specifying the interaction between the user interface and the application code, however, remains something of an issue. Hurley and Sibert (1989) made a recent attempt to solve this problem and demonstrated positive results in a limited domain.

5 ARCHITECTURES

Following Moran's work, discussed above, much debate has taken place about appropriate architectures for separable user interfaces, and a large proportion of the issues of concern have related to the support for separability. In many ways the details of the architecture can be seen as a precise definition of the scope of the user interface.

A very important event in the development of separable user interface architectures was the Workshop held in 1983 in Seeheim (Pfaff, 1985). One group in the meeting, consisting of Jan Derksen, Ernest Edmonds, Mark Green, Dan Olsen and Robert Spence, developed an architecture for the user interface (Green, 1985) reproduced here as Fig. 1.

As Löwgren (1988) pointed out, however, the first proposal of a user interface software architecture of this form was probably that of Edmonds

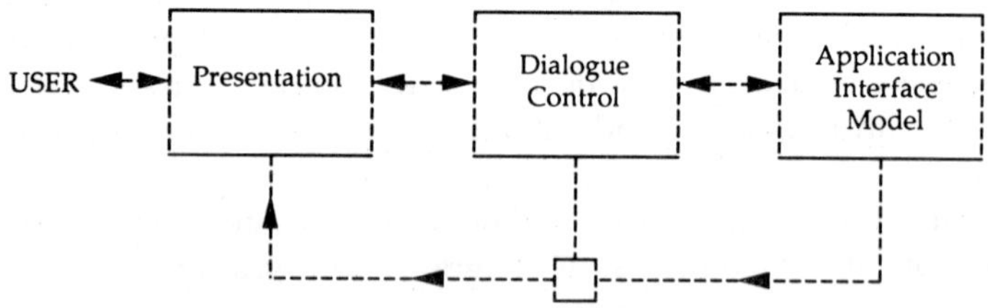

Figure 1. Seeheim Workshop user interface architecture.

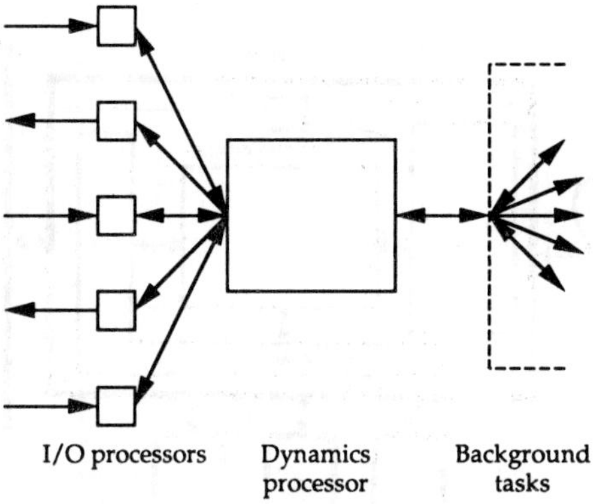

Figure 2. User interface architecture of Edmonds (1982).

(1982) (see Fig. 2), which built directly upon Moran's concept of layers. In this view, the separation between user interface and functional code was precisely at Moran's semantics level, where the objects and manipulations that can be seen as atomic, from a user's point of view, reside.

The Seeheim application interface model went further than either Edmonds' or Green's earlier proposals. The idea was that it might contain, for example, information about the effects of operations in order to assist the user interface in the provision of help. Also, in order to deal with larger amounts of data generated by the functional code, such as dynamic images, a direct path to the display was proposed. In this case, the only functions of the user interface were to open such a path and to decide where it should point to on the screen. This architecture has become widely known as the *Seeheim model* and a good deal of the subsequent debate has used it as the base reference. It is, perhaps, not surprising that this model has been so important because, apart from the earlier architecture from Edmonds, position papers were presented at Seeheim by Thomas and Olsen both of

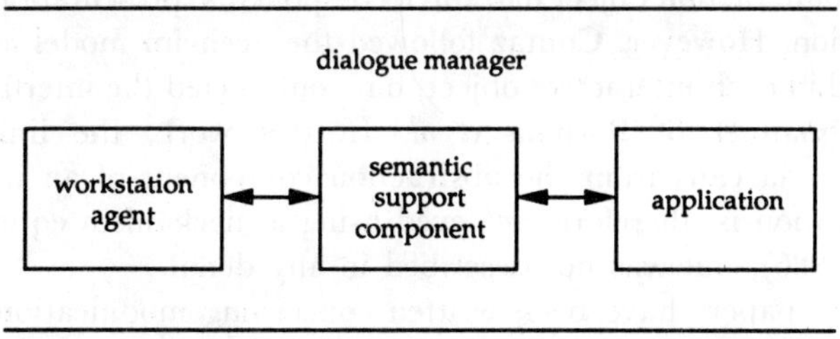

Figure 3. User interface model of Dance *et al.* (1987).

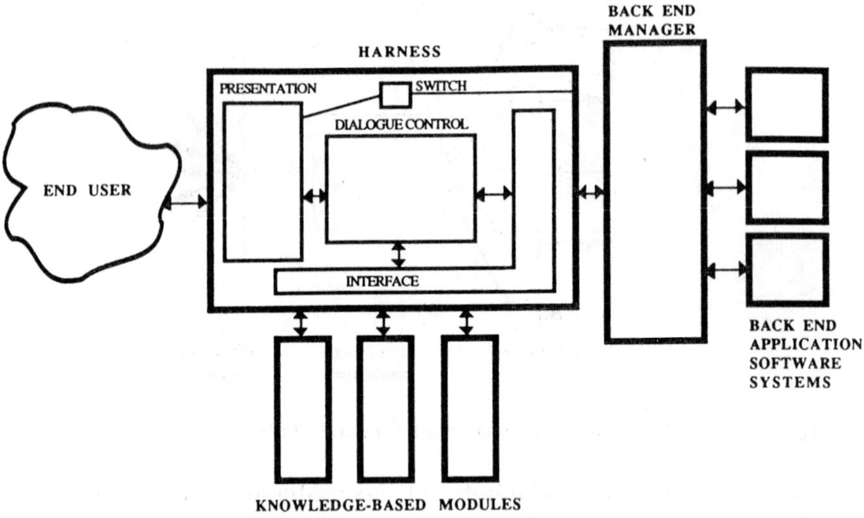

Figure 4. User interface model of Edmonds and McDaid (1990).

whom proposed architectures in the same spirit as that which became the Seeheim model.

Borufka *et al.* (1982) introduced the idea of a user interface structured as a hierarchy of elements, each of the same class. The elements were called 'dialogue cells', each of which consisted of a prompt, a symbol (the input), an echo and a value (derived from the symbol). The idea was that each cell completely described a step in a dialogue. As a component of a dialogue cell could be a call to another cell; the interface could be seen as a hierarchy of cells with the complete interface, at its top level, being itself a dialogue cell. A clear and attractive architecture was thus described although, as the author said, 'The connection to application programs might require special program-dependent interfaces . . .'. Coutaz (1987) reintroduced the same overall architecture, in which the dialogue cell became an 'interactive object'. Each interaction object had three components: presentation, control and abstraction. However, Coutaz followed the Seeheim model at the top level and within each interactive object, but constructed the interface in the hierarchical manner of Borufka *et al.* In this work, the link to the application is via calls from the abstraction component of an interactive object. Separation is, therefore, achieved using a mechanism equivalent to Newman's (1986), but was not described in any detail.

Many other papers have been written concerning modifications to this model, for example, Dance *et al.* (1987) (Fig. 3) and Edmonds and McDaid (1990) (Fig. 4). It is noticeable, however, that most are variations on the

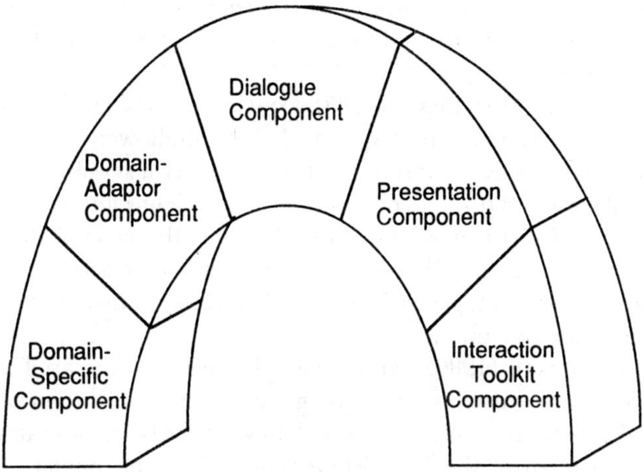

Figure 5. The Slinky model.

Seeheim view, rather than radical departures from it. In fact, a recent re-assessment has confirmed most of those early ideas (Bass *et al.*, 1991). Perhaps the most significant innovation in the Slinky model (Fig. 5), proposed in that review, is the notion that the division of labour between the interface components might be flexible and depend, for example, on the maturity of a particular function. As Newman expresses it, in the last chapter of this book, 'the boundary between user interface and supporting hardware/software is constantly changing'. Nevertheless, the Seeheim concept is still at the centre of the Slinky model. We may assume, therefore, that the climate of opinion remains to favour something of the same type as an architecture for the separable user interface. In particular, it can be seen that the user interface is seen to include a substantial part of the software of a system.

6 PRACTICAL ISSUES OF SEPARABILITY

Certain position papers presented at Seeheim were already addressing practical separability issues. In particular, Olsen (1985) and Sibert *et al.* (1985) considered interdependencies between the layers with some care. One of the working groups, in fact, considered the issue specifically, as reported by Enderle (1985). Their basic conclusion was that separability, even for CAD/CAM applications, appears to be possible given careful design. The group looked particularly at the services provided by the user interface to the functional code, and *vice versa*. This was probably the first attempt to catalogue these difficult concerns (see Table 1 in Enderle's paper, Chapter 6).

Szekely, in his PhD thesis (1988), considered separability in detail. He viewed the interface as, perhaps, a slightly shallower entity than others have done, but this enabled him to identify clearly a set of interaction types. This classification is itself a contribution to the definition of the scope of the user interface. Even if it is not wished to limit the view of the interface in Szekely's way, it is clear that his work is valuable as a contribution to our understanding of that part of the user interface termed the 'presentation component' at Seeheim.

Alty and McKell (1986) made a valuable study of the application model in the Seeheim sense. They demonstrated an application model for a command-driven system and showed how a study of interaction sessions can help to identify the knowledge required in the model. A particular outcome of the empirical study was that they identified a need for a planning component in the application model. Thus, whilst they confirmed the viability of the separable user interface, they demonstrated in practice that the interface can require quite sophisticated components within it.

In another practical case study, Manheimer *et al.* (1989) showed that the separable user interface is a quite realistic concept. It is of interest to note that the mechanisms for coupling user interfaces and functional components vary widely and that, in this case, more than one mechanism was found to be necessary. In applying their Lockheed user interface system LUIS, they found the need for both 'tightly' and 'loosely' coupled relationships:

> 'The tightly coupled routines are linked with the LUIS executable image. A subroutine interface is available for these routines to communicate with the LUIS interface manager, i.e. to send messages to manipulate the ongoing dialogue and to receive messages that inform the application of the state of the dialogue. When a tightly coupled routine is invoked, the user interface is suspended until the application has completed its processing.' (Manheimer *et al.*, 1989).

In another practical investigation, Dance *et al.* (1987) encountered the difficulty of rapid semantic feedback in a separable user interface as discussed at Seeheim (Strubbe, 1985). Suppose that a screen displays three elements: a window, an icon for a file, and an icon for a disc. Consider the difference between the following two situations: if the user drags the window over the disc icon, the icon is simply obscured, whereas if the user drags the file icon over the disc icon, then the latter is, typically, highlighted. The difference represents more or less instant semantic feedback.

It is sometimes argued that this semantic feedback problem is a case against separability, but in fact that case is far from clear. It is true that it would be hard to achieve acceptable performance if tokens had to be passed through the layers to and from the application, in order to achieve it. However, there is no reason why the presentation layer itself should not contain the appropriate knowledge: after all, the example given above does not imply any application action. The difficulty may have arisen because many researchers have been influenced by developments in computer graphics, where closed packages are often used to implement interactions. As even the simple example above makes clear, all levels of a separable user interface must be programmable, in the sense that the system developer may need to build application-specific knowledge into any part of it. This is not an argument against separability, of course, although it suggests caution about the utility of completely general-purpose user interface modules.

The difficulty here is whether the user interface might need too much knowledge (Strubbe, 1985). However, nobody has defined 'too much' in this context. Even as early as 1978, Sutton and Sprague found that more than half of the code in interactive business applications was devoted to the user interface. Size is not the problem, although duplicating application code within the interface would be, of course. It seems that where functional code has to be entered in order to generate semantic feedback and where that feedback is required very quickly indeed, or where it involves large volumes of data, either the direct path, as proposed at Seeheim, or a closely coupled link, as in Manheimer *et al.*, could be used. However, semantic feedback remains an area for investigation.

In work that has aimed to produce new 'front ends' to existing systems, the question of separability has not been an issue. Rather, the problem has been one of *how* to link the separate user interface to the application code. Edmonds and McDaid (1990) have demonstrated an architecture for solving this problem. One important feature was the introduction of a 'back-end manager' to effect the link. This has been described more fully by Prat *et al.* (1990). This work represents a significant step forward in the area of user interface/application interface specification and introduces the notion of an interface that can act as an integrator of systems, front-ending a number of applications and packaging them to provide a single solution to the users' problem.

7 CONCLUSIONS

Issues of separability still remain to be resolved but there is enough evidence now that the separable user interface can be defined. Perhaps the biggest problem that has stood in the way of successful work in the area, is that attempts have sometimes been made to build general-purpose front ends in the belief that (using the Seeheim terminology) only the application model needs to contain knowledge of application issues. In point of fact, even the presentation layer must often be programmed with specific application-dependent knowledge: the separable user interface is not at all ignorant of the functions of the system, as was identified in the Slinky model.

If we return to the definitions of the user interface quoted at the beginning of this introduction, it is interesting to note that the separable user interface can be seen as a concrete elaboration of each of them. Moran (1980) went on to propose that: 'Any aspect of the system that shows through to the user and enters the user's model is a part of the user interface'. The emergence of the separable user interface has occurred partly as an attempt to represent everything 'that shows through to the user' in an identified software module. The degree to which this attempt has been successful remains to be assessed fully, but it is quite clear that the study of separable user interfaces is becoming increasingly important in concentrating our attention on some of the most significant aspects of interactive systems. As Newman and Edmonds point out in the last chapter of this book, the management of design and development teams can benefit significantly from the concept of separability. Thus the concerns of the papers in this book go beyond the technical to the organisation of software production.

In some of the work described in this book the question of separability has ceased to be an issue. User interfaces that serve as front-ends to, and integrate, existing systems and services are separable whatever the purist might desire. Thus for a number of significant reasons, the separable user interface has an important role to play in the future of interactive computing systems.

REFERENCES

Alty, J. L. and McKell, P. (1986). Application modelling in a user interface management system. In: *People and Computers: Designing for Usability.* M. D. Harrison & A. F. Monk (eds), Cambridge.

Bass, L., Little, R., Pellegrino, R., Seed, S., Seacord, R., Sheppard, S. and Szcur, M.R. (1991). The Arch Model: Seeheim Revisited. Paper presented for the User Interface Developers' Workshop at CHI '91, 2–26.

Black, J. L. (1977). A general purpose dialogue processor. *Proceedings of the National Computer Conference* 397–408.

Bolt, R. A. (1984). *The human interface.* Lifetime Learning Publications.

Borufka, H. G., Kuhlmann, H. W. and ten Hagen, P. J. (1982). Dialogue Cells: A Method for Defining Interactions. *IEEE Computer Graphics and Applications.* 25–33.

Coutaz, J. (1987). PAC, an object oriented model for dialog design. In: *Human–Computer Interaction — INTERACT '87.* H. J. Bullinger and B. Shackel (eds). Elsevier Science, 431–436.

Dance, J. R., Granor, T. E., Hill, R. D., Hudson, S. E., Meads, J., Myers, B. A. and Schulert A. (1987). The run time structure of UIMS-supported applications. *Computer Graphics*, 21, 2, 97–101.

Denert, E. (1977). Specification and design of dialogue systems with state diagrams. In: *Proceedings of the International Computing Symposium, Liège.* Elsevier, North Holland, 417–423.

Edmonds, E. A. (1974). A process for the development of software for non-technical users as an adaptive system. *General Systems*, 19, 215–217.

Edmonds, E. A. (1981). Adaptive man–computer interfaces. In: *Computing Skills and the User Interface.* In: Coombs, M. J. and J. L. Alty (eds). Academic Press.

Edmonds, E. A. (1982). The man–computer interface: a note on concepts of design. *International Journal of Man–Machine Studies*, 16, 231–236.

Edmonds, E. A. and Guest, S. P. (1977). An interactive tutorial system for teaching programming. In: *IERE Proceedings 36 — Computer Systems and Technology*, IERE, London.

Edmonds, E. A. and McDaid, E. (1990). An architecture for knowledge-based front-ends. *Knowledge-Based Systems,* 3, 2, 221–224.

Enderle, G. (1985). Report on the interface of the UIMS to the application. In: G. E. Pfaff (ed.), *User Interface Management Systems*, Springer Verlag, 21–29.

Florentin, J. J. (1977). Automatic generation of interactor programs. In: *Proceedings of the International Conference on Displays for Man–machine Systems, Lancaster.* IEE Pub. No. 150. Institute of Electronic Engineers, 126–129.

Foley, J. D., Wallace, V. and Chan, P. (1984). The human factors of computer graphics interaction techniques. *IEEE Computer Graphics and Applications*, 4, 13–48.

Gaines, B. R. and Facey, Pl. V. (1977). BASYS — a language for programming interaction. *IERE Proc. 36, Computer Systems and Technology*, 21–29.

Green, M. (1981). A methodology for the specification of graphical user interface. *Computer Graphics*, 15, 99–109.

Green, M. (1985). Report on dialogue specification tools. In: *User Interface Management Systems.* G. E. Pfaff (ed.). Springer Verlag, Berlin, 9–20.

Hekmanpour, S. and Ince, D. C. (1987). Evolutionary prototyping and the human–computer interface. In: *Proceedings of INTERACT 87.* H. J. Bullinger and B. Shackel (eds). Amsterdam: North Holland, 479–484.

Hurley, W. D. and Sibert, J. L. (1989). Modelling User Interface — Application Interactions. *IEEE Software*, January, 71–77.

Jacob, R. J. K. (1986). A specification language for direct manipulation user interfaces. *ACM Transactions on Graphics*, 5, 283–317.

Lafuente, J. M. and Gries, D. (1978). Language facilities for programming user–computer dialogues. *IBM Journal of Research and Development*, 22, 145–158.

Löwgren, J. (1988). History, state and future of user interface management systems.

SIGCHI Bulletin, 20, 32–44.

Maher, P. K. C. and Bell, H. V. (1977). The man machine interface — a new approach. In: *Proceedings of the International Conference on Displays for Man–Machine Systems*. IEE Pub. No. 150. Institute of Electronic Engineers, London, 122–125.

Manheimer, J. M., Burnett, R. C. and Wallers, J. A. (1989). A case study of user interface management system development and application. In: *Procedings CHI '89*, ACM Press, New York, 127–132.

Moran, T. (1980). A framework for studying human–computer interaction. In: *Methodology of Interaction*. R. A. Guedij, P. J. W. Ten Hagen, F. R. A. Hopgood, H. A. Tucker and D. A. Duce (eds). Amsterdam: North-Holland, 293–302.

Moran, T. (1981). The command language grammar, a representation for the user interface of interactive computer systems. *International Journal of Man–Machine Studies*, 15, 3–50.

Newman, I. A. (1978). Personalised user interfaces to computer systems. *Proceedings of the European Computing Congress, London*, Online, London, 473–486.

Newman, W. (1968a). A graphical technique for numerical input. *Computer Journal*, 11, 63–64.

Newman, W. (1968b). A system for interactive graphical programming. *Proceedings of the Spring Joint Computer Conference*. 47–54.

Olsen, D. R. (1985). Presentational, syntactic and semantic components of interactive dialogue specifications. In: *User Interface Management Systems*. G. E. Pfaff (ed.). Springer Verlag, Berlin, 125–133.

Olsen, Jr, D. R. (1990). Propositional production systems for dialog description. *Proceedings of CHI '90*. 57–63.

Parnas, D. L. (1969). On the use of transition diagrams in the design of a computer interface for an interactive computer system. *Proceedings of the National ACM Conference*. ACM Publications, New York. 379–385.

Pfaff, G. E. (ed.) (1985). *User interface management systems*. Springer Verlag, Berlin.

Prat, A., Lores, J., Fletcher, P. and Catot, J. M. (1990). Back-end manager: an interface between a knowledge-based front end and its application subsystem. *Knowledge-Based Systems* 3, 2, 225–229.

Shneiderman, B. (1987). *Designing the User Interface*. Addison-Wesley.

Sibert, J., Belliardi, R. and Kamran, A. (1985). Some thoughts on the interface between user interface management systems and application software. In: *User Interface Management Systems*. G. E. Pfaff (ed.). Springer Verlag, Berlin, 183–192.

Stalling, W. (1974). Some aspects of an interactive dialogue-generation facility. In: *Proceedings of the International Conference on Systems, Man and Cybernetics*, IEEE Service Center, New Jersey, USA, 495–498.

Strubbe, H. J. (1985). Report on role, model, structure and construction of a UIMS. In: *User Interface Management Systems*, G. E. Pfaff (ed.). Springer Verlag, 3–8.

Sutherland, I. E. (1965). *SKETCHPAD: a man–machine graphical communication system*. MIT Lincol Laboratory, Lexington, MA. Technical Report TR-296.

Sutton, J. and Sprague, R. (1978). *A study of display generation and management in interactive business applications*. IBM San Jose Research Laboratory, San Jose, CA. Technical Report RJ2392 (31804).

Szekely, P. (1988). *Separating the user interface from the functionality of application programs*. PhD Thesis, CMU–CS–88–101, Carnegie–Mellon University.

2. Early Work

A Graphical Technique for Numerical Input

William M. Newman

Reprinted from: *Computer Journal*, Vol. II, pp 63–4, 1968

This paper introduces the 'Light Handle', which demonstrates the concept of a logical input device. Almost all modern user interface software employs the concept extensively, a typical example, as Newman points out in Part 7, is the familiar widget.

A Graphical Technique for Numerical Input*

W. M. NEWMAN

Computer Technology Group, Imperial College, London, UK

1 INTRODUCTION

Most display consoles nowadays include a teleprinter as standard equipment, and the on-line input of numerical data is normally a matter of hitting the right keys in the right sequence. There are a few conditions where this method is unsatisfactory: for example, the teleprinter keyboard may be awkwardly placed, and the user may spend much of his time moving between it and the display screen. A more serious drawback of keyed numerical input is that it cannot be used to achieve continuous variation of parameters in the manner of a shaft encoder or a tracker-ball. Many display installations do not possess any input devices of this type, and a graphical technique has been developed to achieve a similar effect using a light pen. This technique has been called the *Light Handle*, since it simulates the effect of winding a handle or rotating a knob. Any coordinate-input device such as the RAND tablet (Davis and Ellis, 1964) or the SRI mouse (English *et al.*, 1967) could be used to control the Light Handle.

2 USING THE LIGHT HANDLE

The appearance of the Light Handle is as shown in Fig. 1. The user simply points the pen somewhere within the border and swings it in an approximately circular path. Rotation in a clockwise direction causes the displayed value to increase, and anticlockwise to decrease. Any movement outside the border has no effect. Each time the value changes it may be

* The work described in this report was supported by Science Research Council Contract No. B/SR/2071.

THE SEPARABLE USER INTERFACE
ISBN 0-12-232150-2

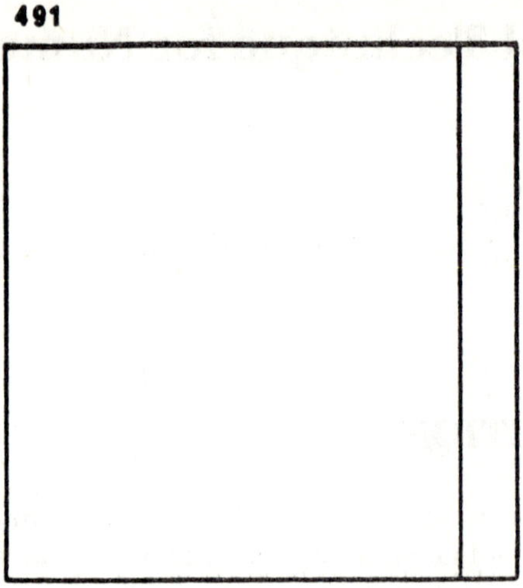

Figure 1. General appearance of the light handle (actual size).

passed to the main program as an input parameter. Alternatively, the light handle may be used to set up a constant, by disregarding all but the final value.

The rate at which the value alters depends on the horizontal position of the centre of rotation. It can be made to change rapidly by rotating in the region of the left-hand border, as shown in Fig. 2. For slower variation, the centre of rotation can be transferred to the right-hand side, as in Fig. 3. Extreme accuracy can be achieved by moving the pen up or down the right-hand column; here, one inch of movement changes the value by four units.

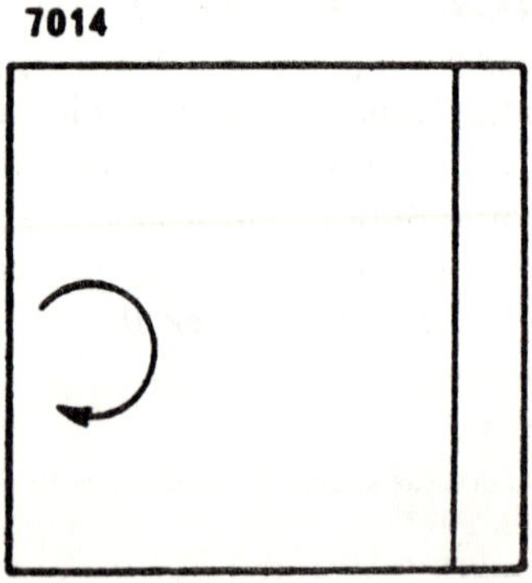

Figure 2. Clockwise rotation near the left-hand edge causes rapid increase in value.

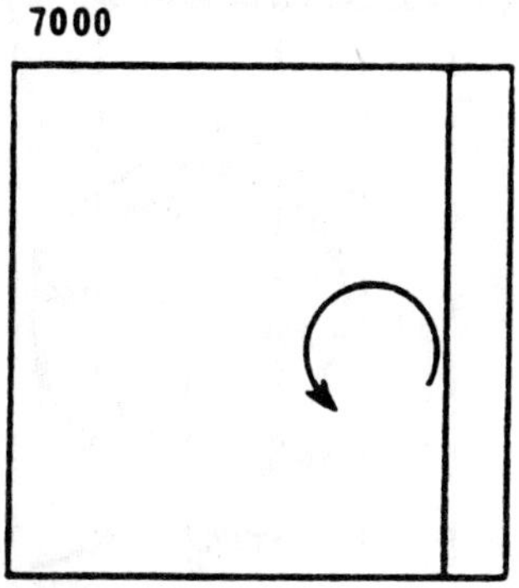

Figure 3. Anticlockwise rotation near the right-hand edge causes slow decrease in value.

Except in the right-hand column, the rate of change of the value is also dependent on the speed of movement of the pen. This 'square-effect' was first suggested by Sutherland (1966) for use with shaft encoders, and has been found to give an added degree of control to the light handle. Thus a single, fast rotation through 360° near the left-hand edge can change the value by 50 000 units or more, and by this means large constants can be set up very rapidly.

3 INTERNAL DETAILS OF THE LIGHT HANDLE

The light handle was developed on a DEC PDP-7 computer and Type 340 Display. The display has a screen size of approximately 10″ × 10″, and a raster unit of about 0.01″. An area of 256 × 256 raster units, or approximately 2½″ × 2½″, is devoted to the light handle. A fresh pen position is fed to the light handle program every 20 ms and, provided that this position lies within the border, the change ΔV in the displayed value is determined from the following expression:

$$\Delta V = \Delta y |a\Delta y|^k 2^{b-z}$$

where a, b are constants, Δy is the change in y, $z = \lceil x/32 \rceil$, i.e. the largest integer $<x/32$, $k = 0$ if (x,y) lies within the right-hand column, 1 otherwise, and x and y are measured in raster units. The program to carry out this computation, together with its display file, occupies about 120 words of memory.

The reader will notice that this program creates the effect of a number of vertical scales or *potentiometers* arranged parallel to one another within the square border. The scale of each potentiometer is double that of its left-hand neighbour, and the 'square-effect' is applied to all but the right-hand

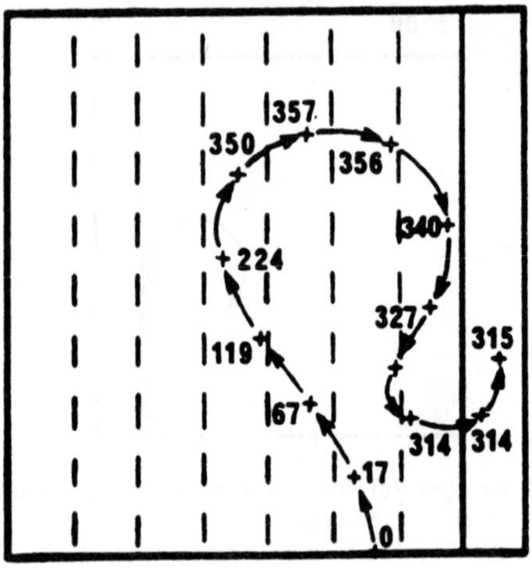

Figure 4. Variation in displayed value during a typical sweep of the pen. The boundaries of the 'potentiometers' are shown as broken lines.

one. The use of pen coordinates to given a potentiometer effect has been described by Rose (1965).

Thus the basic movement recognized by the program is linear vertical movement: horizontal movement on its own has no effect on the displayed value. Rotation of the pen position is detected as movement up one potentiometer and down another, with the cumulative effect of either increasing or decreasing the value. This is illustrated by Fig. 4. Other patterns of movement can be used to achieve the same effect as rotation. For example, a quick flick upwards followed by a slow return to the original position will leave the value increased, and repetition of this manoeuvre has the same effect as clockwise rotation.

4 PERFORMANCE

Once the basic principle of the light handle has been mastered, it becomes a very simple and natural method of numerical input. As mentioned above, it can be used in two modes, depending on whether the value is sampled continuously or only when setting-up is complete. In the first mode it simulates the action of a shaft encoder, and appears to be quite capable of matching the performance of such a device. In the second mode it is capable of setting up a number in about 5 s, and can be used instead of typing the number. Its relative performance in this context depends on many factors, such as the user's proficiency at typing, the siting of the typewriter keyboard and the pattern of use. Experience so far has shown that the light handle can be operated at about one-half the speed of a typewriter.

The principal asset of the light handle is that it provides the programmer with a shaft encoder without the expense of extra hardware. It also offers him a number of advantages over the typewriter, although it cannot match the speed of the latter. For example, it avoids the need to check each character for validity; limits can easily be set on the displayed value, to control the range of the final result; and the value may be incremented by any desired step size. It has the added advantage to the user of not diverting his attention from the display screen. For these reasons it appears to be a valuable tool for the display programmer.

REFERENCES

Davis, M. R. and Ellis, T. O. (1964). The RAND tablet: a man–machine graphical communication device. *Proceedings of the Fall Joint Computer Conference*. 325–331.

English, W. K., Engelbart, D. C. and Berman, M. L. (1967). Display selection techniques for text manipulation. *IEEE Transactions*, HFE-8, 5–17.

Rose, G. A. (1965). Light-pen facilities for direct view storage tubes. *IEEE Transactions*, EC-14, 637–639.

Sutherland, I.E. (1966). Computer graphics: ten unsolved problems. *Datamation*, 12, 5, 22–27.

A System for Interactive Graphical Programming

William M. Newman

Reprinted from: *Proceedings of the Spring Joint Computer Conference,* pp 47–54, 1968.

This paper introduces the 'Reaction Handler', which was the user interface software component within the system. It was programmed by using a network definition language. Given states called procedural components, written in conventional languages, for application functions. It was notable that the user interface was in control of the system.

A System for Interactive Graphical Programming*

W. M. NEWMAN**

Harvard University, Cambridge, MA, USA

1 INTRODUCTION

A system is described in this paper for developing graphical problem-oriented languages. This topic is of great importance in computer-aided design but has hitherto received only sketchy documentation, with few attempts at a comparative study. Meanwhile displays are beginning to be used for design, and the results of such a study are badly needed. What has held back experimentation with computer graphics has been the difficulty of specifying new graphic techniques using the available programming languages; the method described in this paper appears to avoid this difficulty.

2 DEFINING A PROBLEM-ORIENTED LANGUAGE

2.1 Notation

Any description of an interactive process must define the response of the system to each input. For this reason it is convenient to describe graphical problem-oriented languages in terms of *actions* and *reactions*. An *action* is simply an input which may produce a response; the corresponding *reaction* defines this response, and in addition any unmanifested effect of the action on the state of the machine. The same action may cause a different reaction on different occasions: for example, movement of the light pen may affect

* The work described in this report was supported by Science Research Council Contract No. B/SR/2071.

** Formerly at the Centre for Computing and Automation, Imperial College, London.

THE SEPARABLE USER INTERFACE
ISBN 0–12–232150–2

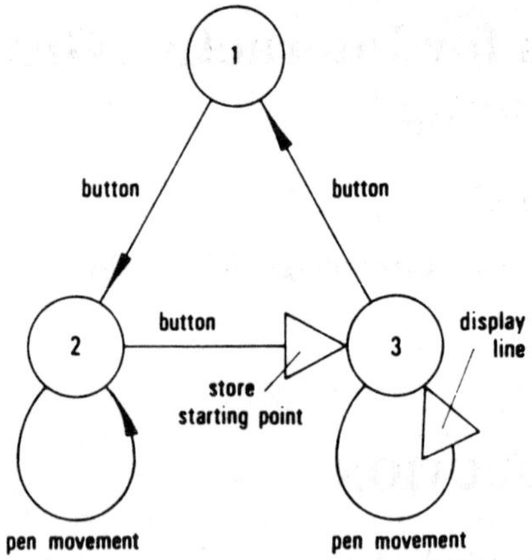

Figure 1. A state diagram representing rubber-band line-drawing.

the display in a number of different ways. It is therefore convenient to treat the system as a finite-state automaton, and to say that the reaction is determined by the *state* of the program as well as by the action. In other words, the actions are *inputs* to the automaton, which cause it to change state; reactions are the *outputs*.

Just how convenient this is for describing interactive processes is illustrated by the following example. A 'rubber-band' line (Sutherland, 1963) can be created by means of a light pen and one push-button, in a sequence of five operations:

(1) press button to start pen tracking;
(2) track pen to starting point of line;
(3) press button to fix starting point;
(4) track pen to end point; and
(5) press button to fix end point and stop tracking.

The 'rubber-band' effect is created by displaying a line joining the starting point to the pen position throughout stage 4.

Figure 1 shows a state diagram representing this sequence. Each branch represents an action, and the resultant reaction is specified in the 'arrowhead'. Only valid actions are included: for example, pen movements are meaningless in state 1 and are therefore omitted. The inclusion or exclusion of an action may add semantic properties to the diagram. This is shown by the 'pen movement' branches on states 2 and 3, which imply pen tracking during those states and make explicit reference to tracking unnecessary.

The state diagram has been used in this way as the basis of a method for defining problem-oriented languages. A particular advantage of this technique is the way an *immediate* reaction can be associated with each action in a sequence: this is of great importance in graphical programs. On the other hand, the state diagram offers no direct method of attaching semantic functions to groups of actions, and is therefore of little use for describing phrase-structured grammars. This is less of a drawback than it seems. An interactive problem-oriented language need not possess a complex structure to function efficiently, and benefit can often be gained from simplifying the language as much as possible. Roos (1966), for example, has noted the difficulty experienced by some engineers in using the relatively simple languages of the ICES system.

The basic function of the state diagram, as illustrated in Fig. 1, is to indicate the actions which may validly occur during each state, and the reactions and changes of state which they will cause. A number of additions have been made to this basic notation. Normally, branching takes place when a user action matches an action defined in the diagram. Branching may, however, be overridden by the result of a *test routine* included in the branch definition. Furthermore, branching may be initiated by the program itself by means of *system actions*: thus the result of a procedure may determine to which of several states the program will branch. A procedure of this kind is called a *program block* and is attached to a state rather than to a branch; it is executed every time the corresponding state is entered. Program blocks need not terminate in a system action, but may instead be used to provide some sort of continuous background activity.

These are the essential additions to the notation. One other has been included for convenience in programming 'conversational' systems, in which each input message produces a predetermined output message. This message can be coded within the reaction procedure or program block, but it is convenient to be able to state it separately as an output string or *response*. States therefore possess a response as well as a program block, and reactions are similarly defined as two components, a response and a procedure. The procedure is represented as an *instruction for execution* (*IEX*).

The suggested form of these additions to the notation is shown in Fig. 2; a somewhat similar notation has been used by Phillips (1967) to describe real-time control programs. Figure 2 illustrates how the first example could be extended to permit the removal of lines and initialization of the program. These two functions are controlled by the commands DELETE and RESTART; as explained below, commands may be typed at the console typewriter, or may be arranged to appear on the screen as light-buttons. After giving the command DELETE, the user points the light pen at each line to be removed. Deletion is carried out by a test routine DLAST, which also tests whether any other lines remain on the screen. When none remains, or the user gives the command DRAW, the program changes state.

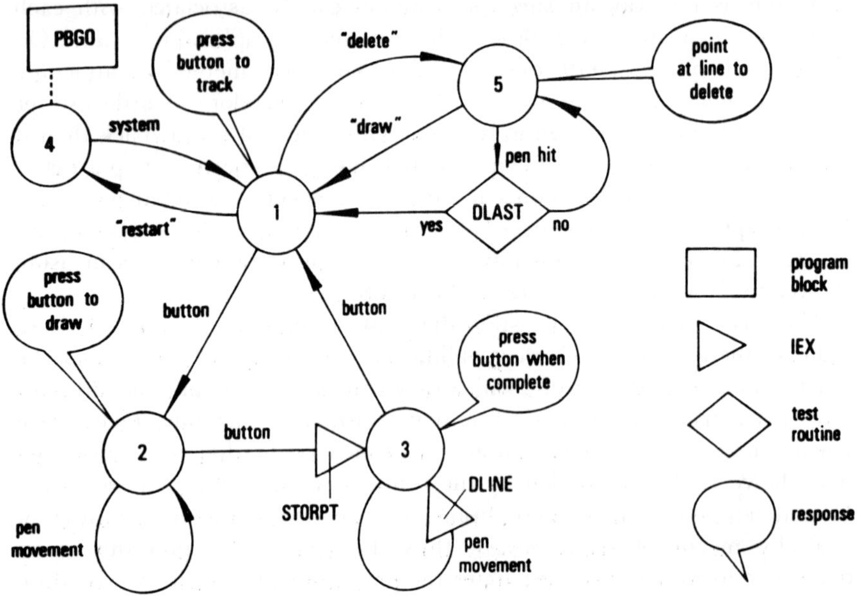

Figure 2. An extended diagram including responses, and with provision for drawing and deleting lines and for initialization.

RESTART causes the program to enter the initial state 4, execute its program block PBG0 and return to state 1 when initialization is complete.

2.2 The language

A *network definition language* has been developed so that problem-oriented languages, defined in the form of state diagrams, can be compiled into interactive programs. W. R. Sutherland has shown that programs can be described directly to the computer in graphical form, and this technique has obvious applications to the input of state diagrams. However, much of the information in these diagrams is in character form, and would be difficult to describe in purely graphical terms. For this reason, and because it is more suited to off-line preparation, a character-based language was preferred. The following remarks and examples are intended to give a general impression of this language, which is described elsewhere in some detail (Newman, 1967a).

The state diagram is described by defining each state in turn; each such *state definition* is followed by a list of the branches from that state and their properties. The ordering of the state definitions, and of the *branch definitions* within a list, is immaterial. State and branch definitions are constructed from *statements*, each defining one property, as in the following examples:

RESP	PRESS BUTTON
PB	PB22
IEX	REPROG

These define a response 'Press button,' a program block called PB22 and an instruction for execution named REPROG, respectively.

Each state has three properties (*name*, *response* and *program block*) and each branch has seven. For convenience, however, the language permits certain statements to be omitted if the value of the property is null, meaningless or zero. The only statements which are syntactically necessary are those defining the names of states and the actions of branches. The remaining statements in a state or branch definition must follow these, but can be given in any order.

Some care has been taken to avoid explicit references to peripherals in the language. As a result, state diagrams are largely *device independent* and compile into similarly device-independent programs. For example, a 'pen movement' action may originate as movement of a light pen or tracker ball, as a pair of typed coordinates, or even as two numbers read off a tape. Any such compatible set of actions is called a *category*, and the definition of an action must include the category name in the first statement. Some actions, such as typed commands, require a further property to define the message content. A command RESTART would be defined thus:

ACT	0
MES	RESTART

The first statement indicates an action of category 0, which includes light-button hits as well as typed commands; the second defines the message content. Numerical names have been used for categories so that extensions to the category list can be made more easily.

Table I shows the state diagram of Fig. 2 coded by means of the language into a *network definition* and illustrates the use of the *state entry* to define a change of state. If no state entry is mentioned in a branch definition, the state remains unaltered.

3 COMPILING AND EXECUTING AN INTERACTIVE PROGRAM

3.1 Bilingual programming

The network definition language contains no facilities for coding the procedures named in state diagrams. It is intended rather to be used in

Table I. The example of Fig. 2 coded into network definition language.

		Comment
STAT	1	*State 1 definition*
RESP	PRESS BUTTON TO TRACK	State 1 response; 'Press button to track'
ACT	0	Branch definition; action of category 0 (command)
MES	RESTART	Message 'restart'
SE	4	State entry; i.e. branch leads to state 4
ACT	0	Branch definition; command 'delete' leads to state 5
MES	DELETE	
SE	5	
ACT	10	Branch definition; category 10 (button)
SE	2	Pressing button leads to state 2
STAT	2	*State 2 definition*
RESP	PRESS BUTTON TO DRAW	State 2 response
ACT	7	Branch definition; category 7 (pen movement)
ACT	10	Branch definition; pressing button leads to state 3
IEX	STORPT	STORPT stores pen position as starting point when button is pressed
SE	3	
STAT	3	*State 3 definition*
RESP	PRESS BUTTON WHEN COMPLETE	
ACT	10	Branch definition; pressing button leads to state 1
SE	1	
ACT	7	Branch definition; pen movement
IEX	DLINE	DLINE computes and displays fresh line at every pen movement
STAT	4	*State 4 definition*
INIT		Initial state; program starts here
PB	PBG0	Program block PBG0, executed on entering state 4
ACT	5	Branch definition; category 5 (system)
SE	1	Completion of PBG0 leads to state 1
STAT	5	*State 5 definition*
RESP	POINT AT LINE TO DELETE	
ACT	0	Branch definition; command 'draw' leads to state 1
MES	DRAW	
SE	1	
ACT	6	Branch definition; category 6 (pen hit)
TEST	DLAST	Test routine DLAST deletes indicated line
SE	1	If last line, branch to state 1

conjunction with a procedure-oriented language, each language being used for the tasks to which it is most suited. Some readers may disagree with this approach, which requires the programmer to be bilingual. The fact remains that procedure-oriented languages onto which powerful control facilities have been grafted rarely make for easy programming. It therefore seems reasonable that interactive programs should be written in two languages, one procedure-oriented and the other *control-oriented.*

This bilingual approach permits an interactive program to be created as three separate components, namely, the *control component*, *procedure component* and *supervisor*. The supervisor contains routines for handling interrupts and maintaining the display; at its nucleus is a program which analyses and interprets inputs. This program, the *Reaction Handler*, is basically a table-driven syntax analyser (Cheatham and Sattley, 1964). The tables to which it refers are ring structures and include a model of the state diagram, created by compiling the network definition with a *Network Compiler*. These tables form the control component of the program. They contain references to the test routines, program blocks and instructions for execution, which constitute the procedure component and are compiled separately.

The decision to use ring structures for the Reaction Handler tables was made for a number of reasons. It permited null-valued entries to be omitted from the tables, and others such as message and response definitions to be of variable length. It meant that a package of routines would be available for building data structures for computer-aided design. It also allowed a much more flexible approach to the design of the Reaction Handler, since the tables can be easily extended or rearranged. The ring-processing package, which has been described in another paper (Newman, 1967b), was based on the ASP language of Gray (1967). It differs from the earlier ring languages of Roberts (1964) and others in the ease with which dynamic alterations can be made to the structure. In particular, elements can be attached to rings or removed from them without altering the element size, since the connections are made by *ring starts* and *associators* which need not be contiguous with the element. This flexibility has made it possible to write an on-line, incremental network compiler.

3.2 The network compiler

The essence of an incremental compiler, as described by Lock (1965), is that each statement is independently compiled into executable form, and can later be modified without complete recompilation. Normally this means assigning a number to each statement so that it can be referenced. In the Network Compiler it was found sufficient to assign names to the states and branches; individual statements could then be referenced by the property name. Branch naming has since been discarded in order to save space, and it is therefore no longer possible to refer back to individual branch definition statements. Users have not found this to be a great disadvantage.

The first statement in a state or branch definition causes the Network Compiler to set up a corresponding ring element; the two classes of element are called *state elements* and *branch elements*. An extra word is provided in the state element to hold the state name. Each further statement in a definition has the effect of attaching to the element a *definition ring* defining the named property. The manner in which rings define properties is shown diagrammatically in Fig. 3. The value of any property of an element can be found by selecting the definition ring with the appropriate *attribute* in the associator, and ascending it to the ring start; the element attached to this ring start contains the value.

Statements defining state entries are treated in the same fashion: the ring to which the branch element is attached leads to the named state element. Each state element has such a *state entry ring*, whose constituent elements

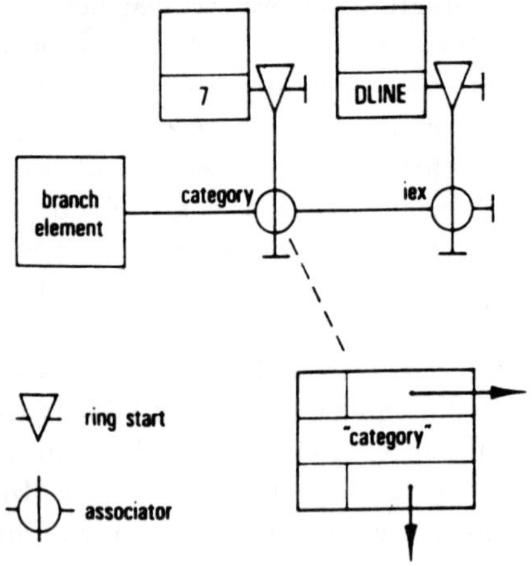

Figure 3. Defining properties by means of definition rings. This shows the ring structure defining a branch of category 7 with an IEX called DLINE. An associator is shown in detail.

define the set of branches leading to this state. A second ring, the *permitted action ring*, starts from each state element and defines the set of branches leading from that state; this set includes branches which return to the same state and therefore possess no state entry. Figure 4 shows part of the ring structure resulting from compiling the network definition of Table 1.

As mentioned above, the Network Compiler is designed for on-line use, and may be operated from the teleprinter or from the display using light-buttons. The teleprinter has proved the more convenient for on-line compilation, but the light-buttons and displayed responses provide a valuable aid, particularly to the novice. The compiler will also accept paper tapes prepared off-line. It has error-checking facilities, and will halt at any erroneous command on the tape until the correct version is typed.

3.3 The reaction handler modes

A program under the control of the Reaction Handler may be in one of three modes: these are *interrupted mode*, *reaction handling* (or *RH*) *mode* and *waiting mode*. *Waiting mode* does not imply inactivity, but that the program has reached one of the states in the state diagram and is ready for an action to occur. It may therefore be engaged in computation (user waiting for computer) or looping on a dynamic stop (computer waiting for user).

During waiting mode any action by the user will cause the program to switch to *interrupted mode*, and a *stimulus* to be passed to the Reaction Handler. The stimulus specifies the device involved and may also refer to a block of data or *message*, such as a teleprinter character or a pair of light-pen

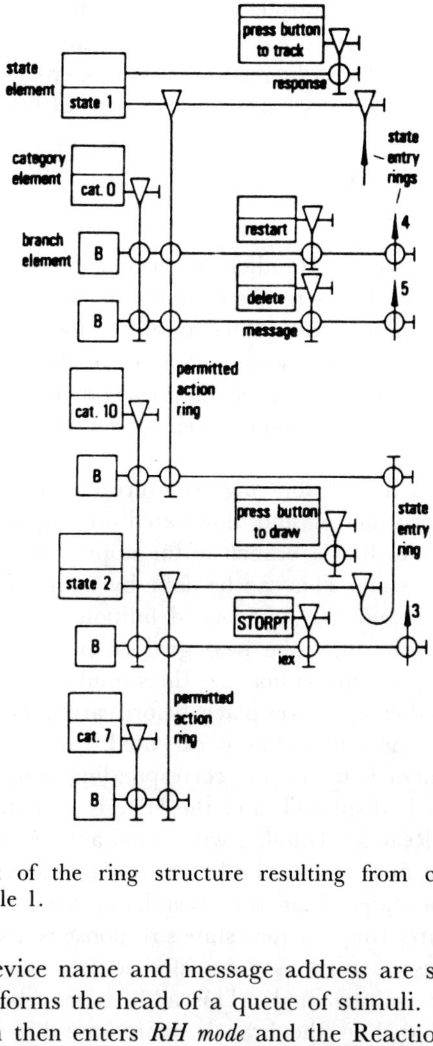

Figure 4. Part of the ring structure resulting from compiling the network definition of Table 1.

coordinates. Device name and message address are stored in a five-word element which forms the head of a queue of stimuli.

The program then enters *RH mode* and the Reaction Handler processes the first stimulus in the queue. Stimulus processing is a form of syntax analysis, whose goal is to match the stimulus to an entry in the appropriate table. If this goal cannot be reached, the stimulus represents an ungrammatical action. If, however, the goal is reached, the table may specify a fresh goal to be attained. Eventually the process stops, either when it fails to reach a goal or when it arrives at an *ultimate goal* where no further goal is specified. The Reaction Handler then fetches the next stimulus from the queue and processes it; when the queue is empty the program returns to waiting mode.

At any time the Reaction Handler may be interrupted by a user action, and a further stimulus may be added to the end of the queue. To prevent the queue from growing uncontrollably, software flip-flops or *latches* are used to govern the rate at which each device generates stimuli. The light-pen latch, for example, is set when a pen stimulus enters the queue and cleared when it has been processed; while it is set, all fresh pen positions are ignored.

3.4 Stimulus processing

The first task of the Reaction Handler on receiving a fresh stimulus is to establish what category of action, if any, the stimulus represents. This it does by referring to a *category table*. Once an action has been recognized in this way, it is matched against descriptions in a *branch table* of the branches leading from the current state. This second phase determines what reaction and change of state should occur, and it is convenient to describe this phase first.

The branch table is in fact the ring structure created by the Network Compiler, as described above and illustrated in Fig. 4. The Reaction Handler's first goal is to find a branch of the appropriate category which belongs to the current state. This can be done by searching in parallel the permitted action ring and the category definition ring. If any branch elements belong to both rings, the next goal is to find among them an element whose message definition matches the stimulus message. A series of message comparisons therefore takes place; before carrying out a comparison on a branch element, the test routine is executed.

If a matching element is found, the corresponding reaction takes place: the reaction response is displayed, and the IEX is executed. If no match can be achieved, the Reaction Handler will accept any branch element with a 'null' message. The final goal is the branch's state entry. If none exists, there is no change of state. If, on the other hand, the branch element is attached to a state entry ring, the new state's response is displayed, and the program block address is used as a transfer address when the program eventually returns to waiting mode. This address may be modified by a *jump displacement* included in the branch definition: this is a method of achieving multiple entries to a program block. If the state has no program block, the program transfers to a standard dynamic stop address.

The most time-consuming part of this process is the parallel ring search, which becomes particularly undesirable when repeated actions such as pen movements are taking place very frequently. The parallel search is therefore avoided by scanning through the permitted action ring at every change of state. At each branch element on the ring an *activity bit* is set which allows a simple search through the category definition ring to be carried out whenever an action of that category occurs.

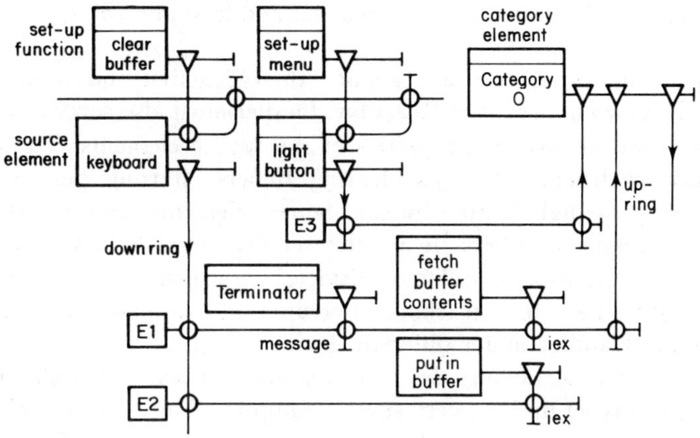

Figure 5. A category-table ring structure, capable of dealing with typed commands and light-button commands.

The first phase of the reaction handling process, in which an input stimulus may be recognized as a particular category of action, is carried out in a similar fashion to the second. During this phase the Reaction Handler uses the *category table*, a fragment of which is shown in Fig. 5. When a stimulus is received, it is first matched with a *source element* containing the same device name as the stimulus. A search is then carried out along the *down-ring* from this element, in an identical fashion to the second-phase search along the category ring. If a matching element is found on this ring, its IEX is executed. The next goal is to find an *up-ring* from this element, leading to a *category element*: this ring is treated in the same fashion as the state entry ring in the second phase. The category element forms a link between the category table and the branch table, and the down-ring which starts at this element is in fact the category definition ring used in the second-phase search.

The first phase of reaction handling performs two important functions. It is capable of concatenating stimuli so that the combined input string can be treated as a single action by the second phase; it is also responsible for grouping together actions of the same category. Both functions are illustrated by Fig. 5, which depicts the ring structure for dealing with input commands. Typed commands originate as a string of characters, each of which matches with element E2 and is stored in a buffer. When the terminating character is typed, the IEX of element E1 exchanges the single-character stimulus message for the complete buffer contents, and the second phase of reaction handling commences from the 'category 0' element. Light-button hits produce stimuli containing the complete command as an input message. These match with element E3 and lead immediately to the second phase.

When the program changes state, the old activity bits must be cleared and the new ones set. The Reaction Handler must also carry out various *set-up functions*, defined as properties of the source elements. These functions include such operations as clearing buffers, starting pen tracking and setting up the light-button 'menu'. Source elements are themselves held on a ring, whose members define the set of active devices. The display is treated as a number of different 'devices': light-pen interrupts are separated into light-button hits, tracking interrupts and so forth, and passed to the Reaction Handler under different device names.

In its general layout, the category table closely resembles the branch table, and is set up by a very similar compiler. This *Category Compiler* is also incremental, and accepts table descriptions written in the *Category Definition Language* (Newman, 1967a), which differs only slightly from the network definition language. In general, a complete category table suits most programs, but it is convenient to be able to edit out unwanted categories with the aid of the Category Compiler in order to save space.

4 CONCLUSIONS

At the time of writing, the Reaction Handler system has been in use for only a few months. Nevertheless, it has during this brief period demonstrated a number of valuable features. In particular, the network definition language provides a very efficient means of writing graphical programs, and simple experiments with graphical techniques can now be carried out in a matter of hours instead of weeks. Both the language and the underlying state-diagram concept are extremely simple, and can be used by those with very little programming experience.

The adoption of a bilingual approach has undoubtedly helped to make this possible, and it is interesting to compare other systems of a similar nature. The use of a separate language to define a program's control sequence has been proposed before, but it is rare to find explicit reference to the need for two languages in interactive programming. The ICES system employs what amounts to a bilingual method, in which a *Command Definition Language* is used to define the control sequence. The language is designed around the use of card-image input, however, and is not particularly suitable for interactive programming. *Command Flow Graphs* are used in a similar fashion to state diagrams, but the concept of program states is not employed.

A much more powerful facility for treating problem-oriented languages of a very general nature is provided in the AED system (Ross, a). Language syntax can be described by means of the AEDJR Command Language (Ross, b); the extreme generality which this system permits is attractive, but is probably unnecessary in graphical programs. The Command Language is very complex, and its efficient use obviously requires considerable experience.

The processing of basic characters by the AED system is carried out by the RWORD system. This system is particularly interesting, as it employs the concept of representing programs as finite-state automata. It possesses many of the features of the Reaction Handler, but avoids the explicit definition of program states, a feature which has been found valuable in practice. RWORD instead uses a very neat regular-expression language for defining vocabulary words, and avoids the use of tables in order to speed up program execution. It is clearly capable of producing more efficient programs than is possible using the Reaction Handler's ring-structured category network.

Nevertheless, the Reaction Handler has performed quite satisfactorily as a real-time supervisor. It provides a fast response to all types of user action, including pen movement where a good response is essential. It does so at the expense of a high system overhead, which may reach as much as 20% during pen-tracking. In a display processor, which is idle most of the time, this is quite acceptable.

Less acceptable is the space consumed by the supervisor. The system was developed on an 8K DEC PDP-7 computer and Type 340 display, and in this machine the supervisor occupies nearly 4K. Besides the Reaction Handler, this includes the ring-processing package, a full set of interrupt-handling and output routines, and a software character generator. Some difficulty was experienced in coding the ring-processing routines as pure procedures, due to the lack of index registers on the PDP-7. It seems likely that the size of the supervisor could be greatly reduced by using a machine equipped with index registers and a hardware character generator.

ACKNOWLEDGEMENTS

I wish to thank Mr C. B. Jones for his extensive assistance in programming the system. I am also grateful to Mr Alan Tritter for suggesting including the test routine; and to many members of staff of the Centre for Computing and Automation, Imperial College, and of the Cambridge University Engineering and Mathematical Laboratories, including Professor W. S. Elliott and Messrs G. F. Coulouris, C. A. Lang and R. J. Pankhurst, for their advice and encouragement.

REFERENCES

Cheatham, T. E. and Sattley, K. (1964). Syntax-directed compiling. *Proceedings of the 1964 Spring Joint Computer Conference.*

Gray, J. C. (1967). Compound data structures for computer aided design: a survey. *Proceedings of the ACM 20th Anniversary Conference 1967.*

Lock, K. (1965). Structuring programs for multiprogram time-sharing on-line applications. *Proceedings of the 1965 Fall Joint Computer Conference.*

Newman, W. M. (1967a). *Definition languages for use with the reaction handler.* Imperial College, London. Computer Technology Group, Report 67/9.

Newman, W. M. (1967b). *The ASP-7 ring structure processor.* Imperial College, London. Computer Technology Group, Report 67/8.

Phillips, C. S. E. (1967). Networks for real-time programming. *Computer Journal*, 10, 46.

Roberts, L. G. (1964). *Graphical Communication and Control Languages.* Information System Sciences, Spartan Books.

Roos, D. (1966). *ICES System Design.* Cambridge, MA: MIT Press.

Ross, D. T. (1964). *AEDJR: an experimental language processor.* MIT Electronic Systems Laboratory, Memorandum 211.

Ross, D. T. (1967). The AED approach to generalized computer-aided design. *Proceedings of the ACM 20th Anniversary Conference.*

Sutherland, I.E. (1963) Sketchpad: a man–machine graphical communication system. *Proceedings of the Spring 1963 Joint Computer Conference.*

Sutherland, W. R. *On-line graphical specification of computer procedures.* MIT Lincoln Laboratory, Lexington, MA. Technical Report 405.

On the Use of Transition Diagrams in the Design of a User Interface for an Interactive Computer System

David L. Parnas

Reprinted from: *Proceedings of the National ACM Conference,* pp 379–385, 1969.

This is another early paper employing transition diagrams to represent dialogues. Unlike Newman's work, Parnas linked the dialogue to functional code on the transition arcs, rather than through the states. There was also a difference in intention, in that Parnas did not emphasise the use of the notation for implementation but as an aspect of top level design. It is interesting, however, that the consideration of the user interface at that level was advocated. This is a view that has still not been universally accepted.

On the Use of Transition Diagrams in the Design of a User Interface for an Interactive Computer System*

D. L. PARNAS

Carnegie–Mellon University, Pittsburgh, PA, USA

1 INTRODUCTION

This paper is concerned with the design of the user interface for a general-purpose interactive system. By user interface we mean the aspects of the system's behaviour that a user sees. Several papers (Parnas, 1969; Parnas and Darringer, 1967; Zurcher and Randell, 1968) have argued that the proper procedure for computer system design involves going 'top-down' or 'outside-inwards' — in other words, designing the user interface *first*. The point of those papers has been that interfaces should be an explicit article of attention for designers, not an implication of the implementation decisions which are made. In this paper we wish to discuss problems which arise in designing the top level. In particular, we wish to suggest a concept — the terminal state — and a notation — the terminal state transition diagram — which can be of great use to the designers of a user interface for an interactive system. Further, we shall explore an approach to interface design which is suggested by these representations.

1.1 General-purpose systems

It is important to note that we are concerned with the design of general-purpose systems rather than systems dedicated to a fixed set of languages. The design problem here is a bit more difficult simply because the designer cannot predict the ways in which his system will be used. If the system is successful, there will be those who write subsystems which are used in ways

* This work was supported by the Advanced Research Projects Agency of the Office of the Secretary of Defense (F 44620–67–C–0058) and is monitored by the Air Force Office of Scientific Research.

ISBN 0–12–232150–2

which differ substantially from the usage of the main system or other subsystems. The designer of the general-purpose system must maintain in his design a certain generality and open-endedness which is not needed in the design of a single-language system.

1.2 Current developments concerning the user interface

The main explicit focus in user interface design has been the command language. The development of the command language aspects of the user interface is an interesting topic in itself. Originally, the commands (for the most part these are simply commonly used programs) were not thought of as part of a language, simply as a set of separate but useful programs which were easily available to the user of the system. In response to a growing user need the command system grew by the addition of commands, each program written separately and usually differing in formats and conventions from other commands. The confusion which resulted from such inconsistency motivated the development of command languages in which a specific syntax and set of other conventions was dictated for all commands. At this time, too, demand was made for certain features which would allow the expression of complex commands built up in regular ways from the basic commands. Macros, iteration statements, etc. now appear in command languages. This development should appear quite familiar, for it is simply a recognition that the user requires a general-purpose programming language for use in expressing his requests to the system. The response to this fact has been the statement by many that a command language should include all the features which have been proposed for programming languages. These include lists as parameters, function procedures, and so on.

This paper is intended to point out another aspect of user interfaces which we feel is not dealt with by the above developments. The need for this view of the user interface is a direct result of the interactive nature of the system; interaction has not, to date, been a major consideration in the design of general-purpose programming languages.

2 TERMINAL STATES

The aspect of a user interface which shall concern us is called the 'terminal state transition diagram'. We think of a user as using a terminal of some sort that is connected to the system. At any point in time that terminal is in some specific *terminal state* which is characterized by the set of possible input messages and their interpretations. In any state there will usually be a large number of input messages which a user may type. A large number of these messages will be rejected by the system as meaningless (null interpretation). The remainder will be interpreted by the system in some way (e.g. as a call to a program, or a value of a parameter). We shall include in a terminal state all system conditions (relative to a given user) in which the set of interpreted messages, and the set of interpretations is constant.

The reader must not think here that we are using state in a slightly different sense than is used in the discussion of finite-state automata. There a state is characterized by the set of input messages and their responses. We are allowing the responses to vary within a single terminal state. This is necessitated by the complexity of the systems with which we are dealing. Were we to insist that a state have a consistent response to a given input (e.g. a query about the amount of file space available), the number of states would be so large as to make analysis of the system impossible for all practical purposes. Luckily, the representation which we can handle is adequate for our purposes.

2.1 Terminal state transition diagrams

As a user interacts with the system, the state of his terminal changes. The changes that are made are predictable (barring errors in the system) and can be represented graphically by a state transition diagram which is entirely analogous to the state transition diagram used in describing finite-state machines (Bartee *et al.*).

The state transition diagram is a graph with a node for each terminal state. At each node there is an arc for each possible input stream (or set of input streams with identical interpretations). The arc starts at the node representing the state being described and ends at the node representing the state that the terminal will be in after receiving the input message and giving the response. The input message and the response are described along the arc in the form: input message description/output message description.

It will become apparent from the examples which follow that the user of a system must become aware of the terminal states and the terminal state transition diagram very early in his usage of the system. If he is not aware of what state his terminal is in, and what interpretation his messages will have in that state, the system (however mnemonic the commands) becomes very difficult to use. If explicit attention is paid to the terminal state diagram, and the user is given an explicit description of it, the system can become a pleasure to use.

2.2 Examples of terminal states

In this section we attempt to make the meaning of the foregoing discussion more concrete by means of a few examples of terminal states which might occur in an interactive computer system. These illustrate the way that terminal states occur and are useful in such systems, and will also serve to illustrate some of the errors which can be made if the designer does not pay explicit attention to the terminal state diagram.

2.2.1 Example 1: the initial state

Figure 1 shows a part of a terminal state diagram which includes the node representing the terminal state which occurs after connection is first made with the system and before any input messages are sent by the user. In this state there are usually only a few messages which have a non-null interpretation. These messages include logon messages (messages in which the user identifies himself in some way to the system and indicates the nature of his usage) and (optionally) some messages in which the user requests information about the system in order to decide whether to logon or not. In our example the user can ask if there are any messages stored in the system for all users (broadcast news) and also he can ask for some description of the load on the system. Many other possible requests might be included at this state, but they would serve no purpose in our example. In the example we also show the possibility of two distinct logon messages which lead to two distinct states according to the type of usage. Clearly there could be no more.

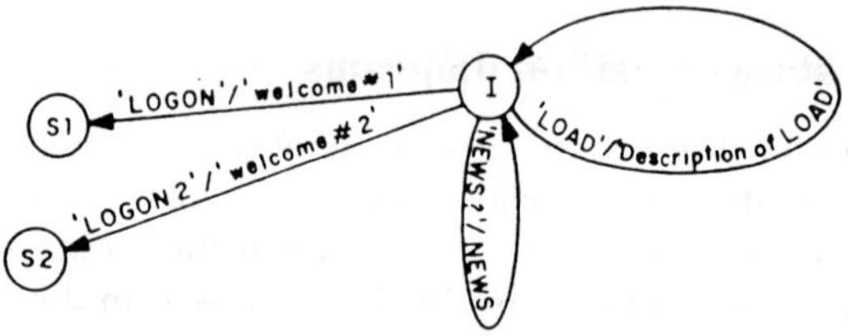

Figure 1. Partial picture of an initial terminal state.

2.2.2 Example 2: a Fortran state

Figure 2 illustrates a part of the terminal state diagram which appears in systems which have an incremental Fortran compiler. The user gets his terminal into this state by a sequence of input messages which inform the system that he wishes to write a Fortran program and have the program checked as he writes it. Our partial diagram shows the arcs corresponding

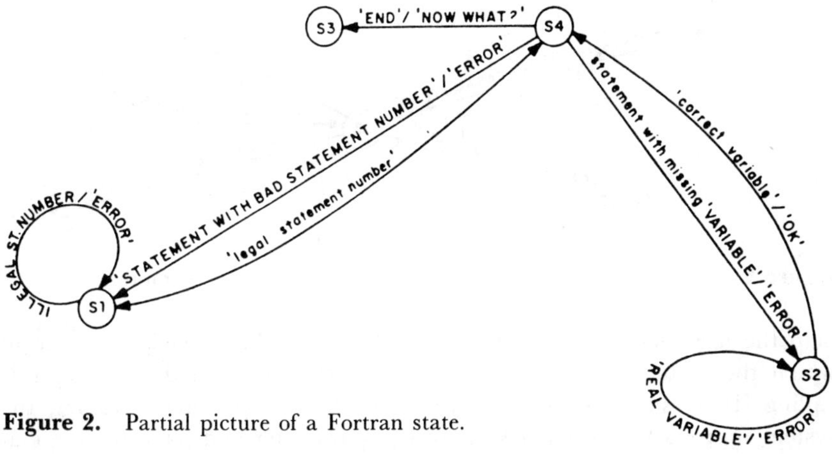

Figure 2. Partial picture of a Fortran state.

to a correct statement (other than END), a DO statement with missing iteration variable, and an otherwise valid statement with an invalid statement number. State S0 represents the state in which whole statements are a valid input. S1 is a state in which the only message with a non-null interpretation is an integer. If the integer is a permissible statement number it is taken as a replacement for the invalid number on the previous statement. In all other cases the user returns to S1. In S2 the user is expected to supply an integer variable to be used as the iteration variable missing from the previous incorrect DO statement. S3 is the state in which the user can request an action to be taken with the just completed Fortran program. Again, this diagram is incomplete; the complexity of an actual diagram will increase with the amount of effort that is put into error diagnosis by the compiler.

It is worth noting that were we counting states in the sense of automata theory (*complete states*), there would be a vast number of states just in what we have called the Fortran state. The set of permissible statements, legitimate statement numbers, etc. changes with each line input, making a set of complete states which is, for all practical purposes, infinite.

2.2.3 Example 3: prompting states

When a user calls upon a program which requires a long string of parameters, there is no need for him to remember the information which is required in this case, the order in which the parameters are to be supplied, and the formats or keywords to be used in supplying the values: the system can be set up so as to prompt him. The prompting may be done for any user or only for a user who calls the program without specifying all the parameters. The state transition diagram which results from this attempt to

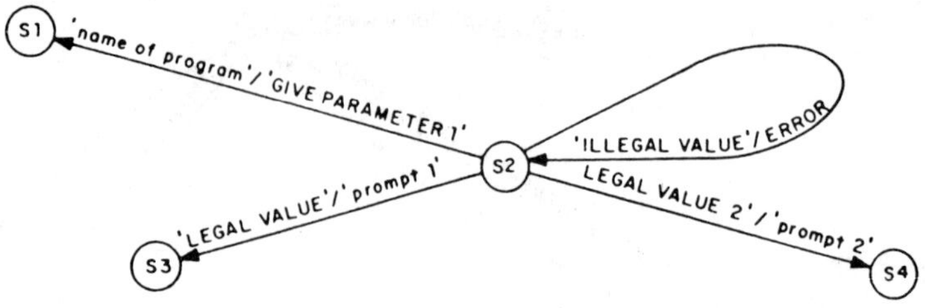

Figure 3. Partial illustration of state transition diagram for prompting.

help the user may look something like Fig. 3. In Fig. 3 S1 is the state in which the system will accept the name of the program that the user is calling. If he supplies the program name but no parameter values, the system supplies a message asking for one parameter and puts the terminal in state S2 in which a valid value for that parameter may be supplied. If an invalid parameter is supplied, an error message is given and the terminal is left in state S2. In the case illustrated some values of the first parameter may imply that values of a second parameter will not be needed. The diagram shows a transition to either S3 or S4, depending on the value of the first parameter. Needless to say, the prompting messages will differ as well. In some cases a system will allow a user to supply values for more than one parameter after being prompted for one. In those cases the diagram will be considerably more complex than that shown.

2.3 Design errors illustrated in state diagrams

In this section we shall exhibit some examples of the types of difficulty which occur in a user interface when it is designed without explicit attention to the terminal state diagram. These user difficulties are rarely insurmountable obstacles for the user. Usually he sees them as a rather annoying set of 'glitches' which make the system more difficult to use than it should be. As a result of these 'glitches' a user will spend an undue amount of time referring to his manuals, will retype information into the system more often than he should have to, and in some cases make an undue number of errors in the system. Very occasionally the latter will result in a user having to start his interaction in the system over again — sometimes he needs to hang up and dial again (errors of this seriousness are rare, mostly because they are top-priority fixes when a system is first tested)*.

* It would be tempting here to give specific illustrations of difficulties on a specific real system. To do so, however, would generate more heat than light. The problems illustrated in this section are (sometimes thinly) disguised examples of problems which have been experienced by the author.

2.3.1 *Almost alike states*

It is quite common to find that a system has a number of distinct terminal states which are very similar. By this, we mean that in those states the majority of the input messages have the same interpretation. The states are distinct because two of the input messages have different interpretations. Such situations generally cause considerable difficulties for a user, who must (1) be aware that there are several states, (2) learn the conditions under which each of the several states is reached, (3) remember the differences between the states as well as which input message is appropriate in which state, and (4) occasionally respond in two distinct ways to apparently identical series of stimuli. As an example, consider a system which has provisions for easy modifications of files. At first glance there appears to be one state in which the system types a '#' and accepts a line number followed by a comma, followed by a line of text. Facilities are available for displaying parts of files, asking for confirmation messages, and so on. In using the system, however, the user suddenly becomes painfully aware that there are at least two distinct states which fit this description. The input stream which signals end of modification in one state is rejected as an erroneous input in the other. Not only does this cause difficulties for the user, but it suggests that the system writers have duplicated (actually, almost duplicated) quite a bit of effort unnecessarily.

2.3.2 *Inconsistent ways of reaching a single state*

In the course of a session with a system, the user may suddenly wish to reach a specific state. He may or may not wish to return to the state he was in at a later time. For example, he may wish to return to a state in which he can inform the system that he wants a certain class of messages suppressed, or enabled if it is now suppressed. In some cases he can reach this state simply by pressing a single button. In other cases (still on the same system) he must press that button three times. In still other cases he will have to give a sequence of specific commands to the system in order to get to the desired state. If he wishes to be able to return to the present point in his computation, he may not be able to make the change at all. In the prompting and error correction examples shown earlier, the diagrams include states in which there is no simple transition back to this state. Generally, each system has a 'break' or other escape mechanism, but the interpretation of that symbol is not consistent from state to state. In many states the use of the 'break' makes it impossible for a user to return to the original state without retyping much of what he has already typed.

2.3.3 *Terminal or almost terminal submachines*

The literature on finite automata defines a terminal submachine as a set of states which, once entered, cannot be exited. Systems have two sorts of difficulties in this regard. First, there may be states which it is impossible to leave by other than the general escape mechanism described earlier. Second, when a subsystem writer wishes to produce a terminal submachine in the user interface, he may find it unnecessarily difficult. We shall have more to say on the second difficulty later. An example of a terminal submachine would be an error-correcting state in some file manipulation command. The system informs the user that the file name he has used is not associated with a defined file and that he must supply the name of a defined file. The user has either forgotten to define his file or assumed that the system would do it for him when he first used the name. In any event he has no appropriate file name that he can use. Any name or message that he gives to the system is rejected as not being the name of an appropriate file and he has no way out of the state. Similar situations can arise in a user-written program which uses formatted input. I have seen one system in which a user attempting to get out of a loop, hit a 'break' repeatedly only to get the message, 'is not in proper format'. He was forced to disconnect from the system.

2.3.4 *Inability to correct errors in long strings of parameters*

In the example of prompting states one can find no way after inputting the fifth parameter to return and change the third parameter. This can on occasion be quite annoying and cause a great deal of duplicate work for the user.

2.3.5 *Conclusions to be drawn from the above examples*

It is very easy to dismiss the above and many other errors as the type of errors that always occur in system designs. They are especially typical of system designs that involve a large number of people. By taking this view it becomes possible to say that they are not illustrative of any particular methodological error. In fact, however, there is a very strong conclusion that can be reached. *The above errors would not have been made if the designers of the system had explicitly designed and documented the terminal state diagram at an early stage in the system design.* These particular errors are too obvious (when viewing a state transition diagram of the system) to be overlooked.

3 USER NEEDS

Before proceeding further, we list some of the demands which the user of a general-purpose interactive system makes on the designer of the user interface.

(1) The user needs a simple state diagram free from transitions which are

both useful and impossible. Notational conventions should (with certain exceptions) be uniform throughout.

(2) The user interface must make it simple for the user to use the system in the manner of a desk tool. Many current user interfaces seem to be designed with the implicit assumption that the terminal will be used in the same way that the console of an open shop batch processor would be used — the user is expected to work on a single task in a predictable way until he can go no further with that task. In fact, the user of a desk tool expects to be interrupted at one task and to be able to switch to another with little effort. He expects to be able to stop on one task and return to it later, perhaps bringing with him some new data for use in continuing his old task. He does not wish to be subjected to any particular discipline (e.g. last suspended–first resumed) in resuming a suspended task. If his suspended task has a database, he would like to be able to have access to that database in a simple way while working on some other task. He would like similar facilities for working and interacting with tasks which he has allowed to proceed in a noninteractive manner.

(3) The user interface should be ample for users who are building subsystems which will be used by others who may be completely unable to use the basic system. The MULTICS design (Corbato and Vyssotsky, 1965; Graham, 1968) shows a great deal of thought about accommodating subsystem writers by allowing restricted access and changes to parts of the supervisor. However, there will always be (and should always be provisions for) persons who wish to create subsystems, but who wish to do so entirely at the user level — knowing nothing of the structure of the supervisor that does not show at the user interface. Among other things, this implies that the user at the Fortran or Algol level must be able to insulate the user of his programs from system messages which would be meaningful to a programmer but not to the user of those programs. In many ways this class of users is likely, in the long run, to be the most important class of users to be provided for in our design. The long-term usefulness of a system depends on its flexibility and the ease with which it expands by the addition of subsystems.

3.1 Applications of terminal state transition diagrams

There are a number of ways in which the concept of terminal state and the terminal state transition diagram can be used to ease and improve the design of user interfaces. Some of the more obvious are the following.

(1) Designers can profit by doing their original design in the design space of state transition diagrams. Many errors that are otherwise hard to find become quite easy to find in this space, and many improvements which

might never be found are easily seen in this notation. If the designer is not comfortable working in this space he can draw the transition diagram of a design produced in some other design space, as a means of gaining these advantages.

(2) Where a system is being built by a relatively large group, the state transition diagram can be a useful means of passing certain aspects of a specification to the subgroups. This is a more concise, less ambiguous form of specification than the English language currently used. The group can either be given a terminal state diagram for their part of the system or, if the design has not yet progressed that far, can be given a set of state transition conventions to which the diagram of their product must adhere.

(3) The state transition diagrams can become a significant part of the system's documentation. Often the initial diagram drawn by the designer can become a part of the user documentation, since it is a compact complete and easy-to-read description of the system from the user's point of view.

(4) There exist algorithms for processing state transition diagrams for the purposes of eliminating identical states, detecting terminal submachines, and so on. Slight modifications of these would detect almost alike states, almost terminal submachines, and violations of established transition conventions. Although it would be preferable if the diagrams remained simple although such automation was not useful, it is comforting to know that there has already been considerable research on these topics.

(5) Although our primary interest in this paper is in the use of these diagrams for designing the top level, there are certain implementation techniques suggested by past uses of state diagrams some examples of which are given in Bartee *et al.* and Heistand (1964). These range from using the diagrams as data for table-driven command interpreters, to encoding the logic implied by the diagrams in boolean equations or even in hardware.

An application which appears less obvious is supplied by a study of the state diagrams of existing systems. In these diagrams there appear to be three types of inputs provided by the user:

(i) calls on programs in some library;
(ii) requests for a change of terminal state; and
(iii) data for a program which has been called.

The first two types of input are usually passed as 'commands' but they actually represent quite different items. It is intriguing to consider a user interface in which the concept of a terminal state is explicit in the interface. In such a system the only commands would be requests for a change in terminal state. Every state in the system would be identified by a label. The user would be able to:

(i) request a transition to a given state by using its label;
(ii) call for a saving of his *complete state*, associating it with a label; the label can be used to return his terminal to that complete state, and also serves as an identifier by which the user or his program may refer to the data associated with his suspended task; and
(iii) call programs from a library.

For a number of reasons, certain transitions and certain suspensions would have to be denied. Transitions might be denied because of either lack of appropriate privilege or lack of sufficient information for the system to make a transition. (The possibility of lack of sufficient information is a direct consequence of our including a large number of complete states in a single terminal state. When the system makes a transition it must have sufficient information to move to an exact state, not just a terminal state.) Suspensions might be denied because they involve an excessive use of storage resources.

In such a system we would not include in the command language all the features of a programming language. Rather, we would include in at least one commonly used programming language the features of a command language. In other words, we would give the programming language the ability to call for state transitions and suspensions, as well as the classical abilities of a command language such as access to the file system. Included in the library associated with this programming language would be the usual programs which have been called commands. However, the user would be able to write programs in his file programming language which would produce arbitrarily complex commands which could then be called just as any program in the library. By means of suspension these complex commands could be written as needed without losing the user's state in the task for which the command was being composed.

Users who write 'commands' or subsystems should be able to define terminal states to the system so that users of the subsystems could use the standard notations for suspension and transition, making use of the facilities already built into the system. Subsystem writers should be able to provide a state transition diagram which establishes local conventions (which might override the outside conventions) and indicates permissible transitions and library calls. If the diagram includes in its possible inputs messages from the main system, the subsystem writer could completely isolate his user from unwanted messages — without knowing the internal structure of the system.

4 CONCLUSIONS

The intent of this paper has been to convince the reader of the importance of designing a user interface early in the design and representing it explicitly. We further hope to have convinced readers that the state transition diagram is as useful a tool in designing the user interface as it has been in designing other parts of computer systems. We have also suggested the possibilities of an interface in which the state transition diagram is explicit rather than implicit.

Certainly the use of the state transition diagram does not aid at all in many aspects of user interface design. We have not even mentioned the appearance of the file system to the user, the primitives for operating on files, and so on. We have not come anywhere near the difficult problem of dealing with the numerical aspects of user interfaces and many other human engineering problems. We only hope that these suggestions aid in dealing with one aspect of interface design. We look forward to seeing discussions of other aspects of top-level design in future papers.

REFERENCES

Bartee *et al. Theory and Design of Digital Machines.* McGraw-Hill.

Corbato, F. J. and Vyssotsky, V. A. (1965). Introduction and overview of the MULTICS system. *Proceedings of the 1965 Fall Joint Computer Conference.*

Graham, R. M. (1968). Protection in an information processing utility. *CACM*, May.

Heistand, R. E. (1964). An executive system implemented as a finite state machine. *CACM*, 7, 669–677.

Parnas, D. L. (1969). More on simulation languages and design methodology for computer systems. *Proceedings of the 1969 Spring Joint Computer Conference.*

Parnas, D. L. and Darringer, J. A. (1967). SODAS and a methodology for system design. *Proceedings of the 1967 Fall Joint Computer Conference.*

Zurcher, F. W. and Randell, B. (1968). Multi-level modeling — a methodology for computer system design. *Proceedings of the 1968 IFIP Conference.*

Specification and Design of Dialogue Systems with State Diagrams

Ernst Denert

Reprinted from: *International Computing Symposium*, pp 417–423, 1977.

Denert built upon the earlier work of Newman and Parnas by introducing two innovations, both of which are arguably necessary. Firstly, he replaced the simple state diagram by the more powerful recursive state diagram and, secondly, he introduced 'task nodes'. With task nodes came the possibility of the dialogue taking different paths according to the outcome of functional questions. Thus, for example, analysis of data can lead to changes in the dialogue, just as readily as user choices can.

Specification and Design of Dialogue Systems with State Diagrams

E. DENERT

SOFTLAB, Munich, Federal Republic of Germany

1 INTRODUCTION

A dialogue system (DS) is a computer system with which one or more partners — either human beings or other computers — exchange information. This communication serves two purposes:

(1) To raise the information potential of the dialogue system or the dialogue partners (DP); and/or

(2) To perform services like printing bills, tickets, etc.

The rules a man–machine dialogue has to follow are much more formal than those for human conversation. Therefore, there is a need for a precise and comprehensible specification of these rules; precision is required by the computer, comprehensibility by the man. The method presented in this paper satisfies both aims. It provides a means for specifying the user interface of a dialogue system in a precise and comprehensible manner and to derive from it a system design which reflects the user interface directly.

Our method is based on a well-known concept from theoretical computer science: the finite automaton. It consists of a finite set of states and a mapping which yields the successor state to the current state depending on a given input. This simple model in its graphical representation, the state diagram, is augmented so that it allows top-down design through the possibility of building a hierarchy of state diagrams.

We consider not only man–machine dialogues but also dialogues between the system and different types of dialogue partners. These dialogues have a star-shaped structure (Fig. 1). Two DPs cannot communicate directly but only via the DS, i.e. we do not consider networks of a universal structure. It should be noted that in this context DP means one *type* of dialogue partner, which may be a human being or some computer system. So, several users

THE SEPARABLE USER INTERFACE
ISBN 0-12-232150-2

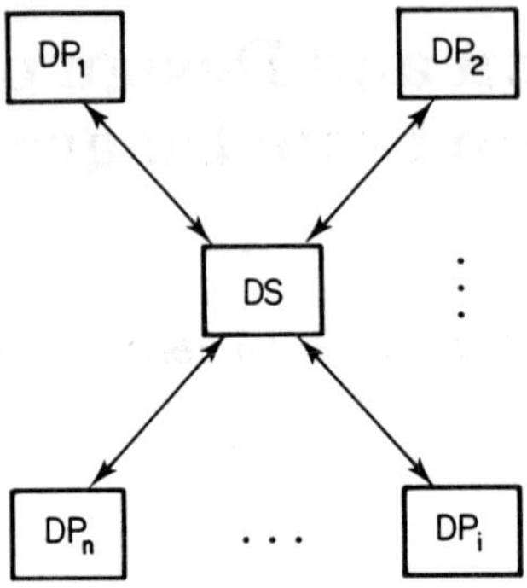

Figure 1. Star-shaped dialogue structure. DS, dialogue system; DP, dialogue partner.

are considered to be one DP and it is assumed that each user has his own (virtual) dialogue system.

The state diagram method for dialogue specification originated in the computer graphics area, where many rather different interaction devices have to be handled in order to get a manageable dialogue system (see Newman, 1968; Stack and Walker, 1971). Parnas (1969) proposes the use of state diagrams for describing the user interface of an interactive operating system.

Based on the ideas in these papers, our concept develops them in the following ways.

(1) The notion of a 'complex state' allows the widely accepted software engineering method of top-down design (or stepwise refinement) for state diagrams.

(2) Our concept not only allows for modelling man–machine communication but also interaction with other computer systems, i.e. it may be used for computer networks.

(3) So-called 'interaction points' denote explicitly where an interaction between the DS and a DP takes place. This is important, among other things, because the load of a teleprocessing system depends heavily on the number of interactions it has to handle per second. Therefore, the design of a dialogue system should clearly reveal how many interactions a particular task requires.

State diagram hierarchies as presented in this paper have already been used in two very different software projects. The first one is an editor for a two-dimensional programming language, PLAN2D (Denert, 1975a), for the manipulation of linked data structures. A PLAN2D program consists of complex line drawings which may be built up and modified with the

PLAN2D editor (Denert, 1975b). This dialogue system is implemented on the ADAGE graphics system and utilizes some of its elaborate interaction devices (light pen, data tablet, analogue dials, buttons and, of course, an alphanumeric keyboard).

The second project is a large teleprocessing system called START, which provides information and reservation services for travel agencies. The START system (which is not yet implemented) will serve about 1000 terminals in travel agencies. To accomplish this task it has to communicate with computer systems of several large companies in the public transport and mass tourism business. In the START system, state diagrams are used for the specification of the user interface, and for the description of the dialogue with other computer systems.

2 AN EXAMPLE

Figure 2(a,b) shows two state diagrams where the second is a refinement of a part of the first. A detailed discussion of the graphical symbols used for drawing state diagrams will be given in Section 3. For the moment, we want only to develop an intuitive understanding of the method to be presented.

The system described in the example always works in one of several modes (named U-, V- or W-mode). When the user drives the system into U-mode (Fig. 2(a)), it first checks whether he is authorized to do so. If not, the system forces an exit from U-mode and sends the user an appropriate message ('You don't have a license for U-mode'). Otherwise, a so-called interaction point (IAP), depicted by a circle, is entered. Such a point symbolizes a wait for an interaction from a dialogue partner. Arrows emanating from an IAP define the set of states that can be reached from that IAP, and the labels at the arrows determine the set of enabled interactions (input commands). Any other input is rejected.

Figure 2(a) is to be interpreted as follows. Transactions T1, T2 and T3 drive the dialogue system into the states TASK1, TASK2 and TASK3, respectively. When the task is accomplished the system returns to the (single) IAP of the U-mode diagram. The U-mode can be left by using one of the transactions V or W, thereby switching to the V- or W-mode.

The difference between a singly and a doubly framed box is of major importance: a singly framed box denotes an action which is executed by the DS without further interactions with the user, whereas a doubly framed box indicates that there exists a refining state diagram elsewhere; for example, the TASK2 box in Fig. 2(a) is refined by the TASK2 state diagram.

Figure 2(b) shows this refinement in the TASK2 state diagram. After

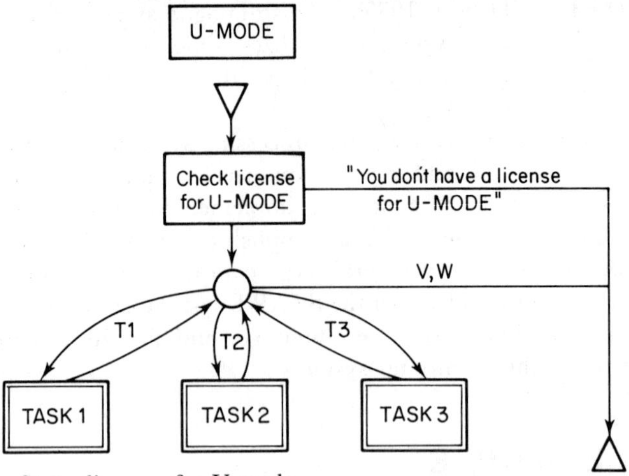

Figure 2(a). State diagram for U-mode.

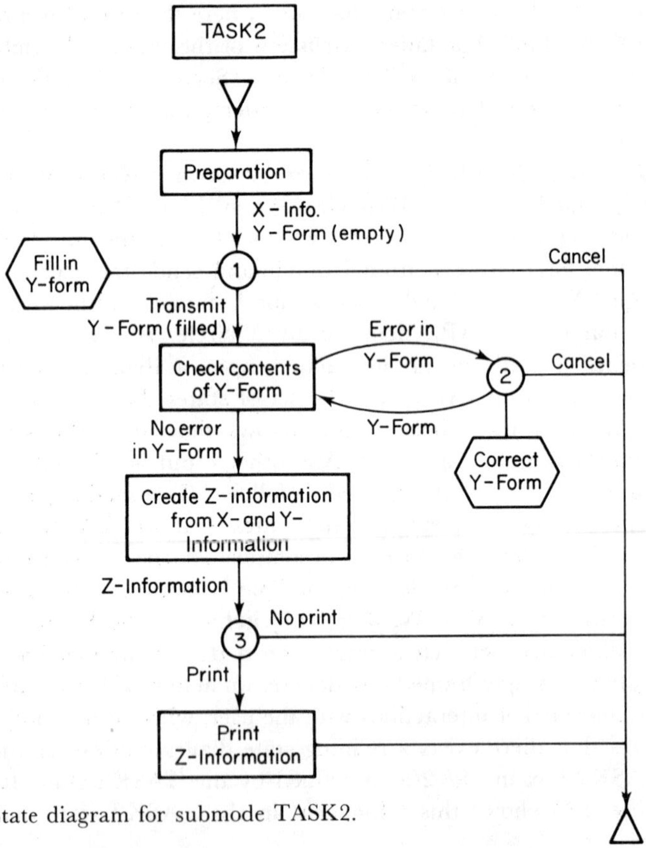

Figure 2(b). State diagram for submode TASK2.

some 'preparation' the dialogue system displays the 'X-info' and the empty 'Y-form' on the screen and passes to interaction point 1 (IAP1). There it waits until the user has filled in and transmitted the 'Y-form'. In addition, at this point the user may cancel TASK2. If errors are found in the 'Y-form' the system forces the user to correct them in IAP2, since the dialogue does not proceed until all errors are removed. Alternatively, in IAP2 the user may again cancel the whole process. Finally, the output ('Z-information') is created and displayed on transition to IAP3. Here the user has to decide whether he wants a hardcopy of the 'Z-information' (transmission of the print command) or not.

3 STATE DIAGRAMS AND STATE DIAGRAM HIERARCHIES

Basically, *state diagrams* (SDs) are directed labelled graphs. The nodes with their labels represent states, and the edges (arrows) state transitions. The latter are labelled with input symbols so that the successor of the current state can be determined when an interaction occurs.

The symbols used for constructing state diagrams are shown in Fig. 3; their meaning is as follows.

(1) Each SD contains exactly one *initial state* and one *final state*. They mark the points of entry and exit, i.e. they determine where the execution of an SD starts and stops. Furthermore, they are needed for embedding an SD which is a refinement of a complex state.

(2) A circle represents a special state termed an *interaction point* (IAP). In

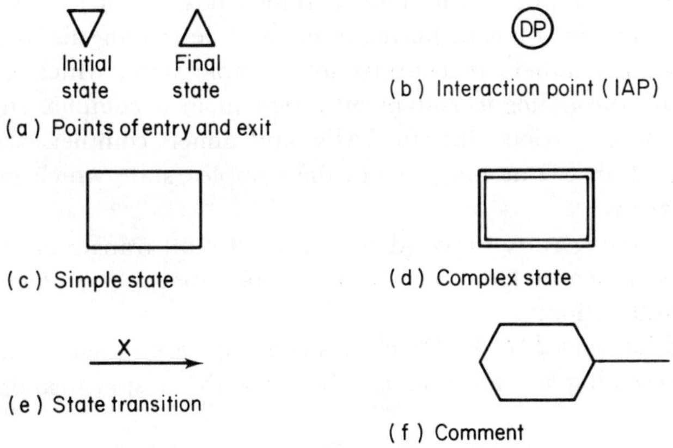

Figure 3. Graphical symbols for the construction of state diagrams.

such a state the system is waiting for an interaction, i.e. an input from a dialogue partner (man or machine). This DP is denoted by some abbreviation within the circle, which may be omitted if no misunderstanding can occur (e.g. an SD describing a user interface deals with only one DP, the user). Notice that an IAP always describes an interaction with one and the same DP.

The explicit representation of IAPs supports the design of a teleprocessing system in some aspects:

an IAP marks the point where the system may switch over to serve another user while it is waiting for a response from the DP of the IAP in question;

the job which the dialogue system has to carry out between two IAPs is a clear candidate for a separate program unit;

the number of interactions per second is an important performance characteristic of a teleprocessing system: in order to predict this figure it is necessary to derive the number of interactions that are needed for fulfilling the user's tasks, and this can easily be done simply by counting the IAPs contained in an SD and its refining SDs.

(3) A *simple state* represents an action which is characterized by the text contained in the box and which is executed without further interactions. (This is not the whole truth: a simple state in a user-interface SD may be refined for system design; then it may contain IAPs for interactions with other DPs (e.g. computers, operators, etc.) but no more user interactions. However, considering a set of state diagrams for a special purpose (system specification, design), no further refinement for a simple state exists, i.e. it is at the bottom of the state hierarchy.)

(4) A *complex state* represents an action which is described by another SD identified by the name in the doubly framed box. It yields a simple, but nevertheless powerful means for designing and describing dialogue systems in a top-down manner. In contrast to a simple state, which is executed immediately, the dialogue system may remain in a complex state for an arbitrarily long period due to IAPs and inner complex states. The embedding of an SD at the place of the complex state which it refines is discussed below.

(5) *State transitions* are depicted by arrows. Of all transition possibilities between the different kinds of states ((1)–(4) above) the following need special consideration:

on transition *to an IAP* the DS always transmits a message to the DP; the arrow representing a transition is labelled with (a specification of) this message;

all errors emanating *from an IAP* must be labelled uniquely with permitted DP inputs in order to enable the system to select the desired transition; inputs not corresponding to one of the transition labels are rejected;

if there is more than one transition *from a simple state* they are labelled with predicates which can somehow be evaluated by the system and used to select one transition; of course, exactly one predicate must evaluate to true, and at most one of the arrows may be unlabelled, thereby stating that the corresponding transition has to be taken if none of the other predicates evaluates to true;

all arrows pointing *to a complex state* are (conceptually) tied to the initial state of the refining SD;

arrows emanating *from a complex state* are (conceptually) connected with those arrows ending at the final state of the refining SD which are labelled identically.

(6) *Comments* are designated by a hexagonal box attached to its point of reference by a simple line.

Now, a *state diagram hierarchy* (SDH) consists of a set of states which may be arranged as a tree. Its leaves are the simple states, whereas the complex states constitute its branch nodes.

4 STATE DIAGRAM HIERARCHIES FOR USER INTERFACE SPECIFICATION AND DESIGN OF DIALOGUE SYSTEMS

We have seen how state diagrams can be developed top-down using complex states. When appropriately designed, the resulting state diagram hierarchy defines several meaningful levels of abstraction. The relations between these levels are defined formally by the rules for substituting complex states by their refining SDs.

In addition, we advocate another hierarchy, namely, a hierarchy of SDHs. There are at least three levels in this second hierarchy:

(1) an SDH describing the *user interface* of a dialogue system;

(2) an SDH constituting the *specification* of the dialogue system, i.e. describing *what* the system does; and

(3) an SDH for the *design* of the system, thereby stating *how* the system fulfils the specification.

Obviously, the most abstract level is the user interface. The specification is derived from it by some sort of refinement, and in a further step the design is obtained from the specification. We cannot give any formal rules for carrying out these refining steps. Instead, we should like to stress that they have to preserve the basic structure of the state diagrams, i.e. that the final design diagrams directly reflect the user interface diagrams. Taking

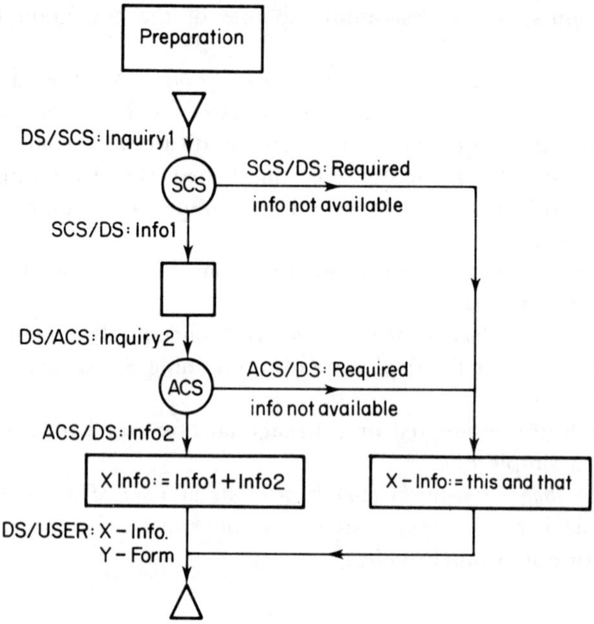

Figure 4. Refinement of the user interface simple state 'Preparation' (Fig. 2(b)) for system specification purposes. DS, dialogue system; SCS, some computer system; ACS, another computer system.

this approach we accomplish Parnas' claim 'that (user) interfaces should be an explicit article of attention for designers, not an implication of the implementation decisions' (Parnas, 1969).

The following are some remarks characterizing the above three levels of abstraction.

(1) SDHs for the user interface should, of course, contain only details relevant to the user, who should not be bothered with implementation features. Especially, interaction points must solely designate interaction with the user: IAPs with other computer systems are not appropriate at this level.

(2) The specification of a dialogue system may involve interactions with other computer systems. Figure 4 illustrates this point; it contains two IAPs each specifying an interaction between the DS and another system. Note that we introduce a somewhat formal notation for labelling the edges. 'DS/SCS: inquiry 1' means that the DS sends to SCS an inquiry 1. Therein lies some redundancy, since this label is attached to an edge pointing to an IAP with SCS which implies that some message is sent from DS to SCS. We accept this redundancy because we explicitly want to state the sender and receiver of a message.

Figure 4 further illustrates that a simple state in the user interface may become a complex state in the specification. In some cases, it also makes sense to refine an edge, i.e. to replace an arrow by a whole state diagram when developing the specification from the user interface.

If the action a simple states represents cannot be described sufficiently by the text in the simple framed box, a more detailed specification may be given elsewhere either in some informal way or by an algorithmic notation. Such a refinement of a simple state must by no means contain an interaction with some dialogue partner.

(3) Part of the system design could evolve from enrichment of the specification with implementation-dependent details, e.g. access to data structures, files on I/O devices. Considerably more experience with this level of refinement has to be gained.

5 IMPLEMENTATION OF STATE DIAGRAM HIERARCHIES

An SDH can easily be implemented by almost mechanical translation into some programming language using the following technique. The states are numbered in Dewey decimal notation, i.e. the states in a diagram are numbered arbitrarily and prefixed with the number of the refined state, if any. Consider Fig. 5: The main diagram has three states numbered 1, 2 and 3. The mode A diagram has four states the numbers of which are prefixed with 2 (the number of the refined state, mode A), giving the state numbers 21, 22, 23 and 24.

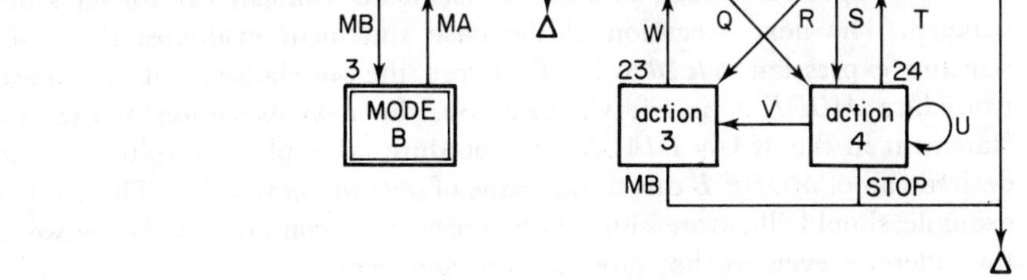

Figure 5. SDH with state numbers in Dewey decimal notation.

```
proc MAIN DIAGRAM = void:
begin state := 1;
    do case state
        in (initialisation; state := 2)
            MODE A,
            MODE B
        out goto exit
      esac
    od;
exit:
end;

proc MODE A = void:
begin state := 21;
    do case state - 20
        in (action 1; state := if P then 22 else 24 fi),
           (action 2; state :=  if RESTART then 1
                                elif R then 23 else 24 fi),
           (action 3; state := if MB then 3 else 21 fi),
           (action 4; state :=  if STOP then 0
                                elif T then 22
                                elif U then 24 else 23 fi)
           out goto exit
        esac
    od;
exit:
end;
```

Figure 6. Implementation of the SDH of Fig. 5 using Algol 68 notation.

The edge labels in both diagrams are considered to be predicates which are evaluated either from user inputs or from other data. Note that we do not distinguish between simple states and interaction points here: both are merely considered to be states.

Now, we implement the two diagrams in Fig. 5 as given in Fig. 6, guided by the following rules and using Algol 68 notation. A global integer variable *state* always holds the current state number. The structure of each diagram is translated into a **case** statement, with each case corresponding to one state. This **case** statement is embedded in an infinite loop (**do . . . od**) which can only be left via the **out** clause of the **case** statement.

Consider a transition from mode A to mode B. Assume that the system, being in mode A, somehow arrives at *state 23* where it first executes *action 3*. Then the input *MB* occurs and as a consequence the *state* variable gets the value 3. The next execution of the **case** statement evaluates the case-selecting expression *state 20* to 17. Therefore, the **out** clause is taken and the procedure *MODE A* is left via **exit**. So, the next execution of the *case* statement in the *MAIN DIAGRAM* procedure takes place, resulting in the desired call of *MODE B* due to the value of *state* which is still 3. This simple example should illustrate sufficiently the way of communication between the different levels in the state diagram hierarchy.

The example presented should have convinced the reader that the structure of a state diagram is transformed easily and almost mechanically in a program. In the absence of a **case** statement, a language feature like the Fortran computed **goto**, the Algol 60 **switch**, or a PL/I label array may be used. Changes in a state diagram, e.g. inserting or deleting a state, cause only limited effort in changing the corresponding program.

Because of the unique *state* variable no ambiguity concerning the state of the system can arise. This is especially useful for testing and debugging, because the *state* variable helps strongly in localizing an error.

6 CONCLUSIONS

We have presented a graphical method using state diagrams for describing dialogue systems which is both precise and comprehensible and which has proven its usefulness in two very different software projects. It not only allows for modelling of man–machine communication but also interaction with other computer systems, i.e. it may be used for computer networks. The notion of a complex state allows a top-down design of state diagrams resulting in a state diagram hierarchy. Several SDHs each corresponding to another phase in a software project (user interface definition, system specification, system design) constitute a second kind of hierarchy which needs further investigation. Finally, an implementation technique has been sketched. It offers a reliable and easily modifiable realization method for state diagram hierarchies.

ACKNOWLEDGEMENTS

The author gratefully acknowledges several fruitful discussions he had with colleagues at SOFTLAB, especially Ch. Floyd, U. Maiborn and P. Schnupp.

REFERENCES

Denert, E. (1975a). PLAN2D — a concept and syntax of a two-dimensional programming language (in German). Dissertation, Technical University of Berlin, Cybernetics Faculty.

Denert, E. (1975b). A method for the design and implementation of an interactive software system using PLAN2D editors and ADAGE graphics systems (in German). Technical University of Berlin, Cybernetics Faculty, Pub. No. 75–23.

Newman, W. M. (1968). A system for interactive graphical programming. *Proceedings of the Spring Joint Computer Conference*, 47–54.

Parnas, D. L. (1969). On the use of transition diagrams in the design of a user interface for an interactive computer system. *Proceedings of the National ACM Conference.* 379–385.

Stack, T. R. and Walker, S. T. (1971). AIDS — advanced interactive display system. *Proceedings of the Spring Joint Computer Conference.* 113–121.

3. First Generation User Interface Systems

BRIDGE: An Interactive Dialogue-Generation Facility

William Stallings

Reprinted from: IEEE Transactions on Systems, Man, and Cybernetics, pp 402–406, May 1975.

This paper describes an early interactive programming system for generating dialogues or software user interfaces. It is somewhat of the style of a report generator and is intended to be used by non-computing professionals.

BRIDGE: An Interactive Dialogue-Generation Facility

W. STALLINGS

Center for Naval Analyses, Arlington, VA, USA

1 INTRODUCTION

Perhaps the most significant trend in the computer field is the explosive growth in man–computer systems. The demand for computer access by persons who are not computer professionals has resulted in the development of countless types of man–computer dialogues, including airline reservation systems, hospital information systems, computer-assisted instruction (CAI), intelligent terminal data entry systems, and so on. One aspect of this trend is that man–computer dialogues are becoming increasingly sophisticated: dialogues that require training and employ obscure 'action codes' are being replaced by dialogues that can be used immediately, without training, and that converse with the user in his own frame of reference and terminology. Another aspect of this trend is the broadening range of applications supported by man–computer dialogues. The ultimate goal is to allow the untrained (in computer programming) user to program his own tailor-made applications. Already a number of dialogues exist that support user programming in a restricted sense.

The rapid growth of man–computer dialogue systems is reflected in the data processing industry. There is a clear trend away from wholly batch systems and towards transaction-oriented on-line systems (Martin, 1973). The design of such systems is evolving away from the philosophy of 'inside-out' (computer to user) and toward the philosophy of 'outside-in' (user to computer): more attention is paid to the idea that the system should conform to the user's needs and capabilities rather than vice versa. On the whole, programming is still done by programmers, but the industry has recognized the need for end-user programming capabilities, and some steps have been taken in that direction.

THE SEPARABLE USER INTERFACE
ISBN 0–12–232150–2

The trend in man–computer systems can be summarized as follows: there are more types of dialogue, covering a broader range of tasks (including programming), with greater sophistication, requiring less training, employing more familiar terminology and resulting in less user dependence on computer professionals.

2 BRIDGE

The increasing demand for new man–computer dialogues draws with it a demand for dialogue-generation tools. Tools are needed to allow fast generation, demonstration, evaluation and iteration of dialogues during their development phase. What is needed is a dialogue program generator that generates the code for a man–computer dialogue, much as a report program generator generators the code for producing a report.

Most of the work on dialogue program generation has been done in the field of CAI. A large number of course-writing languages are already in use (Allen, 1973; Dowsey, 1974; Frye, 1968; Zinn, 1968). Experience has shown that these languages do indeed meet a need. The time required to create instructional material, which can run as high as 100–200 hours per hour of dialogue, is drastically reduced using one of these languages (Simonsen and Renshaw, 1974).

Dialogue program generators for a much broader range of dialogues are needed. This paper reports on a project for the development of a general-purpose dialogue program generator, Basic Resource for Interactive Dialogue generation (BRIDGE). BRIDGE is an interactive programming system the purpose of which is to provide an easily learned efficient tool for generating dialogues. The remainder of this paper discusses the nature of the dialogues that BRIDGE is intended to create, and the facilities that BRIDGE provides for their creation.

3 DIALOGUE TYPES

Any general-purpose dialogue-generation system should certainly be able to match the capabilities of existing CAI languages. The system should provide for the creation of course material, the specifications of correct, part correct, and wrong answers, maintenance of student scores and records, and so on.

A general-purpose dialogue-generation system should allow the creation of dialogues for users who are concerned with a specialized domain of activity. Business professionals would like to talk about fields and forms

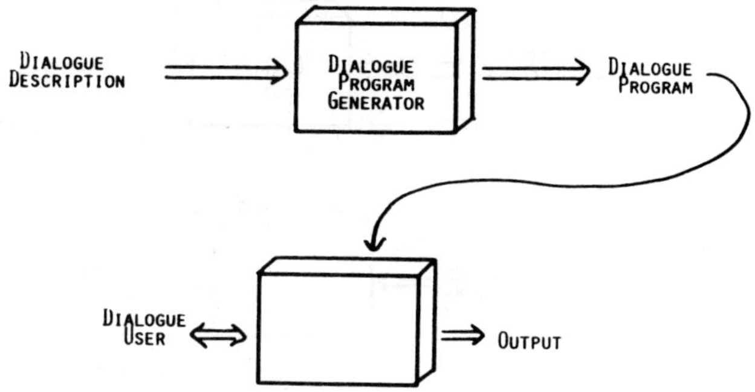

Figure 1. Dialogue program generator.

and folders and files. Doctors would like to talk about symptoms and patients' histories. Physicists would like to talk about particles. All these people would like to query: to ask questions and obtain information that is in the system; and they would like to update: to insert or alter information in the system. A dialogue-generation system should support the creation of dialogues that communicate in terms of a domain model, which is understandable to those who are familiar with the domain but are not necessarily familiar with the use of computers.

The aforementioned dialogue types require what might be called a simple dialogue program generator. A simple dialogue program generator is

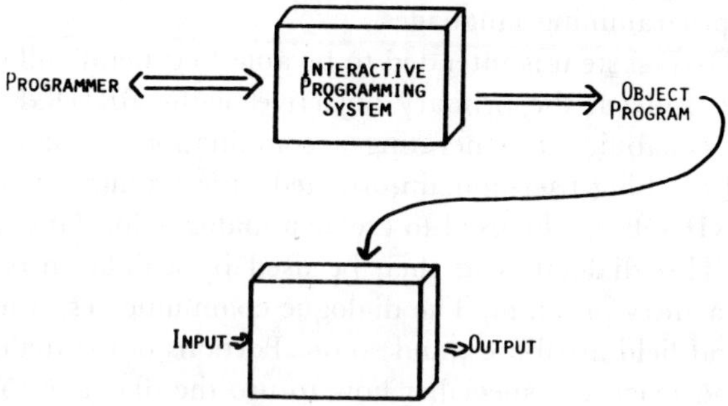

Figure 2. Interactive programming system.

capable of accepting a dialogue-description, either in batch form as in Fig. 1, or interactively, and producing a dialogue program that may be executed to provide the requested dialogue.

In addition, a general-purpose dialogue-generation system should allow the creation of programming dialogues. Interactive programming systems,

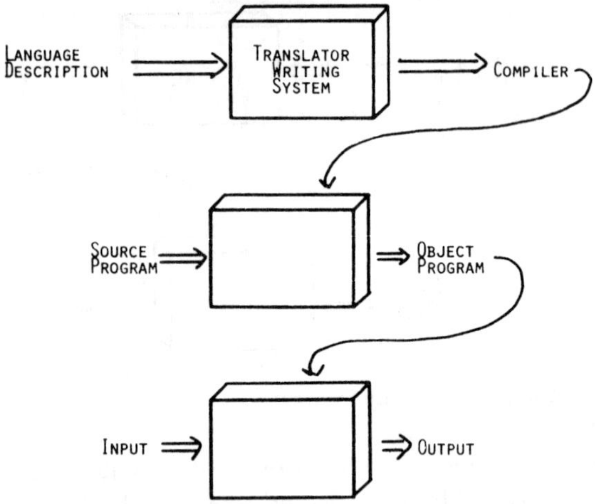

Figure 3. Translator writing system (compiler–compiler).

as depicted in Fig. 2, are becoming increasingly popular. Interactive versions of Cobol, Fortran and PL/I are widely used and, of course, there is APL. Translator writers, used to define noninteractive programming languages, are also gaining acceptance. Again, a translator writer may be noninteractive, as in Fig. 3, or interactive. Combining all these concepts, it is reasonable to expect that our general-purpose dialogue program generator will include interactive translator-writing capabilities for creating interactive programming languages.

The BRIDGE system is intended to be able to generate all of these types of dialogues. Indeed, the primary objective of the BRIDGE project is to develop the capability of generating a combination of these dialogues — namely, self-teaching user-domain-oriented programming dialogues. As an example, BRIDGE can be used to create a dialogue for data entry program generation. This dialogue can then be used by a data entry specialist to create a data entry program. The dialogue communicates in terms of forms and fields and field attributes, and so on. Portions of the dialogue are CAI in nature and teach the specialist how to use the dialogue to program his data entry application. When the dialogue is completed, a data entry program has been created. This program can then be used for on-line data entry at a terminal. This example will be elaborated in a later section.

Figure 4 summarizes the BRIDGE system. At (a), there is a BRIDGE user who creates a dialogue program. This program can then be run as a job in the BRIDGE system at (b). A dialogue user uses this dialogue to produce some output, which appears at (c). The output may be simply data, for example, a report of a CAI session, or the output may be a batch

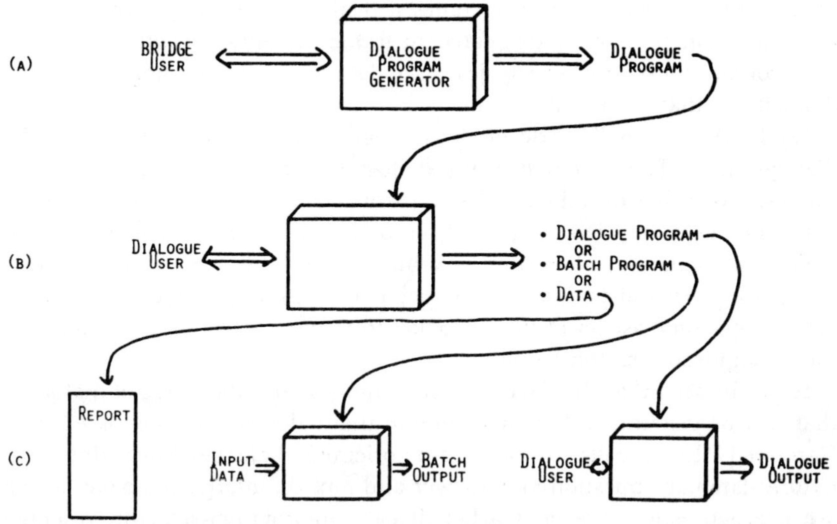

Figure 4. BRIDGE.

program that can be run as a job against some input data to produce batch output, or the output may be a dialogue program (as in the data entry example) and that, too, can be run as a job in the BRIDGE system.

4 DIALOGUE CHARACTERISTICS

We have been describing the capabilities of BRIDGE in terms of the types of dialogues that it can generate: CAI, user-domain, programming, or a combination. As a first cut, a BRIDGE system has been implemented that includes to some extent the capability to generate all these types of dialogues. There is another orthogonal dimension along which BRIDGE's capabilities may be displayed. That dimension is concerned with the interaction characteristics of the dialogue to be generated: what sorts of things can the dialogue user do and what sorts of things can the computer do? The first-cut system imposes certain limitations in this area. The interaction possible with a BRIDGE-created dialogue can be characterized by the following.

(1) The dialogue is frame-oriented. The computer half of the dialogue consists primarily of display units, or frames, containing text and/or graphics of which the structure has been predefined. The sequence in which frames are presented depends on the history of dialogue user responses to prior frames.

(2) The dialogue interface includes a display, which is partitioned into windows. One window is dedicated to frame presentation; other windows may contain messages, directories, user data, a listing, or summary of the dialogue to that point, and so on.

(3) In the 'normal' mode of the dialogue, frames are presented to the dialogue user. The user half of the dialogue consists of responses to these frames: answering questions, selecting from alternatives, entering data.

(4) The user may seize the initiative by interrupting the dialogue with a variety of commands. The user may interrupt to alter a previous response (edit), to query and update data associated with the dialogue, to seek CAI concerning some aspect of the dialogue, to request a report or summary of the dialogue so far, and so on.

It can be seen that the BRIDGE system does limit the range of dialogues that can be generated. The main line of the dialogue corresponds to what Carbonell (1970) calls ad hoc frame-oriented dialogue. Such things as natural-language question-and-answer and mixed initiative dialogue, which are characteristics of what Carbonell calls information-structure-oriented dialogue, are missing. The provision for several interrupt modes in BRIDGE-created dialogues is a first step in that direction.

5 USING BRIDGE

BRIDGE is itself a man–computer dialogue. The long-range objective concerning the capabilities of BRIDGE is that it be able to generate dialogues with a broad range of dialogue characteristics; in the short range, a BRIDGE system has been implemented that limits the characteristics of the generated dialogues. Similarly, the long-range objective concerning the use of BRIDGE is that it be accessible to and useable by persons who are not programmers; in the short range, the implemented system compromises on this objective. The use of the first-cut BRIDGE system is characterized by the following.

5.1 Frame creation and editing

The usual sort of frame creation and editing facilities are provided. The BRIDGE user can create frames containing text and/or graphics; he can create frames the contents of which depend on the state of the system at the time of frame presentation. Frames can be edited by insertion, deletion, patching together of pieces of several frames, and shifting pieces of a frame relative to each other.

5.2 Data structures

The BRIDGE user can define data structures for storage of user responses and other data. These structures are similar to the associative data structures of Wilkes (1972), and the structures developed in the GOLD STAR project (Fillat and Kraning, 1970). The intent is to provide the BRIDGE user with a simple device for storing entities, expressing relations among entities, and operating on entities.

5.3 Intraframe logic

The BRIDGE user can specify the syntax of the response sequence for each frame. This is accomplished using the BRIDGE procedural language, which includes **if–then–else**, **do–while** and **case** constructs. He can also specify actions to be taken if a legal response is given, including operations on data and on the display. The BRIDGE language makes a clear distinction between flow-of-control elements used to specify syntax or the logic of a procedure, and computation elements used to specify the 'actions' portion of a procedure. This characteristic of BRIDGE corresponds to and is inherited from TRAIL, the systems programming language being used to implement the BRIDGE system (Lechner and Stallings, 1973; Theberge and Beaverstock, 1974).

5.4 Interframe logic

The BRIDGE procedural language is also used to specify the sequencing from frame to frame. The sequence of frames presented, of course, may depend on user responses to frames already presented.

5.5 Dialogue documentation

A standardized method of documenting the results of a dialogue is available in BRIDGE, consisting of 'review-frames' and 'listings'. A review frame summarizes, in the desired format, the responses to a group of frames. A review frame is automatically presented to the dialogue user after the corresponding group of frames has been seen. This reminds the user of what he has just done. A listing is a complete history of all user responses to a dialogue. It is intended to be the primary documentation of a dialogue activity, and also to be a device by which the dialogue user can refer to prior responses that he wishes to change.

5.6 Dialogue semantics

The BRIDGE user specifies the semantics of the programming dialogue by specifying how to transform dialogue user responses into executable form. That is, for each response or group of responses, he constructs a BRIDGE procedure that defines the semantics of those responses.

5.7 CAI

The BRIDGE user can develop a set of CAI packages to go with his dialogue. A package is invoked at a specified point in the dialogue if the user requests instruction at that point. Since each package is a complete subdialogue, all the dialogue-generating capabilities of BRIDGE can be used for developing the package.

5.8 Dialogue testing

A BRIDGE user can test an incompletely specified dialogue. He can request execution of the dialogue starting at any point. When execution is interrupted because of a missing frame or procedure, for example, the system goes into an incremental execution mode. The BRIDGE user can then enter commands and operators to step the dialogue along. He can also cause the system to 'skip over' an unspecified portion of the dialogue and resume execution.

6 EXAMPLE

In this Section, we elaborate the data entry example mentioned earlier, discussing each of the three stages depicted in Fig. 4.

6.1 Use of BRIDGE

A BRIDGE user wishes to create a dialogue for data entry program generation. He is concerned with the type of data entry in which a clerk, sitting at a terminal, transcribes data from a batch of forms into the system. He wishes to create a dialogue that will allow a business manager to define a data entry procedure tailored to his particular installation.

The BRIDGE user sits at a keyboard/CRT terminal. The BRIDGE system will guide him in specifying a complete dialogue definition. He begins by defining a data structure to describe a form. The structure is an array with a fixed number of columns and a variable number of rows. Each row corresponds to one field on a form. The row contains the name of the field and a list of its attributes, such as length, data type, etc.

The BRIDGE user then creates some frames to ask for information about the form. The frames consist of questions such as, 'How many fields on the form?', 'What is the length of field ————?', and so on. He writes a little procedure for each frame that defines the correct syntax of responses to that frame. He also writes a procedure that sequences through the frames until all the fields have been defined.

In addition, the BRIDGE user must define the 'semantics' of the dialogue he is generating. That is, he must define what happens at (C) as a function of the dialogue taking place at (B) (see Fig. 4). In this example, all that is required is a procedure that defines a data entry dialogue for a particular form. This will be clearer when we discuss (C) later.

Finally, the BRIDGE user may wish to add some frames and procedures to define a CAI dialogue that will explain data entry definition to a user at (B).

6.2 Use of BRIDGE-created dialogue

At this stage, we have a dialogue user who wishes to define a data entry procedure for the forms used in his office. He will also use a keyboard/CRT arrangement.

The dialogue begins with a sequence of frames explaining the use of the dialogue. Then the user is asked how many forms he has. The system will create one data structure (array) for each form. For each form, the system cycles through a series of frames that asks the user to define and describe all the fields on the form. This completes the dialogue.

6.3 Use of dialogue-created program

The program created at (B) is itself a dialogue — a data entry dialogue. Actually, the logic for this program was defined at (A). The user at (B) simply provided some parameters for the program. Examples in which the logic is essentially defined at (B) could be presented.

The data entry program works as follows. The user at (C) also has a keyboard/CRT terminal. Using the form definition created at (B), the system will sequence through the fields on the form and ask the user to enter the data for each field. When the form is full, the dialogue starts over and accepts the data for the next form, and so on.

This example, though simple, illustrates all the principal capabilities of BRIDGE. The BRIDGE user created a dialogue that was self-teaching; the user of the dialogue needed no instruction or training other than that provided by the dialogue itself. The dialogue was user-domain-oriented: the dialogue user dealt only with concepts familiar to him — fields and forms. Also, it was a programming dialogue; the dialogue user actually wrote a data entry program.

7 CONCLUSIONS

We have demonstrated to our own satisfaction that BRIDGE as just described is far easier to use for implementing dialogues than a conventional programming language. The dialogue designer need not be concerned with a great many of the messy details. The various tools used are fairly natural for the task at hand and provide adequate expressive power. Nevertheless, the BRIDGE user would need either prior programming experience or special training to use the system. Later versions of BRIDGE are planned that will be progressively easier to use and at the same time contain progressively more general dialogue-generation capabilities.

REFERENCES

Allen, J. R. (1973). The cybernetic centaur: advances in computer-assisted instruction. *Computers and Humanities*, Sept., 373–387.

Carbonell, J. R. (1970). AI in CAI: An artificial-intelligence approach to computer-assisted instruction. *IEEE Transactions on Man–Machine Systems*, Dec., 190–202.

Dowsey, M. W. (1974). Easy author-entry systems: a review and a prototype. *International Journal of Man–Machine Studies*, July, 401–419.

Fillat, A. I. and Kraning, L. A. (1970). *Generalized organization of large data-bases: a set-theoretic approach to relations*. MIT, Cambridge, MA. Tech. Rep. MAC-TR-70.

Frye, C. H. (1968). CAI languages: capabilities and applications. *Datamation*, Sept., 34–37.

Lechner, R. J. and Stallings, W. W. (1973). A minisystem programming language. In: *Proceedings of the ACM National Conference, 1973*, 174–182.

Martin, J. (1973). *Design of Man–Computer Dialogues*. Englewood Cliffs, NJ: Prentice-Hall.

Simonsen, R. and Renshaw, K. (1974). CAI — boon or boondoggle? *Datamation*, Mar., 90–102.

Theberge, H. and Beaverstock, E. (1974). Narrowing the generation gap between virtual machines and minicomputers. In: *Proceedings of the National Computer Conference, 1974*. 285–287.

Wilkes, M. V. (1972). Associative tabular data structures. *International Journal of Computing and Information Science*, 225–233.

Zinn, K. L. (1968). Programming conversational use of computers for instruction. In: *Proceedings of the ACM National Conference, 1968*, 85–92.

The Man–Machine Interface — A New Approach

P. K. C. Maher and H. V. Bell

Reprinted from: *Displays for Man–Machine Systems*
IEE Conference Publication No. 150, pp 122–125, 1977

This paper specifically introduces the notion that the user interface module should be viewed as a virtual machine. One of their interesting observations is that it can be convenient to organise the functional code, in this case a database, for the benefit of the user interface. Whilst there may be conflicting requirements here, it is clear that they cannot be adequately resolved if user interface design follows firm decisions about the design of the functional code. There are therefore, clear implications for design and development methods.

The Man–Machine Interface: a New Approach

P. K. C. MAHER and H. V. BELL

Plessey Company Limited, Plessey Radar, Liverpool, UK

1 INTRODUCTION

The number and scope of computer applications has increased rapidly over the past decade. In a large number of these applications an operator is required to direct the computer to carry out actions, the results of which are then displayed to the operator for further consideration. The application systems range from the simple to extremely complex. On the one hand, there is an order entry system which normally consists of a visual display unit (VDU) having proforma and cursor positioning facilities, while on the other, there are large air traffic control systems with many terminals to allow the controllers to process flight plans and radar track information. These all have in common the need to pass information from man to machine, and vice versa.

This 'man–machine interface' (MMI) has to be realized both physically and conceptually. Numerous experiments and simulations have been carried out over the years to find the 'right' man–machine interface — largely related to the physical problems — and on a 'one-off' basis for individual application projects. This paper takes the most common physical man–machine interface, the keyboard and VDU, and examines a new approach to the realization of the conceptual interface in software.

There is a need for a method of standardizing MMI software design which requires very little development effort to implement on a wide range of computers, with various languages and which also allows development staff time to 'learn' a new computer with grace. This need emerges from the fact that training of development staff in the quirks and nuances of proprietary foundation software is expensive and takes time. Also, it is not sensible to design a totally logical model of an application system in isolation and then to expect to map it onto the host computer without

THE SEPARABLE USER INTERFACE
ISBN 0–12–232150–2

problems. Both considerations are important in budget-conscious applications.

Analysis showed that it was both feasible and effective to devise and develop a standard aid to help with the MMI aspect of system design. The solution lay in building a software model of a computer which would process, in real time, a specially designed instruction set, related to the most commonly needed man–machine commands and responses.

The application of this technique in the first instance was a real-time simulation of a system control cell for a mobile military communications system. The original package was developed on an ICL 1900 and was transferred subsequently to a PDP 11 which was used as the basis of the simulator. The language used was Fortran IV.

2 DESIGN REQUIREMENTS AND FEATURES

The main design requirements of the aid were that it:

(1) could be used on different machines;

(2) could be easily expanded;

(3) could have features special to MMI applications;

(4) could interface easily with host computer proprietary software and programs written in a conventional programming language;

(5) could be used to develop quickly new MMI commands and responses; and

(6) would be easy to debug.

2.1 The design concept

A pictorial representation of the system structure is shown in Fig. 1. The software comprises three main areas:

(1) a virtual machine and associated virtual store which 'lives' in the host computer;

(2) machine–independent instruction blocks coded in a special language which can be designed to perform any function (Fig. 2); and

(3) a simple database management system (DBMS) package providing boolean selection for accessing or amending the database held on backing store.

2.1.1 Size

The following are the approximate program sizes:

Virtual machine 1000 Fortran statements

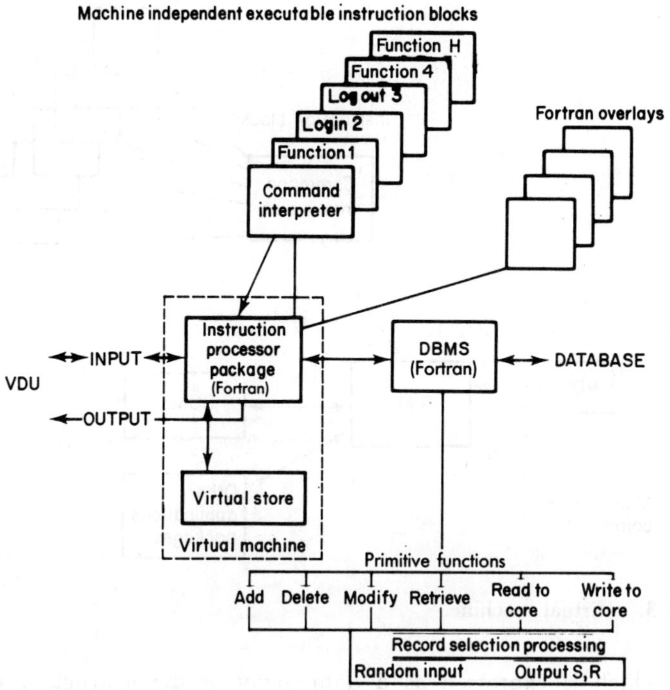

Figure 1. System structure.

INTRODUCTION INDEX	FUNCTION CODE	VIRTUAL STORE LOCATIONS		NEXT INSTRUCTION	
32	3	12	37	33	: COMMENT
33	3	6	35	34	: LOCK FILE
34	6	23	99	0	
35	3	15	99	26	
36	6	23	99	0	

Figure 2. Example of instruction format.

Virtual store	400-word array
DBMS	750 Fortran statements

2.1.2 Virtual machine

The virtual machine (VM; Fig. 3) has a current repertoire of 24 instructions. In this implementation the instruction processor facility is a Fortran program. The function of this program is to execute VM instruction blocks. Each block or group of blocks performs some required function. Most instructions executed either manipulate data in the virtual

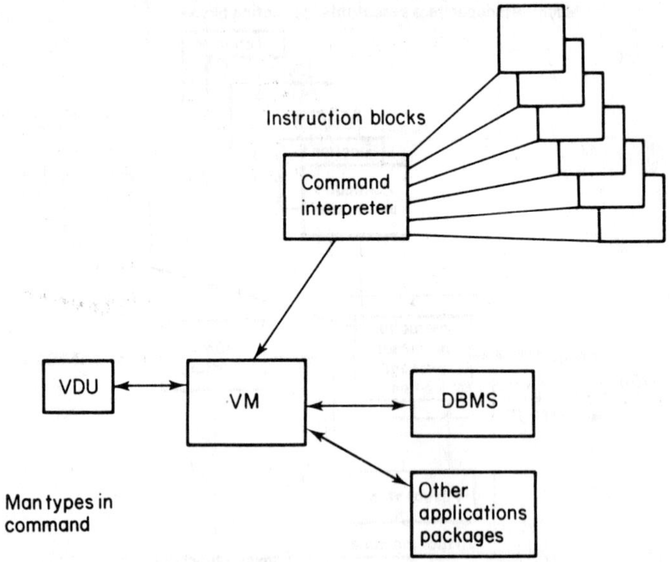

Figure 3. Virtual machine.

store (which is expressed as a data array of the instruction processor program), or call normal Fortran subroutines, overlays or schedule other tasks.

2.1.3 DBMS

The DBMS is data independent in that:

(1) there is no limit to the number of files which can be declared;
(2) files are referenced by an integer number;
(3) the number of records in each file is arbitrary;
(4) the record format can vary.

The DBMS provides relatively sophisticated data selection on any field or fields.

2.1.4 System response time

The MMI was implemented on a system using a PDP 11/40 with two 2.5-Mb disks for program overlay and database storage. The execution time of VM instructions is on average equivalent to 5 Fortran statements. The reaction time from input of a command to playout of a report or database update obviously depends on the number of disk accesses required. The range experienced with a *heavily overlayed system* so far is 2–10 seconds from command input to start of report playout and 3–35 seconds to completion of playout.

2.1.5 Debugging

An optional on-line trace program keeps a transaction file of the last 100 instructions executed. A dump program permits this file to be displayed in a readable format. To supplement this, a DBMS interface dump program is also available. The effect of this is to do away with the normal off-line test stage and immediate on-line testing can proceed instead.

Changes to the program instruction blocks are performed using the standard proprietary edit program and consequently there is no need for recompilation and linking. The effect is a very reduced debug phase and very little development for a comprehensive software support system.

3 CASE HISTORY

The application of the design aid, in the first instance, was to the task of developing a man–machine interface suitable for the controller of a mobile communications system. The user wanted to derive knowledge of operational routines before the system as a whole became available to him. A simulation was set up to gain an insight into the problems associated with input and report formats and their influence on the organization of the database. The need for easily changed MMI commands and display formats and minimal software debugging time was evident if continuity in the experiments was to be achieved.

3.1 The user

The user is used to having a well-defined method of working, in an organized environment, well-disciplined and having a definite reporting structure. He is intelligent but not necessarily familiar with computers or trained in keyboard operation. The job entails the control of a number of mobile switching centres which use voice and telegraph communication. The database provides a picture of the physical state and deployment of the system and gives the controller information to allow him to assess the effect of redeploying facilities to meet traffic demands. Accesses to and updating of the computerized database took up some 20% of the time available. The user interface was a teleprinter and VDU.

3.2 Input format

The user, understandably, was extremely interested in the format of the command language and input data. Meaningful abbreviations were chosen in preference to plain text in the case of the command identifiers. Parameter data format was also selected by the same criterion. For example, a connection between two switching centres was a combination of the centre identity codes. The delimiters preferred between elements of a command were either a space or comma in preference to a new line. Provision was made for multiline commands, and this facility was frequently used by experienced operators.

3.3 Report formats

Report generation was limited to an 18-line page. During the preparation and presentation of these displays, numerous comments were made about the heading data abbreviations, positional relationships of the data and intelligibility. All of these resulted in changes which were required to be made and debugged rapidly.

3.4 Validation of input data

The validation of input data, in order to make the software 'man proof', was a major element of the task and was divided into two stages. The first was to check the syntax and character count and type of data. Following this, the parameter character values or sets were checked in relation to their existence being allowed within the database. The first stage can be detected early in the process. The extreme case of the second can take considerably longer, especially when relationships within the database are implied. Some user staff found it difficult to understand why the second-stage errors took longer to find than their stage one counterparts. Error reports which identified the faulty parameter, together with a system of having to retype the command from the point at which the fault was detected, caused less operator frustration than those which required him to retype the complete line.

3.5 Response time

Response time played an extremely important part in the application. In this case it was not simply 'to keep up with the Joneses' that a fast response was required. Observation showed that the pattern of operations was determined by the response time provided. This confirms the premise that an intelligent operator will adapt his pattern of work to suit the response time. All concerned agreed that a response time of 2 seconds was desirable. Where this was impractical because of the nature of the task, 'comfort' messages were helpful in maintaining the operator's confidence that his task was being processed.

3.6 Operator training

To cater for both the trained and untrained operator, a method of full prompt *on request only* at any stage of input was implemented. This enabled the trained operator to make full use of his skill and avoid the frustration of the menu-type system, and at the same time provided enough data to help the untrained operator. Two types of prompt were provided. The first was a general prompt which showed the format of the complete command, and the second was a prompt which identified the next parameter only. In general, both the trained and untrained operators preferred the latter method of prompting.

3.7 Organization of the database

The database was organized as a logical model of the physical system (Fig. 4). This enabled an operator to scan vertically through the files using a sophisticated boolean selection system. This, together with a display and page command, enabled selections so made, to be displayed in single record sequence, or up to eight selected fields to be displayed in pages of up to 15 records. This facility highlighted a database organization conflict between that which is eminently suitable for display generation and that which is suitable for applications software which updates a system model. It was anticipated and borne out in practice, that data structures which are suitable for vertical scanning make complex report generation difficult. No satisfactory resolution of this conflict was possible within this project.

12–02–15 JUNE 1976 PAGE 1 of 75

DISPLAY FROM FREQ. BAND 2

TRANSMIT	RECEIVE	LINK ID	TIME OPEN
702.3	320.7	008406	121842
—	—	—	—
—	—	—	—
—	—	—	—
—	—	—	—
—	—	—	—
—	—	—	—
—	—	—	—

INPUT COMMAND FORMAT

DD, TX, RX, LI, TO

Figure 4. Typical report format and input command.

4 CONCLUSIONS

We have gained considerable experience in the use of this system. So far we have implemented some 45–50 functions. These range from Retrieval, Display and amendment database primitives to complex second-level Macro Operations on multifiles. In certain cases these include the generation of complex reports which require access to several files and which are dependent on data relationships. From this experience we can identify the following advantages:

(1) the system does work as designed;

(2) it is easy to debug and requires very little in the way of support software to make this possible;

(3) programmers require only a short training period even with the first crude version of the package;

(4) it is extremely flexible and easily expandible if new or different instructions are necessary.

However, there are some improvements that could be made:

(1) execution time is relatively slow and this would be reduced by a much larger virtual store and fewer overlays;

(2) VM instruction code forms are primitive and a simple conversion program would make these much more readable.

ACKNOWLEDGEMENTS

The authors wish to acknowledge the assistance of their colleagues in various aspects of this work and the permission of the Directors of The Plessey Company Limited to publish the paper.

REFERENCES

Bell and Maher, Operational control of Ptarmigan Communication System. *IEE Conference Publication No. 139.* Institute of Electronic Engineers.

Martin, *Design of Man–Computer Dialogue.* Englewood Cliffs, NJ: Prentice-Hall.

Language Facilities for Programming User–Computer Dialogues

J. M. Lafuente and D. Gries

Reprinted from *IBM Journal, Research Development.*
Volume 22, Number 2, pp 122–125, 1978.

This paper described an extension to Pascal that provides 'dialogue frames', each of which could include a procedural block for functional actions. This is the same structure as that employed earlier by Newman but, this time, a conventional language is extended. The extensions are described in detail.

Language Facilities for Programming User–Computer Dialogues

J. M. LAFUENTE AND D. GRIES

1 INTRODUCTION

Typical applications of interactive user–computer dialogue systems include the collection of business data (key data entry), question-answering sessions typified by computer-aided instruction (CAI) systems, and interactive database systems, such as may be used in banks or airline reservation systems. These systems can be characterized as follows.

(1) The system is in a state (often called a *frame* in CAI systems; e.g. Feingold, 1967; IBM, 1969) in which text is displayed to the user, and the user answers questions, pushes buttons or types in values. The system monitors the user input for validity and consistency and asks the user to supply additional values if necessary. This process may cause changes in the format and content of the text being displayed but, basically, the system is in one state or frame.

(2) After values have been satisfactorily keyed in, the system performs some computations based on these values. It then selects another (or the same) frame and returns to step (1) to resume the dialogue in the new frame.

Previously, such systems have been implemented in assembly language or in Fortran or other high-level languages. Some work has been done to make language more amenable to programming dialogue systems. For example, some have considered attention-handling (Johnson, 1968; Cotton, 1971) constructs such as:

```
ON LIGHTPEN DETECT THEN GO TO LABEL1;
IF KEY 5 THEN CALL KPROG5;
```

while others (Newman, 1968; Stack and Walker, 1971) have suggested state diagrams for describing and restricting interactions. Most of the techniques used in the design and implementation of such dialogues have been summarized adequately by Martin (1973).

THE SEPARABLE USER INTERFACE
ISBN 0–12–232150–2

However, the design and implementation of such dialogues is still a long, arduous task, partly because the programmer must describe everything — how text is to be displayed, how user inputs are to be monitored, etc. — in a procedural fashion. For example, if there are restrictions on the combination of two input values required from the user, then the test for these restrictions must be programmed as a sequence of procedural statements.

In this paper, we propose extensions to the programming language Pascal (Jensen and Wirth, 1975; Wirth, 1971) that are designed to ease the description of interactive dialogues. First, we provide for the description of the layout of information to be displayed for a frame, in a device-independent manner. This means providing for a description of the logical units of information — the *items* — that may appear on the display screen. Essentially, an item is a Pascal variable with some additional characteristics, such as the position on the screen, the text, the format of values that the item can have, whether or not the value can be modified by the user, and so forth. Our notation also provides for grouping items into logical units called *subframes*, which can be used in more than one frame.

Second, we extend Pascal to allow the inclusion of *behaviour rules* for a frame, which are, essentially, the specifications of the interactive dialogue. A behaviour rule is either a boolean expression that describes a constraint on items and their values (e.g. whether or not the user is to select one or more options from the item), or it is a statement that expresses the conditions under which an error should be reported, a value should be changed by the system, the text being displayed should be changed, the dialogue is to terminate, etc. The important point is that these behaviour rules are specified nonprocedurally. Thus, the programmer need not be concerned with the order in which the rules are executed. Moreover, the compiler can ensure that the rules are consistent and can disregard rules that are superfluous.

We restrict our attention to facilities for implementing *alphanumeric* user–computer dialogues (as distinguished from dialogues involving the manipulation of graphical entities, such as lines, points, etc.). Our intent is not to give a complete, rigorous, formal definition but to outline briefly ideas which we believe are interesting and useful for programming such dialogues. More work needs to be done if a full language is to be designed and implemented. We do give some hints on implementation where appropriate, and more information can be found in Lafuente (1977).

Pascal has been chosen as a base notation for expressing our ideas because of its simplicity and clarity of definition, its block structure, and its flexible data type constructs. As will be seen, our extensions blend quite well with the Pascal concepts and syntax. We assume the reader is familiar with Pascal.

```
                 BANK OF NEW YORK

                   NEW ACCOUNT

Enter information.  Hit ENTER when done.
NAME:
SEL. SERVICE NO.:              SEX:   *MALE
                                      *FEMALE
NO. CHILDREN:
SALARY:                        STATUS: *SINGLE
SPOUSE'S SALARY:                       *MARRIED
```

Figure 1. A typical frame.

We do assume several simple and hopefully obvious extensions to Pascal, such as the use of the break character ‘_’ in identifiers. Its scope and block structure rules are also assumed to hold for frames and subframes (which are defined later).

We make use of the operators **cor** and **cand** (conditional **or** and conditional **and**), which can be used in place of **or** and **and** to ‘short-circuit’ evaluation of a ‹*condition*› or boolean expression:

a **cor** *b* ≡ **if** *a* **then true else** *b*
a **cand** *b* ≡ **if** *a* **then** *b* **else false**

The reader must realize that we have left much to his imagination, and we rely heavily on his knowledge of current systems. For example, we assume a device-independent, two-dimensional description of a display screen, with rows numbered 0 through 40 (say) and columns numbered 0 through 100 (say), each element of which can contain a character. The interface between this grid and a real display must be specified in some ‘job control language’ that we do not describe. The fact that a light-pen is triggered when pointing at a certain place on the screen is described in the language as ‘selecting’ the option being displayed at that point. Similarly, pushing a button is referred to as selecting an option; how the interface is realized is beyond the scope of this paper.

2 SHORT EXAMPLE

Before proceeding with a description of the language extensions, we present and discuss a small example to illustrate some of the language features and their use.

Figure 1 shows a frame as the user might see it on a display screen. He is to key in the obvious information requested — name, selective service number if the user is male, number of children, salary and spouse's salary. The user must also select either *MALE or *FEMALE and either *SINGLE or *MARRIED. When finished, he is to depress the ENTER button on the keyboard.

Shown on this screen are *display* items, each consisting only of text, *key-in* items, each consisting of text and a field for a value to be entered by the user, and *menu* items, each consisting of text together with a set of options from which the user makes a selection. The two display items are declared as follows:

```
var title: display text 'BANK OF NEW YORK';
    heading: display text 'NEW ACCOUNT' at (0,16),
        'Enter information. Hit ENTER when done.' at (2,0)
```

The tuple following **at** indicates the row and column numbers where the text is to be placed relative to the origin of the item ((0,0) is the default). The position of the item itself on the screen is not established by this declaration.

There are five key-in items, which are declared below. For each, we give the type of value to be keyed in, the position of the field for the value (relative to the item origin), the text, and a format under which the value is to be read in. In all of these cases, the relative position of the text is assumed to be (0,0).

```
var name:    key-in char at (0,6) text 'NAME:' format A20;
    sel_ser: key-in integer at (0,18)
             text 'SEL. SERVICE NO.:' format I9;
    nchild:  key-in integer at (0,14)
             text 'NO. CHILDREN:' format I10;
    salary:  key-in real at (0,8) text 'SALARY:'
             format F15;
    salary2: key-in real at (0,17)
             text 'SPOUSE''S SALARY:' format F15
```

Finally, we define the menu items *sex* and *status*:

```
type options1 = set of (MALE, FEMALE);
var sex: menu options1 at (0,6) text 'SEX:';
type options2 = set of (SINGLE, MARRIED);
var status: menu options2 at (0,8) text 'STATUS:'
```

Note that in a menu item we specify a *set* of options, which are essentially string constants. The first option is displayed at the indicated position with respect to the item origin, with an asterisk preceding it; the remaining options in successive rows immediately below.

Suppose that these variables have been declared, either locally within a frame or globally. We now add to the definition of the frame the *contains* clause, which describes where each of these items is to appear on the screen (the top leftmost position in row 0, column 0):

contains *title* **at** (0,17); *heading* **at** (2,3);
name **at** (5,3); *sel_ser* **at** (6,3);
sex **at** (6,31); *nchild* **at** (8,3);
salary **at** (9,3); *salary2* **at** (10,3);
status **at** (9,31)

We now wish to specify the following constraints and relations among the items defined above:

(1) (*requirement*) at least one option must be selected from *sex*; a value must be entered for *salary*;

(2) (*limit*) only one option can be selected from *status* and *sex*;

(3) (*requirement*) *nchild* must have a nonnegative value (which is disregarded unless the user is married);

(4) (*requirement*) if the user is male, then a value must be entered for *sel_ser*;

(5) (*exclusion*) if the user is female, then a value should not be entered for *sel_ser*;

(6) (*requirement*) *salary2* is required if the user is married and *salary* is less than $10 000;

(7) (*binding*) the item *salary2* is to appear on the screen only if the user is married;

(8) (*terminate*) process the given information when the ENTER key is depressed.

To express these constraints and relations, we write behaviour rules for the frame as follows:

require *sex*, *salary*;
with *sex*: **allow only 1 option**;
with *status*: **allow only 1 option**;
require *nchild* ≥ 0 **if** MARRIED **in** *status*;
require *sel_ser* **if** MALE **in** *sex*;
exclude *sel_ser* **if** FEMALE **in** *sex*;
require *salary2* **if** MARRIED **in** *status* **cand**
salary < 10000;
let *salary2.d* **be** MARRIED **in** *status*;
terminate if ENT_KEY

The *.d* part of the notation *salary2.d* refers to the *display/no-display* property of item *salary2*, i.e. whether or not it is to be displayed to the user. The last rule indicates that the dialogue is to terminate when the user depresses the ENTER key, provided that there are no errors; if a rule is violated, however, an error message is given to the user and the dialogue is not terminated.

This small example is intended to give an idea of what we are proposing. We now go into more detail: Sections 3, 4, 5 and 6 discuss items, subframes, frames and behaviour rules, respectively.

3 ITEMS

Like a variable of a program, an item may contain a value of a specific type, and this value may be changed during the execution of a program. However, unlike a variable, an item has attributes that determine where and how it is to appear on a two-dimensional display. An item *declaration* describes the type of value that the item can have, an initial value (if desired), and the position of that value relative to the origin of the item. It may also describe additional text to be displayed along with the value. Finally, an item may be associated with an input or output file; in this case, the item can be considered as a 'window' through which the file can be viewed by the user.

We describe four kinds of items in this section: *display*, *key-in*, *menu* and *attention*. A fifth, the *list* item, is similar to the menu item; it specifies a list of values, instead of a set of values, and is useful when the order of selection of options is important. The list item is not needed in our examples; hence it has been left out. A sixth, the *table* item, although quite useful, is fairly complicated and is not needed for a general view of our ideas; its description has been relegated to Appendix A.

The overall syntactic structures of an *‹item type›* and an *‹item declaration›* are given below. As usual, the brackets '[ ]' denote an optional syntactic entity. The reader should realize that not all parts of an *‹item type›* may be present for a particular item kind. To keep our description simple, we give a grammar that 'covers' a more exact grammar for the language (which is given in Appendix B). When discussing each item kind, it will become clear which parts are allowed and which are not.

‹item type›::=*‹item kind›‹type›*[*‹position›*]
          [**text** *‹string›‹position›*
            {,*‹string›‹position›*}]
          [**initial** *‹expression›*]
          [**file** *‹id›*]
‹item kind›::= **display** | **key-in** | **menu** | **attention**
‹position› ::= **at** (*‹row number›*, *‹column number›*)
‹type› ::= a Pascal data type
‹item declaration› ::= *‹id›*: *‹item type›*

We consider the **file** *‹id›* part separately, after the various item kinds have been discussed.

Before proceeding with a discussion of the specific item kinds, let us make some general observations. First, a ‹*position*› gives the relative row and column numbers where the value or text string is to be placed. An item declaration does not indicate where the item is actually to appear on the display; this is specified for each frame by means of a **contains** clause to be defined later. If ‹*position*› is omitted, (0,0) is assumed.

Secondly, the **initial** ‹*expression*› gives an initial value for the item. The type of the ‹*expression*› is assumed to match the ‹*type*› of the value of the item.

Thirdly, any item has three properties that affect its appearance and behaviour, and these properties may change as the dialogue progresses, as follows.

(1) The *selected/unselected* property indicates whether or not the item contains a value. We say that the *status* of an item is *selected* or *unselected*. An item is unselected until it receives a value by an assignment in the program, by means of the *initial* clause in its declaration, or by user's input. Provision should also be made for an item to be *deselected* (set to unselected status) by the user (perhaps by pointing again to it with a light pen).

(2) The *enabled/disabled* property indicates whether or not the user is permitted to act on the item — enter a value, etc.

(3) The *display/no-display* property indicates whether or not the item is to appear on the display device. Thus an item may appear or disappear from view, depending on actions by the user or the program.

The programmer must have the means for testing and changing these properties. To do this, we use the Pascal notation for referencing fields of a record. Thus, for an item x:

$x.s$ is a boolean value that describes the selected/unselected property of x, i.e. $x.s$ = **true** if x is selected, **false** otherwise;
$x.d$ is **true** if x is to be displayed, **false** otherwise;
$x.e$ is **true** if the user is allowed to act on item x, **false** otherwise.

Thus, the assignment $x.d := y.s$ can be interpreted as 'if y is selected, then display x; otherwise, do not display x'. We are now ready to discuss the individual kinds of items.

3.1 Display item

A *display* item is used to present information consisting of text and a value to the user. The program may change the value, but the user may not. Thus, the enabled/disabled property $x.e$ of a display item x is always **false**. The example of Section 2 contained two display items whose declarations contained no ‹*type*›. Thus the items were used only to present information to the user, and no values were associated with them. Another declaration of a display item with both text and a value is:

> **var** *x*: **display** *integer* **at** (0,16)
> **text** 'current_number:' **at** (0,0),
> 'maximum: 9' **at** (1,0) **initial** 0

Whenever and wherever item *x* is displayed, it will look as follows (except that its value, initially 0, may have been changed by the program):

```
current number: 0
maximum: 9
```

3.2 Key-in item

A *key-in* item *x* (say) is similar to a display item except that the user is allowed (usually expected) to enter a value for it, as long as its enabled/disabled property is **true**. He can do this by positioning the cursor on the display screen at the place where the value for *x* belongs (or, alternatively, by aiming the light pen there) and then typing in a value. Upon typing in such a value, *x* automatically assumes status *selected*, i.e. *x.s* is set to **true**. Presumably, the user would also have means for deselecting the item — for erasing its value completely — thus setting *x.s* to **false**. In this case, the value of the key-in items is undefined. The programmer can also do this simply by writing *x.s* := **false**.

Consider the item declaration:

> **var** *y*: **key-in** *integer* **at** (0,16)
> **text** 'current number:' **at** (0,0)

When first displayed, it will look like 'current number:'. After the user keys in the value 6 (say), the item value becomes 6, *y.s* is set to **true**, and the screen is changed to 'current number: 6'.

3.3 Menu item

A *menu* item is used to describe a set of options from which the user may make zero or more selections. In the ‹*item type*› specification (see the beginning of Section 3), the ‹*type*› must be a Pascal set type. The value of a menu item is always a subset of the set of values defined by the ‹*type*›. Consider, for example, the following declaration:

> **type** *colour* = **set of** (*red*, *white*, *blue*);
> **var** *z*: **menu** *colour* **at** (1,2)
> **text** 'Which colour do you like?' **at** (0,0)

In Pascal, *colour* is a set type which denotes the powerset of the set of values {*red*, *white*, *blue*}. The value of z can be any subset of the base type {*red*, *white*, *blue*}. Facilities exist in Pascal for adding a member of {*red*, *white*, *blue*} to z and for testing whether z contains a value from {*red*, *white*, *blue*} (for example, *red* **in** z yields **true** or **false** depending on whether *red* is in z or not). These facilities are available to the programmer in designing and coding the dialogue.

For a menu item z, $z.s$ corresponds to whether the value of z is nonempty ($z.s$ = **true**) or is the empty set ($z.s$ = **false**). When the above item z is displayed, it will look like:

Which colour do you like?
  *red
  *white
  *blue

Thus, the options are displayed beginning in the same column, in successive rows, with the first option beginning at (1,2) (with an asterisk preceding it). If the user now selects '*red' and '*blue', the display will be changed to reflect this fact (perhaps by brightening the selected options). Then $z.s$ = **true** and the value of z is the set {*red*, *blue*}. Similarly, by aiming the light-pen at an already selected colour, the user could delete it from z.

To summarize, the value of a menu item z is a subset of the set of options defined by the ‹*type*› in the declaration of z, and $z.s \equiv card(z) > 0$ (the cardinality of z is greater than 0). All options of the specified ‹*type*› are displayed in a standard format, with the ones currently in z indicated in some manner. The user may select an unselected option (add it to z) or deselect a selected option (delete it from z). The programmer may reference the value of z (change z, test whether an option is in z, etc.) as he would normally use a variable of type *set*.

3.4 Attention item

An *attention* item is declared in the same fashion as a menu item (except that the item kind is **attention**). The ‹*type*› must be a scalar or subrange type. The difference between the two kinds of items lies in how their corresponding values are treated. The value of an attention item is always a scalar from the set of values defined by ‹*type*› (or undefined, if no option has been selected). The item is always restored to unselected status whenever the system becomes ready to accept the next user action.

The reason for attention items is to allow the use of special buttons or keys or to make it simple for the programmer to specify an immediate system response when a phrase on the display screen is pointed at with a light pen. Any number of such keys, buttons or phrases may be specified as options of an attention item. After the user pushes a button or selects a phrase, the system may record the input and then deselect the option (that is, set the status of the item to unselected). The user may then choose another option.

Consider, for example, an attention item declared as follows:

type *choices* = (PROCEED, RESET, TERMINATE);
var *x*: **attention** *choices* **at** (1,2)
  text 'What would you like to do next?'

When the above item is displayed to the user, it will appear as follows:

What would you like to do next?
 *PROCEED
 *RESET
 *TERMINATE

The programmer may wish to specify a system response for each option as follows. When the user selects *PROCEED, the current frame dialogue is to terminate, information entered by the user is to be recorded, and the next frame is to be presented. If *RESET is selected, all key-in items in the current frame are to be 'reset' (i.e. their status set to unselected) and the user is to type in new values. Finally, if *TERMINATE is chosen, the dialogue is to terminate. In any case, $x.s$ is set to **true** after the user action, until the system is ready to accept the next user action, at which time $x.s$ = **false** and the value of x is again undefined.

3.5 Associating a file with an item

In many data-directed interactive applications it is necessary to read information from a file, present the information to the user (usually in tabular form), accept changes from the user, and then rewrite the file with the updated information. A table item, described in Appendix A, is part of the mechanism for doing this, and a more detailed discussion appears there. However, the association of a file with an item is interesting enough to be explained here.

If a file attribute **file** f appears in the declaration of a key-in item x, then f must be an identifier denoting a Pascal input or output sequential file. We say that item x is *bound* to the file f. The value of x is always the value of the buffer variable $f\uparrow$ whose value can be used and changed by file operators. Thus, item x becomes a 'window' through which file f can be viewed. In the case of an input file, the programmer can read the components of the file using the Pascal operators *reset* and *get*, whereas an output file can be written using the operators *rewrite* and *put*.

A simple example will illustrate these ideas. Suppose *oldf* is a file of real numbers to be inspected. The user looks at each value, changes it if necessary, and then pushes a key, which causes the value to be appended to an output file *newf*. We declare two items *k1* and *a1* and a procedure *read_file* as follows:

```
type oldf = file of real;
     newf = file of real;
var k1: key-in real at (2,15)
        text 'Change value if necessary.' at (0,0),
             'Depress key 1 when done.' at (1,0),
             'Next value is:' at (2,0)
        input file oldf output file newf
        format F10.2;
    a1: attention (KEY12);
        .
        .
        .
procedure read_file;
begin if not eof(f) then
        begin put(newf); get(oldf)
        end
end
```

In this example, *k1* is a key-in item bound to files *oldf* and *newf*, and *a1* is an attention item containing only the option KEY12, which denotes, say, hardware key number 12. Procedure *read_file* is invoked each time the user depresses this key (this is specified by the programmer with a *terminate* behaviour rule, described in Section 6). This procedure writes the current value of *k1* (which is also the value of *oldf*↑ and *newf*↑) into *newf* and reads the next value from *oldf*, which is then displayed to the user automatically by virtue of the attribute **input file** *oldf*.

4 SUBFRAMES

The subframe notation is used to group together a set of items (and/or other subframes) as a logical unit. In addition to items declared locally, the subframe may contain items and other subframes declared globally. It must specify where (on the display screen) each of the included items and subframes is to be placed. This, of course, is relative to the row and column where the subframe being defined is to be placed. It may also contain

```
BANK OF NEW YORK  JULY 4, 1976
                  1:30 P.M.
```

Figure 2. A subframe.

behaviour rules (see Section 6) which describe restrictions and interrelations on the items of the subframe.

A subframe type is thus similar to a Pascal record type in that it allows the programmer to view a collection of objects as a single value. The syntax is:

‹*subframe type*› ::= **subframe** ‹Pascal *declaration*›
[‹*item inclusion part*›]
[‹*behaviour rules*›] **end**

In the ‹Pascal *declaration*› the programmer can declare items (and other subframes) which are local to the subframe. The ‹*item inclusion part*› lists all items and subframes (including local ones) which are considered to be part of the subframe, together with their position with respect to the subframe:

‹*item inclusion part*› ::= **contains** ‹*id*› **at** ‹*position*›
{; ‹*id*› **at** ‹*position*›}

As an example, suppose we want a subframe to contain the information in Fig. 2, where the items *date* and *time* have already been declared globally. The subframe *y* would be given by:

var *y*: **subframe**
banktext: **display text** 'BANK OF NEW YORK';
contains *banktext* **at** (0,2);
date **at** (0,20);
time **at** (1,20)
end

5 FRAMES

A *frame* describes a set of dialogues between the system and the user. It is similar in concept and definition to a Pascal procedure without parameters, except that it also describes how information is to be displayed to the user and how the user is to interact with the program.

A frame definition may contain declarations of local variables, items, subframes, functions and procedures to be used in the frame. In addition, it may contain:

(1) a procedure *initialize*, which is automatically invoked (if declared) upon entry to the frame in order to perform necessary initialization;

(2) a *contains* clause, as described above in the discussion of subframes; this specifies the items to be displayed together with their position and other attributes (format, intensity, text of the error message if an illegal value is supplied, etc.);

(3) a set of *behaviour rules* (described in Section 6), which describes the user interaction with the program (for this frame), restrictions on this interaction, and conditions for termination of the frame dialogue; and

(4) a procedure *terminate*, which is automatically invoked (if declared) upon termination of the dialogue, just before the frame itself is terminated.

The 'execution' of a frame thus proceeds as follows. First, procedure *initialize* is executed. Then the items are displayed to the user and a dialogue takes place. Upon its termination, procedure *terminate* is executed (if it exists) and the frame itself terminates (control is returned to just after the point of invocation).

Let us illustrate this with a simple example in which a global item is used in two frames in different ways. Suppose, for example, that the following items were declared globally:

```
var accno: key-in char at (0,16)
        text 'ACCOUNT NUMBER:';
    balance: key-in real at (0,9)
        text 'BALANCE:' format F10.2
```

In one frame, say *F1*, the item *accno* is displayed to the user and he must specify a value, which the system then uses to search a file for information concerning his bank account:

```
frame F1;
  contains accno at (3,3)
        intensity high format 16
        format msg 'Invalid value — respecify';
  procedure initialize;
  begin accno.s := false
  end
endframe
```

When this frame is presented to the user, item *accno* will appear at position (3,3). The **intensity** attribute specifies that the item is to be brightened (high intensity) in this frame. The **format msg** attribute specifies an error message to be given to the user if the value entered for *accno* is not a six-digit number.

In another frame, *F2*, the same item is to be displayed to the user but at a different position and with different attributes. The purpose of this frame is to allow the user to request a bank 'operation' (for example, to show his account balance). Thus we declare the local item *op_type* and include the global item *accno*:

```
frame F2;
  var op_type: attention (KEY1, KEY2, KEY3);
  contains accno at (5,5); op_type;
  rules let accno.e be false;
        terminate if op_type.s
  end
  procedure terminate;
  begin case op_type of
    KEY1: begin balance := get_bal;
              balance.d := true
          end
    .
    .
    .
  end
endframe
```

The **let** rule prevents the user from changing the account number (the item is disabled). When the user selects the option KEY1, the procedure *terminate* is automatically invoked; the function *get_bal* obtains the account balance, which can then be displayed to the user in another (or the same) frame.

We see from this example that different attributes and behaviour rules that affect an item can be specified in each frame where the item is to be used. Consequently, whereas the basic characteristics (item kind, data type, initial value, etc.) of an item do not change, the behaviour and appearance of an item can vary from one frame to another.

As a convenience for the programmer, we relax the syntax rules and allow frame attributes to be specified directly in the declaration of local items or subframes (thus eliminating the need for a **contains** clause for local items). For example, instead of writing:

```
frame F1;
  var x: key-in char at (0,12) text 'ENTER NAME:';
  contains x at (1,2) format A15;
  .
  .
  .
endframe
```

one can, equivalently, write:

```
frame F1;
  var x: key-in char at (1,14) text 'ENTER NAME:'
        at (1,2) format A15;
    .
    .
    .
endframe
```

5.1 A Pascal program

Finally, we need to extend the definition of a Pascal program to include a *‹frame definition part›*, which consists of one or more frame definitions. We can now think of a program as a description of a class of *application dialogues* and all the processing steps required to support any such dialogue. The processing is specified by procedure declarations and by the *‹statement part›* of the program. The *‹statement part›* contains statements to be executed initially and statements to invoke frames and to determine the order of presentation of frames.

6 BEHAVIOUR RULES

As the user acts on items of a frame, the appearance of the frame changes depending on the behaviour rules that have been specified for the frame. For example, entering data for an item may cause a message to be displayed, pressing a key may result in tutorial information being given, and pointing to an item option with a light-pen may cause part of another item to be brightened or dimmed or to disappear altogether. With complicated relationships, a simple user action can cause the appearance of the frame to change quite radically, so much so that the user no longer sees it as the same frame. Nevertheless, the basic notion is that it *is* the same frame, at least as far as the programmer perceives it. The user, however, does not need to think in terms of frames.

Three types of behaviour rules can be used to guide the interactions with the user during a frame dialogue. The *binding rule* is used to specify the conditions under which the value (and status properties) of a variable should be changed by the system; the *requirement rule* is used to specify the conditions that must be *true* before the frame dialogue may terminate; and the *terminate rule* is used to specify when termination is to occur.

6.1 Binding rule

The binding rule has the general form:

let *‹variable›* **be** *‹expression›* [**if** *‹condition›*]

The conventional rules about matching types of *‹expression›* and *‹variable›* in an assignment apply here also. After each response by the user, all **let** rules are processed (in an undetermined order and perhaps several times each) as follows: if a *‹condition›* of a **let** rule is **true**, then the *‹expression›* is evaluated and assigned to the *‹variable›*.

After processing all the **let** rules, for any rule with its *‹condition›* **true**, the *‹variable›* will have the value of the *‹expression›*.

We realize that with these semantics, **let** rules may be difficult to implement efficiently. Different ordering of processing of the rules can produce different results, the processing may not terminate, and there may be inconsistencies that cannot be resolved. For example, consider:

let $x.s$ **be not** $x.s$ **if not** $x.s$; **let** $x.s$ **be not** $x.s$ **if** $x.s$

or

let a **be** $b + 1$; **let** b **be** $a + 1$

Proposals have been made for languages in which the order of execution is not given explicitly (Homer, 1966; Tesler and Enea, 1968; Foster and Elcock, 1969). In particular, Foster and Elcock (1969) describe a compiler for a generalized language consisting of such 'assertions'. We believe that the use of **let** behaviour rules can be restricted so as to allow efficient processing and safe checks for termination, without harming flexibility too much. One simple restriction is that it be possible to order the rules so that the *‹variable›* of **let** rule i does not appear in rules 1 through $i - 1$. We adhere to this restriction in this paper.

6.2 Requirement rule

The rule

require *‹condition›*

is used to indicate that *‹condition›* must be **true** before the frame dialogue may terminate. Should termination be signalled when *‹condition›* is **false**, a message is displayed to the user, who must then respecify entries so that *‹condition›* is **true**.

6.3 Terminate rule

The rule

terminate if *‹condition›*

indicates that when *‹condition›* is **true**, the current frame interactions are to terminate and control is to return to the point in the program where the current frame was invoked. After performing computations, the program may invoke another (or the same) frame, or terminate execution.

As examples of these basic types of rules, we rewrite some of the behaviour rules of the example presented in Section 2. Remember, for an item *x*, *x.s* refers to the selected/unselected status, and *x.d* to its display/no-display status:

require *sex.s*; (a *sex* option must be selected)
require *salary.s*: (a *salary* must be given)
require *card(sex)* = 1; (exactly one of MALE and FEMALE must be chosen)
require *card(status)* = 1;
require not (MARRIED **in** *status*) **cor** *nchild* ≥ 0;
require not MALE **in** *sex* **cor** *sel_ser.s*;
require not FEMALE **in** *sex* **cor not** *sel_ser.s*;
let *salary2.d* **be** (MARRIED **in** *status*);
terminate if ENT_KEY

6.4 Some syntactic sugar

Although the three types of rules above are powerful enough, some syntactic sugar can increase the ease of writing behaviour rules. One abbreviation is simply to use the item name *x* instead of *x.s*. For example, '**require** *salary*' makes perhaps more sense than '**require** *salary.s*', which means that the item *salary* must be selected. To illustrate other syntactic extensions, we give below a set of formats for new rules and show immediately below how each could be written in the skeleton syntax given above:

require *‹condition1›* **if** *‹condition2›*
≡ **require not** *‹condition2›* **cor** *‹condition1›*

(exclusion rule) **exclude** *v1*, *v2* **if** *‹condition›*
≡ **require not** (*v1.s* **or** *v2.s*) **if** *‹condition›*

(limit rule) **limit is 1 of** *sex*
≡ **require** *card(sex)* ≤ 1

require at least 1 of *sex*

≡ **require** *card(sex)* ≥ 1

(option limit rule) **with** *‹id›*: **allow only** 1 **options**
≡ **let** *card*(*‹id›*) ≤ 1

(implication rule) **with** *‹id›*: *‹condition›* **implies** *red, blue*
≡ **let** *‹id›* **be** *‹id›* + [*red*] **if** *‹condition›*;
let *‹id›* **be** *‹id›* + [*blue*] **if** *‹condition›*

(option exclusion rule) **with** *‹id›*: *‹condition›* **excludes** *blue*
≡ **let** *‹id›* **be** *‹id›* − [*blue*] **if** *‹condition›*

Another convenient extension is the *enter* behaviour rule, which allows a procedure to be invoked directly without terminating the frame dialogue:

enter *‹id›* **if** *‹condition›*
≡ invoke procedure *‹id›* if *‹condition›* is *true*;
upon return from the procedure, resume the frame dialogue.

As can be seen, the language allows the programmer to say the same thing in many ways. The language designer must search for a minimum set of rules with maximum flexibility (if such a thing is possible). It is probably better to have just a few ways of describing behaviour rules rather than too many.

7 A LARGER EXAMPLE

As an example of a dialogue program, suppose that a financial institution wishes to computerize some of its operations. We show below part of the application program.

The program is structured as a sequence of frames *F1*, *F2*, . . . Frame *F1*, shown in Fig. 3, allows the user to select one of the bank functions and, accordingly, to proceed to another frame to perform the desired function (new account, deposit or withdrawal). Frames *F2* and *F3* (Figs. 4 and 5) allow the user to enter the required information in order to open a new account and are typical of applications requiring the collection of a large amount of interrelated information, with very little processing.

```
                    BANK OF NEW YORK

Select transaction desired:
        *OPEN ACCOUNT
        *DEPOSIT
        *WITHDRAWAL
```

Figure 3. Frame *F1*.

```
                BANK OF NEW YORK

                  NEW ACCOUNT

Enter information.  Hit ENTER when done.
NAME:
PERMANENT ADDRESS:
MAILING ADDRESS - Same as above?  *YES
   ENTER ADDRESS:                 *NO

STATUS:  *MARRIED
         *SINGLE
```

Figure 4. Frame *F2.*

```
                BANK OF NEW YORK

                  NEW ACCOUNT

Enter information.  Hit ENTER when done.
NAME:
SEL. SERVICE NO.:              SEX:  *MALE
                                     *FEMALE
NO. CHILDREN:
SALARY:
SPOUSE'S SALARY:
```

Figure 5. Frame *F3.*

7.1 Program

```
program bank;
  var title: display text 'BANK OF NEW YORK';
  R: subframe
      return: attention (RETURN);
      rules terminate if return.s end
    end;
 a1: attention (OPEN ACCOUNT, DEPOSIT, WITHDRAWAL)
    at (1,8) text 'Select transaction desired:';
 d1: display text 'NEW ACCOUNT';
 heading: subframe
          inf: display at (4,3)
            text 'Enter information. Hit ENTER
            when done.';
        contains d1 at (2,19);
      end;
 name: key-in char at (0,6) text 'NAME:';
 status: menu set of (MARRIED, SINGLE) at (0,9)
      text 'STATUS:';
```

```
                    BANK OF NEW YORK

                      NEW ACCOUNT


NAME:

The new account No. is:
                                          *RETURN
```

Figure 6. Frame *F4*.

```
accno: display at (0,24)
        text 'The new account no. is:';
frame F1; . . . endframe;
frame F2; . . . endframe;
          . . .
begin
  start: F1;
  case a1 of
        NEW ACCOUNT: F2; F3; F4;
        DEPOSIT: F5;
        WITHDRAWAL: F6;
  end;
  go to start
end
```

First, we declare global variables which can be referenced in any of the frames. Subframe *R* will be used in frame *F4* (Fig. 6) to return control to frame *F1*; selecting the RETURN option would terminate the dialogue in frame *F4*, whereby the program would then cause frame *F1* to be presented.

Subframe *heading* is used to display text at the top of the screen in frames *F2* and *F3*. It consists of *d1*, which is also used in frame *F4*, and display item *inf*.

7.2 Definition of frames

Frame *F1* is shown in Fig. 3. It is defined as follows:

```
frame F1;
  contains title at (0,17) intensity high;
           a1 at (2,2);
  rules terminate if a1.s
  end
endframe
```

This frame contains two global items: display item *title* and attention item *a1*, which is used to select the desired function to be performed. The **case** statement in the program is used to present the next frame, depending on the option selected.

Frame *F2* is shown in Fig. 4, and is defined as:

```
frame F2;
  var addr1: key-in char at (0,19)
                text 'PERMANENT ADDRESS:';
      d3: display text 'MAILING ADDRESS –';
      m1: menu set of (YES, NO) at (0,16)
            text 'Same as above?';
      addr2: key-in char at (0,15) text
               'ENTER ADDRESS:';
  contains title at (0,17); heading; name at (5,3);
           addr1 at (6,3); d3 at (7,3); m1 at (7,21);
           addr2 at (8,6); status at (10,3);
  rules require name;
        require at least 1 of addr1, addr2;
        require addr1 if YES in m1;
        require addr2 if NO in m1;
        with m1: allow only 1 options;
        exclude addr2 if YES in m1;
        with status: allow only 1 options;
        terminate if ENT_KEY
  end;
  procedure initialize;
  begin reset_frame; m1 := [YES]
  end
endframe
```

The global items *title*, *name* and *status* and the subframe *heading* are included in this frame. One of the two addresses must be supplied, depending on whether YES or NO is selected. If neither option is in *m1*, then it is valid to enter either address or both. Actually, the rule **require** *addr1* is superfluous because it can be inferred from the other rules.

Upon entering the frame and before the frame is presented to the user, the procedure *reset_frame* causes the status of all items in *F2* to be set to unselected. Then, the item *m1* is initialized to [YES]. We have not defined the procedure *reset_frame* here; this could be a 'built-in' procedure provided by the implementation.

Frame *F3* is shown in Fig. 5, and is as follows:

```
frame F3:
  var sel_ser: key-in integer at (0,18)
```

```
                text 'SEL. SERVICE NO.:' format I9;
        sex: menu set of (MALE, FEMALE) at (0,6) text 'SEX:';
        nchild: key-in integer at (0,14)
                text 'NO. CHILDREN:' format I10;
        salary: key-in real at (0,8) text 'SALARY:' format F20;
        salary2: key-in real at (0,17)
                 text 'SPOUSE''S SALARY:' format F15;
    contains title at (0,17); heading; name at (5,3);
            sel_ser at (6,3); sex at (6,31); nchild at (8,3);
            salary at (9,3); salary2 at (10,3);
    rules with sex: allow only 1 options;
          require sex, salary;
          require nchild ≥ 0 if MARRIED in status;
          let name.e be false;
          require sel_ser if MALE in sex;
          exclude sel_ser if FEMALE in sex;
          let salary2.d be MARRIED in status;
          require salary2 if MARRIED in status cand salary < 10000;
          terminate if ENT_KEY
    end;
    procedure initialize;
    begin reset_item(sel_ser, sex, nchild, salary, salary2)
    end;
    procedure terminate;
    begin accno := new_acc; file_acc
    end
  endframe
```

This frame is very similar to the example shown earlier in Fig. 1. As in frame *F2*, the items *title* and *heading* are included here. The items *status* and *accno* are referenced here but will not be displayed to the user. The item *name* contains the information supplied by the user in the previous frame, but it cannot be changed here. Initially, the procedure *reset_item* (not defined here) sets the status of all key-in and menu items (except *name*) to unselected.

The relations among the items are expressed by the behaviour rules. For example, selective service number is required only from male applicants. To determine loan eligibility, the bank wants to know the spouse's salary if the applicant's salary is less than $10 000. Further, *salary2* makes no sense if the applicant is not married; therefore, *salary2* appears on the screen only if MARRIED was selected in frame *F2*. When all these relations are satisfied, the user can depress the ENTER key, which causes a new account to be produced and filed by the local procedures *new_acc* and *file_acc* (not defined here).

Frame *F4* is shown in Fig. 6, and has the form:

```
frame F4;
  contains title at (0,17); d1 at (2,19); name at (7,3);
           accno at (9,3); R at (12,41);
  rules let name.e be false
  end
endframe
```

This frame is used to display the new account number to the user after all specified information has been collected in frames *F2* and *F3*. The item *name*, which appears in frames *F2* and *F3*, also appears here but at a different location. Selecting the RETURN option causes a return to the program, according to the **terminate** rule specified in subframe *R*; frame *F1* will then be displayed again.

8 IMPLEMENTATION PROBLEMS

The efficient implementation of behaviour rules may be a point of contention about the applicability of this work. In this section, therefore, we discuss briefly implementation problems and give hints at solutions. A more detailed explanation of these problems, and a discussion of techniques and algorithms to solve them, appear in Lafuente (1977).

To begin with, a set of behaviour rules may be inconsistent, and to check for this possibility the compiler should contain a compile-time analysis procedure. For example, suppose that the following rules are given to describe the frame behaviour:

```
require sel_ser if MALE in sex;
with sex: allow only 1 of MALE, FEMALE;
let sex be sex + [FEMALE] if sel_ser.s
```

The problem is that selecting the MALE option leads to an inconsistency. Another situation that must be detected is when a termination condition can never occur or would lead to an inconsistency.

These kinds of problems can be analyzed with a graph model of interactions. A graph representation of the above rules is illustrated in Fig. 7, where the nodes of the graph represent items and options, and the edges represent constraints and dependencies. Associated with each node x is a *possible status* property *ps*, as follows:

if $node(x).ps = 1$, then x must be selected;
if $node(x).ps = 0$, then x cannot be selected;
if $node(x).ps = 2$, then x can be in either status.

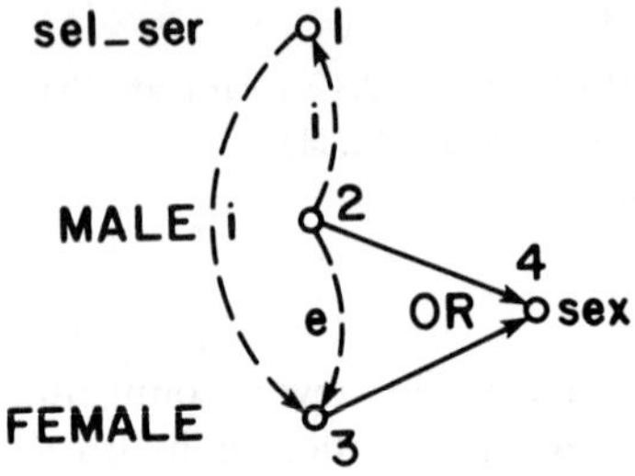

Figure 7. Graph representation of behaviour rules.

Shown in the graph are implication links (labelled *i*) and exclusion links (labelled *e*), which express relations between the possible status of nodes. The graph is constructed as the rules are parsed. For example, the first rule above produces the link $2 \xrightarrow{i} 1$. A rule such as **require** *x* does not produce a link; it simply causes the possible status of node *x* to be set to 1. The specification of

require *x*; **exclude** *x*

would result in the inconsistency $node(x).ps = 1$ and $node(x).ps = 0$.

It is not always necessary to test conditions after every user action. Here, the graph model also helps, since it is possible to determine which user inputs have an effect on each system response (such as the display of a message or the termination of the dialogue). Furthermore, certain combinations of user's inputs are irrelevant, in the sense that, although they may occur, they cause no change in the observable state of the system. A run-time procedure that takes advantage of these observations to implement behaviour rules efficiently is contained in Lafuente (1977).

9 CONCLUSIONS

We have presented extensions to Pascal to provide a language for programming alphanumeric user–computer dialogues. In this language, interactive behaviour rules can be defined nonprocedurally by an application programmer, leaving the task of checking for inconsistencies and setting up the control logic to the system. This type of language, therefore, can reduce much complicated coding of interactive applications.

The extensions were designed to be natural and to blend well with the concepts and syntax of Pascal. We feel that, in general, block-structured languages with flexible data-type definition facilities are good candidates for the embedding of interactive behaviour specifications.

We saw, for example, how items were defined with a simple extension of

Pascal types, how subframes were simple extensions of Pascal records, and how frames were defined in a way similar to Pascal procedures. We also saw how the scope rules for variables in blocks and procedures extended very nicely to items in frames and subframes.

It is, of course, possible to extend other languages to allow the specification of interactive dialogues, but the extensions may not be as elegant. A possible way to extend Cobol is discussed in Lafuente (1977).

In the description of our language, we have deliberately omitted some language features for the sake of simplicity. For example, in a real implementation, the language may be extended to contain abbreviations, more item and frame attributes, and more functions to manipulate table items. Also, a graphics protocol could be designed to lay out the information on the frames interactively.

REFERENCES

Cotton, I. W. (1971). Languages for graphic attention-handling. In: *Advanced Computer Graphics*. R. D. Parslo and R. E. Green (eds). New York: Plenum Press.

Feingold, S. L. (1967). PLANIT — a flexible language designed for computer–human interaction. *AFIPS Conference Proceedings*, 31, 545.

Foster, J. M. and Elcock, E. W. (1969). ABSYS1: an incremental compiler for assertions: an introduction. *Machine Intelligence*, 4, 423.

Homer, E. D. (1966). An algorithm for selecting and sequencing statements as a basis for a problem-oriented programming system. In: *Proceedings of the 21st ACM National Conference*, New York, NY.

IBM (1969). *COURSEWRITER III Student Text.* Form No. GC20–1706. White Plains, NY: IBM Corporation.

Jensen, K. and Wirth, N. (1975). *PASCAL User Manual and Report. Lecture Notes in Computer Science 18* (2nd edn). New York: Springer Verlag.

Johnson, C. I. (1968). Principles of interactive systems. *IBM Systems Journal*, 7, 147.

Lafuente, J. M. (1977). The specification of data-directed interactive user–computer dialogues. Ph.D. Thesis, Cornell University, Ithaca, NY.

Martin, J. M. (1973). *Design of Man–Computer Dialogues.* Englewood Cliffs, NJ: Prentice-Hall.

Newman, W. M. (1968). A system for interactive graphical programming. *AFIPS Conference Proceedings*, 32, 47.

Stack, T. R. and Walker, S. T. (1971). AIDS — advanced interactive display system. *AFIPS Conference Proceedings*, 38, 113.

Tesler, L. G. and Enea, H. J. (1968). A language design for concurrent processes. *AFIPS Conference Proceedings*, 32, 403.

Wirth, N. (1971). The programming language PASCAL. *Acta Informatica*, 1, 35.

APPENDIX A TABLE ITEMS

High-level programming languages normally contain data constructs such as arrays, structures and records, which are built up from the basic data types (integer, real, character, etc.). Similarly, our language contains a structured type of item called a *table* item, which is made up of the basic items that we have considered so far. The table item allows the programmer to define a two-dimensional structure of values, with text, position and other characteristics — the number of rows to be displayed, whether the user is to select rows or enter values in a column, etc.

A table item may be viewed as a set of *columns*; each column is defined very much like a key-in or display item (depending on whether or not the user is permitted to enter values into the column), having attributes such as position, format, initial value, etc. The programmer can also specify that the rows of the table are to behave as a menu or as an attention item. Behaviour rules can then be specified to describe selection constraints and relations among the rows or columns of the table.

An example of a table item is shown in Fig. 8. Let us assume that the values contained in the first column can be obtained from a global table *emp_tab*, which was used by an authorized person to specify the employees' names. We then include this column in our new table and add two more columns. When this table is displayed, a clerk is to enter the hours worked each week, and the program will then compute the pay. The table can be defined as follows:

```
var pay_tab: table (20) text 'WEEKLY PAYROLL' at (0,9)
    columns
        hrs: key-in integer at (5,18)
            text 'HOURS' at (−3,−2), 'WORKED'
            initial 0 format I2;
        pay: display real at (5,25)
             text 'PAY' at (−2,1) initial 0 format F6.2;
        contains emp_tab.name at (5,2)
    end
    rows (10) attention
```

This defines a table item *pay_tab* having a maximum of 20 rows; of these, only 10 rows can be seen by the user. The rows are to behave as an attention item (having 10 options). To specify the behaviour of this table, we give behaviour rules for the containing frame:

```
let pay_tab.name.e be false;
require hrs ≤ 40;
let pay be hrs *rate
```

The first rule prevents the user from changing the values in the *name* column. The pay is computed automatically by multiplying the hours worked (which cannot exceed 40) by the global variable *rate*.

Thus, a table item may be used for displaying or updating information, depending on the ‹*item kind*› specified for the columns (and their status properties).

WEEKLY PAYROLL

EMPLOYEE NAME	HOURS WORKED	PAY
F.W. SMITH	20	
J.M. ROBERTS	36	
A.L. ANDERSON	40	

Figure 8. A table item.

If used for updating information, then, at any time during the presentation of the containing frame, one of the rows may be designated as the *current row*. Each value in the current row behaves as a display or key-in item, according to the *‹item kind›* specified for the corresponding column. Only the current row can be acted on by the user.

The programmer can manipulate the information in the table item, change the status properties of the columns, select rows of the table, or designate another row as the current row. For this we need some notation.

A.1 Notation

If T is a table item, the rows are denoted by $T[1]$, $T[2]$, . . ., and, in particular, *T.current_row* is the current row. The variable *T.current_index* is the *current-row index*, i.e. *T.current_row* is equivalent to *T*[*T.current_index*]. To reference elements in each row, we use Pascal record notation. Thus:

$T[i].x$ = the value at row i, column named x

Now, the table item T itself has a value, which is the value that results from treating the rows as a menu or attention item. For example, if **menu** is specified for the rows of T and rows 1 and 3 are the only selected rows, then the value of T is the set $\{1, 3\}$, $T.s$ and 1 **in** T are **true**.

To illustrate, suppose that the user can enter the 'hours worked' in any of the rows of the item *pay_tab* defined above. Prior to entering the information, he must indicate which row he wishes to act on by pointing to it with the light pen. This can be accomplished by adding the behaviour rule:

let *pay_tab.current_index* **be** *pay_tab*

which specifies that the value of the table item (the selected row) is to be assigned to the variable *pay_tab.current_index*.

Alternatively, we could define key number 1 as the 'next key', so that pressing key

1 would compute the pay for the current row and place the cursor at the next row. This can be programmed as follows:

```
var next_key: attention (KEY1);
    .
    .
    .
enter p1 if next_key.s;
    .
    .
    .
procedure p1;
begin pay_tab.current_row.pay :=
        pay_tab.current_row.hrs *rate;
      pay_tab.current_index :=
        pay_tab.current_index + 1
end
```

More flexibility may be needed to manipulate rows of a table item. For example, the following built-in procedures would be helpful:

nrows(T)	gives the number of rows defined so far;
delete(T,i)	deletes row *i* from the table;
insert(T,i)	inserts a row (of undefined values) after row *i*

Moreover, in order to increase the usefulness of table items, the language should provide a mechanism for associating external files with a table item, and it should provide operators for transferring data. We explore these ideas briefly in the next section.

A.2 Associating a file with a table item

We are particularly interested in sequential files of type *record*. We call these *structured sequential files* and define them as follows:

‹*structured sequential file*› ::= **file of** ‹*record type*›

Exactly how the components are allocated in external storage is implementation dependent.

By specifying the attribute **file** (input or output) in the declaration of a table item, the programmer establishes an association between the table item *T* and records of the specified file. In this case, we say that the table item is *bound* to the file.

What we wish to accomplish is, in fact, a generalization of the binding of files to key-in or display items, which was discussed earlier. In this case, a table item *T* bound to a file *f* would be regarded as a work area into which one could read records from *f* (if *f* is an input file) or write records to *f* (if *f* is an output file). Superimposed on this work area is a window through which the user can view the area. The size of this window, say w, is specified in the row specification part of the declaration of T, and represents the number of rows that the user sees. Let p be the current number of rows and s the size of the table (maximum number of rows). The programmer can manipulate values in rows $T[1]$, $T[2]$, . . ., $T[p]$, while the user has access only to w or p rows, whichever is smaller.

The implementation may provide facilities for scrolling, for reading (writing) records from (to) a file, and for associating the file information with the table item. The operators for reading and writing would be generalizations of the Pascal operators *get(f)* and *put(f)*. We omit the details and refer the reader to Lafuente (1977) for more information.

APPENDIX B SYNTAX

We present here a summary of our syntactic extensions to Pascal:

‹frame definition part› ::= *‹frame definition›*
  {; *‹frame definition›*};
‹frame definition› ::= **frame** *‹id›*: *‹frame body›* **endframe**
‹frame body› ::= *‹label declaration part›*
  ‹constant definition part›
  ‹type definition part›
  ‹variable declaration part›
  ‹item inclusion part›
  ‹behaviour rules›
  ‹procedure declaration part›
‹item type› ::= *‹item kind›* [*‹type›* [**at** (*‹row›*, *‹col›*)]]
  ‹attribute specification› | *‹table item type›*
‹item kind› ::= **display** | **key-in** | **menu** | **attention**
‹attribute specification› ::= [*‹text specification›*]
  {*‹item attribute›*}
‹text specification› ::= **text** *‹string›* [**at** (*‹row›*, *‹col›*)]
  {, *‹string›* [**at** (*‹row›*, *‹col›*)]}
‹type› ::= ‹Pascal *type›* | *‹subrange set›* | *‹value set›*
‹Pascal *type›* ::= a Pascal standard type, scalar type or set type
‹subrange set› ::= *‹constant›* .. *‹constant›*
  {, *‹constant›* .. *‹constant›*}
‹value set› ::= (*‹constant›* {, *‹constant›*})
‹table item type› ::= **table** (*‹size›*)
  ‹attribute specification›
  ‹column specification part›
  ‹row specification part›
‹column specification part› ::= **columns** {*‹id›*:*‹item type›*;}
  [*‹item inclusion part›*] **end**
‹row specification part› ::= **rows** (*‹size›*) [*‹row kind›*]
‹row kind› ::= **menu** | **attention**

‹subframe type› ::= **subframe** {*‹id›*: *‹type1›*;} [*‹item inclusion part›*] [*‹behaviour rules›*] **end**

‹type1› ::= *‹subframe type›* | *‹item type›*

‹item inclusion part› ::= **contains** *‹item specification›* {; *‹item specification›*}

‹item specification› ::= *‹id›* {, *‹id›* } {*‹frame attribute›*}

‹frame attribute› ::= **at** (*‹row›*, *‹col›*) | **intensity high** | **format** *‹format specification›* | **format msg** *‹string›*

‹behaviour rules› ::= **rules** *‹rule›* {; *‹rule›*} **end**

‹rule› ::= *‹requirement rule›* | *‹binding rule›* | *‹terminate rule›* | *‹enter rule›*

‹requirement rule› ::= **require** *‹condition1›* [**if** *‹condition›*]

‹condition1› ::= *‹condition›* | *‹name part›*

‹name part› ::= *‹item name›* {, *‹item name›*}

‹binding rule› ::= **let** *‹variable›* **be** *‹expression›* [**if** *‹condition›*]

‹terminate rule› ::= **terminate if** *‹condition›*

‹enter rule› ::= **enter** *‹id›* **if** *‹condition›*

‹condition› ::= *‹basic condition›* | *‹condition›* **cor** *‹basic condition›*

‹basic condition› ::= *‹logical expr›* | *‹basic condition›* **cand** *‹logical expr›*

‹logical expr› ::= a logical expression | (*‹condition›*) | ENT_KEY

4. User Interface Specification for Separability

Adaptive Man–Computer Interfaces

Ernest A. Edmonds

Reprinted in part from: *Computing Skills and the User Interface*. Editors: M. J. Coombs and J. L. Alty. Academic Press, pp 389–426, 1981.

This paper consolidates earlier work and combines a state diagram notation, in the style of Denert, with the use of grammars to allow for the recognition of complex input objects, such as arithmetic expressions, and subsequent transformations into appropriate forms for passing to the functional code.

Adaptive Man–Computer Interfaces

E. A. EDMONDS

1 INTRODUCTION

The value of considering the man–computer interface as a separate part of an applications computer system has been discussed. Maher and Bell (1977) in fact proposed that the interface should be seen as a virtual machine. The dialogue specification methods discussed below all assume some such view.

The meaning of the term 'dialogue' is intended to include a broad range of types of exchange between users and computers. Whilst these exchanges might well be in terms of character strings (using a keyboard and visual display, for example), they could equally well include the depression of functional buttons, the selection of graphical components from a displayed image or the generation of a diagram. For the purposes of the following exposition it is adequate to consider only character strings as inputs or outputs. The encoding or decoding of such strings, to deal with the broad range of possible media, introduces an extra stage in the process. This is not particularly difficult to deal with in principle at the design level, although it does introduce an extra practical problem.

2 DIALOGUE SPECIFICATION

Parnas (1969) proposed the use of *state diagrams* in order to clarify the specification of dialogues. Figure 1 illustrates this approach. On entering a given node an associated output is generated. The following input is then matched with one of the strings referenced on the arcs leading out of that node and that arc is then followed, leading to the next node. If no match is found the output is repeated and the resulting new input considered as before. *Tasks* are functions to be performed by the computer that do not form part of the interface, e.g. the searching of a database or a calculation. Figure 2 shows an example of a dialogue conforming to the state graph shown in Fig. 1. It is important to notice that the convention of returning to

THE SEPARABLE USER INTERFACE
ISBN 0-12-232150-2

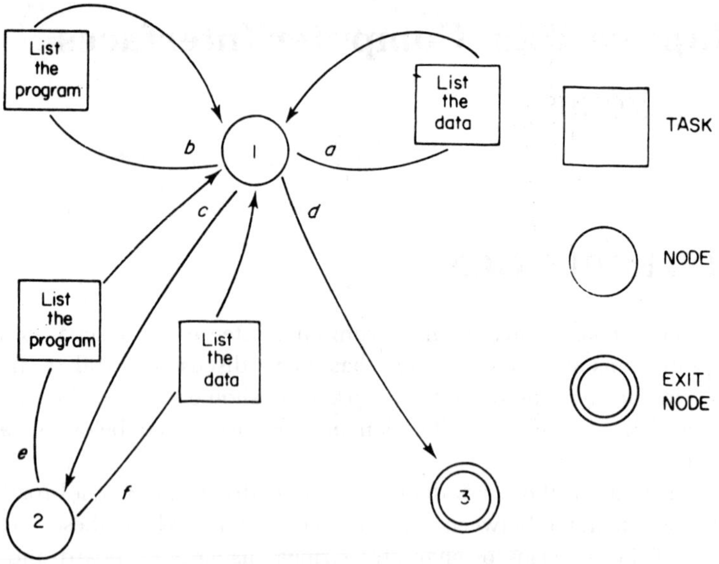

1: ?
2: PROGRAM OR DATA
?
3: BYE

a: LIST DATA
b: LIST PROGRAM
c: LIST
d: EXIT
e: PROGRAM
f: DATA

Figure 1. A state diagram representing a dialogue system.

```
? LIST PROGRAM
  GET IT
  PRINT IT
  STOP
? LIST
PROGRAM OR DATA
? DATA
  abc
  xyz
? EXIT
BYE
```

Figure 2. A dialogue generated using the specification of Fig. 1.

a node when no match is found can to some extent be circumvented by introducing special arcs associated with certain input errors, as in Fig. 3.

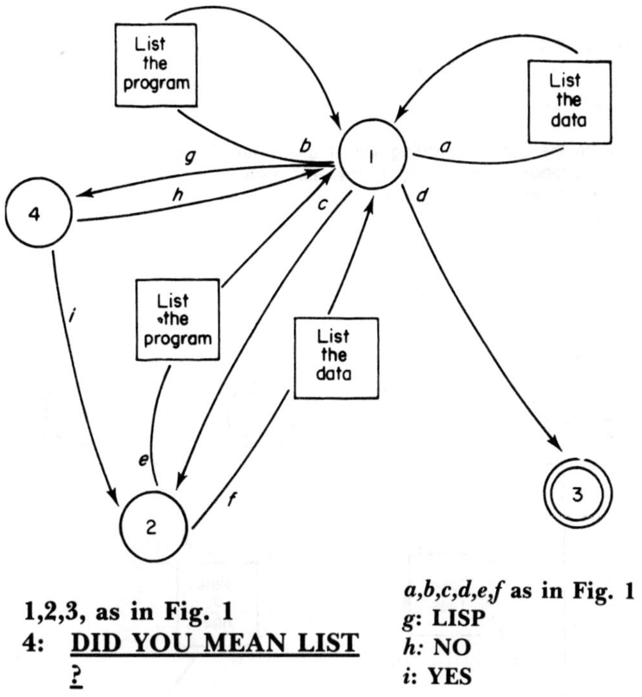

Figure 3. An elaborated version of Fig. 1.

If one considers the set of all possible dialogues that could occur whilst conforming to a given state diagram, then the set must be regular (see for example, Arbib, 1969). Conway (1963) extended the idea of a state diagram in a way that enables a broader set to be represented. Similarly, Denert (1977) used an enhanced type of state diagram in a system for specifying dialogues. Using Denert's approach we introduce complex nodes which are, in effect, calls to other state diagrams.

Any of the state diagrams in a specification may contain complex nodes so that, for example, recursive calls are possible. Figure 4 shows a simple example of state diagrams containing complex nodes. The process starts with the initial state (i.e. 1) of G1. Denert points out that the use of complex nodes leads naturally to a top-down design method, and so might be valuable even when the extra power that they make available is not required.

Edmonds and Guest (1978) devised a notation for representing translation specifically intended for use in man–computer interfaces. The source language is specified in an extended BNF-like, or context-free, style

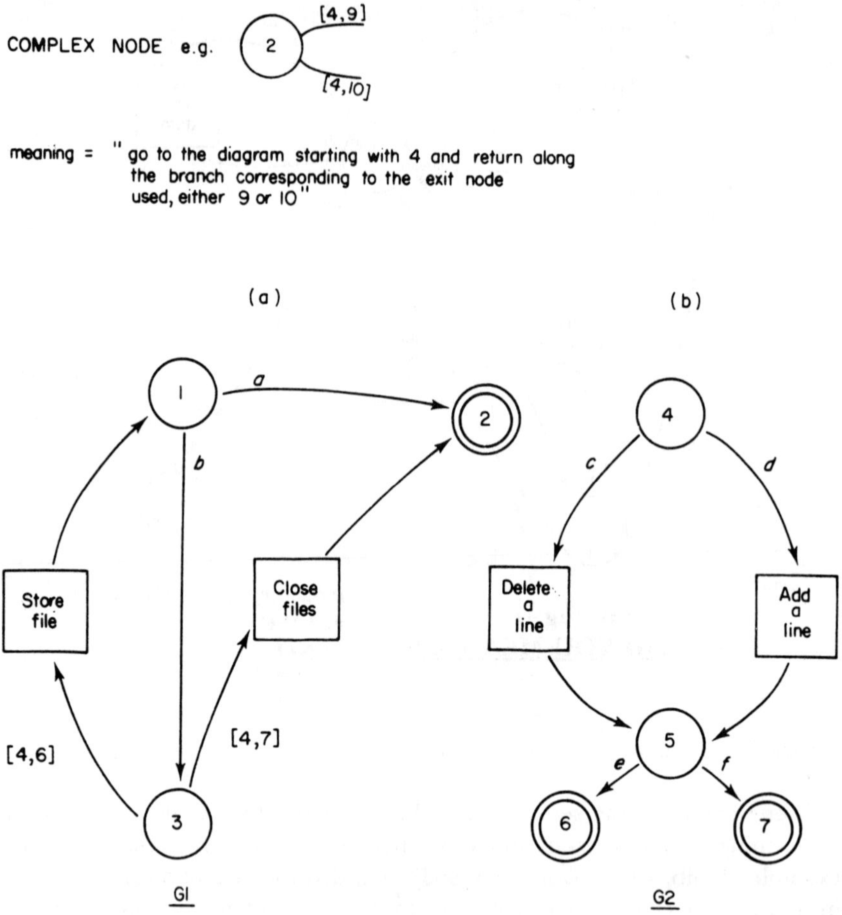

(a) 1: <u>?</u>   *a*: EXIT
2: <u>BYE</u>   *b*: EDIT

(b) 4: <u>ADD OR DELETE</u>   *c*: DELETE
<u>?</u>   *d*: ADD
5: <u>STORE OR CLOSE</u>   *e*: STORE
<u>?</u>   *f*: CLOSE

Figure 4. A state diagram representation using a complex node.

(see for example, Foster, 1970). The significant feature that extends the range beyond context-free languages is an **if–then–else** construct. The statement **if** *A* **then** *B* **else** *C* can be roughly interpreted as meaning '**if** the input string is of the form A **then** try to match it to form B **else** try to match it to form C'. It is thus possible, whilst analysing a string, to take the context of an element partly into account. This can be termed the introduction of 'following context'. Figure 5 illustrates the use of the notation in its simplest form. It is possible to embed instructions relating to the generation of output in the definition. An example of the very simplest variety of output specification is given in Fig. 6. This notation is discussed in greater detail in Section 3.

I INPUT = 'SAY PROGRAM'/'SAY DATA'/'SAY'/'EXIT'/.

Figure 5. An example of input specification ('/' = 'or').

```
I INPUT = 'SAY PROGRAM' ['PROGRAM'] */ -
          'SAY DATA' ['DATA'] /'SAY' ['WHAT?'] / -
          'EXIT'/.
```

Figure 6. An elaboration of Fig. 5 to include output specifications.
*That is, if the input is 'SAY PROGRAM' then the output is to be 'PROGRAM'.

By combining the state graph notation and the translation notation of Edmonds and Guest (1978) a powerful and flexible language can be formed. This language and its use are discussed in detail in Edmonds and Guest (1979). In Fig. 7 the state graph is as in Fig. 1 except that the labels on the arcs now correspond to the specifications indicated, rather than to simple character strings. We will see that instead of a single string causing a given arc to be traversed, any one of a possibly infinite set of strings can now cause that action. It follows that, with the **not** construct available in the language, it becomes possible to associate a set of unrecognized strings with a given arc, e.g. any string starting with a character other than 'Y' or 'N', as illustrated in Fig. 8. It thus becomes possible to include an appropriate message to be output in such cases. The system allows the use of complex nodes in exactly the same way as described above.

A particular feature of this design specification method is the possibility of embedding output instructions in the definition of the source strings for a given arc. This feature can be used to incorporate actions in the definitions of source strings, the output being treated as output from the man–computer interface to the main computer system, i.e. as a task. The specification of output directed to the user can then be generally confined to that associated with the entering of nodes. A simple example using this idea is given in Section 3.

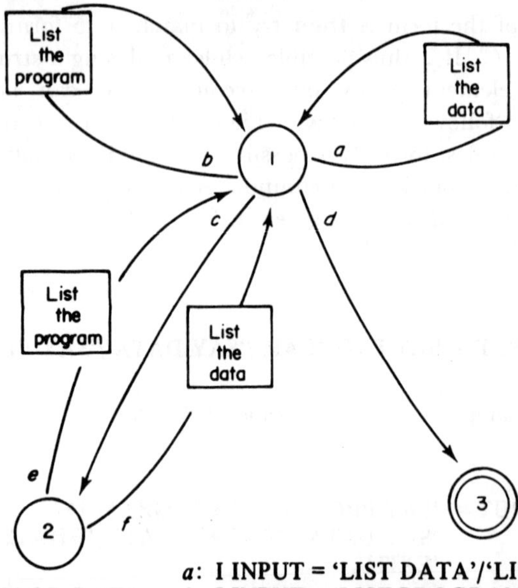

1: ?
2: PROGRAM OR DATA
?
3: BYE

a: I INPUT = 'LIST DATA'/'LIST THE DATA'/.
b: I INPUT = 'LIST PROGRAM'/'LIST THE PROGRAM'/.
c: I INPUT = 'LIST'/.
d: I INPUT = 'EXIT'/'BYE'/'GOODBYE'/.
e: I INPUT = 'PROG'/'PROGRAM'/.
f: I INPUT = 'DATA'/.

Figure 7. A representation of a dialogue system using the method of Edmonds and Guest.

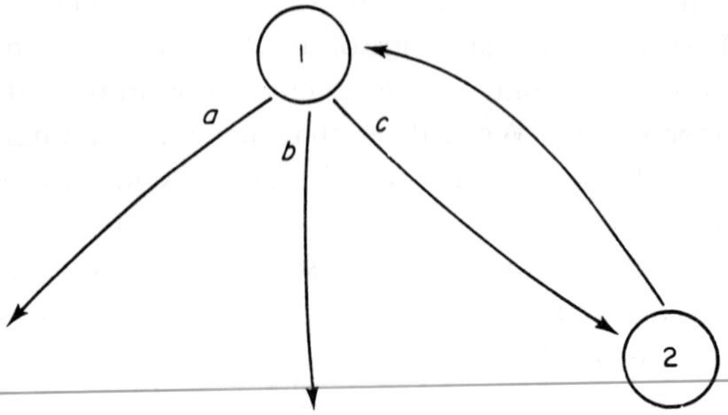

1: DO YOU WANT A CAKE?
2: I DON'T UNDERSTAND.
LET'S TRY AGAIN

***a*: 'Y'/.**
***b*: 'N'/.**
***c*: ¬ 'Y'/¬'N'/.**

N.B. *a*, *b*, *c* are tested in that order ("¬" = "not").

Figure 8. An example of the use of **not** in the input specification. Note that the transition from 2 to 1 is performed on a null input, i.e. it is unconditional and takes place without a request for input from the user.

BNF: <INPUT>::= ADD/DELETE/REPEAT

Displayed menu: ADD
DELETE
REPEAT

Figure 9. An example of language and menu equivalence.

Hall (1977) has pointed out that it is often desirable to arrange for an interface to be attractive to users of varying levels of competence. In particular, he shows how BNF definitions of language structures can lead naturally to the definition of an equivalent sequence of menu lists. Figure 9 illustrates this equivalence. Hall gives four rules for devising menus from BNF forms and vice versa. This approach could be used with the method of Edmonds and Guest described above. Work on the clarification of the relationship between the two methods is proceeding.

Alternative formulations of somewhat similar ideas can be found in Anderson and Sibley (1972) and Losbichler and Mühlbacker (1974). In the latter case certain editing commands to be used for modifying the interface design are incorporated into the formalization. The degree of the need for this depends on the way in which the design method is eventually used in implementation and is discussed below.

3 AN IMPLEMENTATION TOOL

Edmonds and Guest (1979) have constructed an implementation tool that incorporates many of the features of SYNICS and corresponds to the design specification method described above.

Figure 10 shows the state diagram of a simple dialogue. Figure 11 shows the description of the dialogue required by the implementation program. The output to be generated on entering a node is described on the lines following the node number, given in the 'AT NODE' line. This is followed by a list of the node numbers to which control may pass, in the form of 'TO *n* IF', each followed by a description in a BNF-type notation on the input that would cause that branch. The square brackets contain descriptions of messages to be sent to the main system for action before the next node in the interface is entered, as described above. Figure 12 shows a sample dialogue. Although the example shows only a very simple dialogue, the system will accept descriptions of input forms (and associated output) of a class larger than those of context-free languages.

The notation used to describe acceptable input for a given node is based upon that of BNF or context-free notation, and uses the concept of a syntax

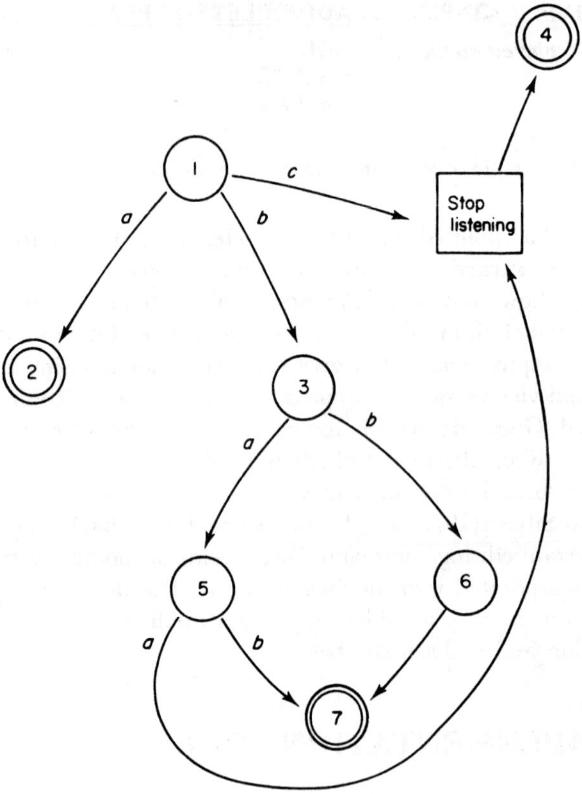

1: ARE YOU WELL
?
2: GOOD. GOODBYE
3: IS IT SERIOUS
?
4: I MUST RUSH. GOODBYE
5. IS IT FATAL
?
6. GOOD
7. LIFE COULD BE WORSE, GOODBYE

a: 'Y'/.
b: 'N'/.
c: ¬'Y'/¬'N'/.

Figure 10. The representation of a dialogue system. Note that the transition from 6 to 7 is unconditional, as illustrated in Fig. 8.

tree (see for example, Foster, 1970). BNF notation specifies how to *generate* strings in a language, and if treated in certain ways can double as a way of

```
AT NODE 1
      ARE YOU WELL
      ?
   TO 2 IF
         'Y'/.
   TO 3 IF
         'N'/.
   TO 4 IF
      ¬'Y' ['STOP LISTENING']/¬ 'N' ['STOP LISTENING']/.
AT NODE 2
      GOOD. GOODBYE
   EXIT
AT NODE 3
      IS IT SERIOUS
      ?
   TO 5 IF
         'Y'/.
   TO 6 IF
         'N'/.
AT NODE 4
      I MUST RUSH. GOODBYE.
   EXIT
AT NODE 5
      IS IT FATAL
      ?
   TO 4 IF
         'Y'/.
   TO 7 IF
         'N'/.
AT NODE 6
      GOOD
   TO 7
AT NODE 7
      LIFE COULD BE WORSE.
      GOODBYE.
   EXIT
```

Figure 11. Figure 10 specified in a form suitable for input to the programs of Edmonds and Guest.

specifying how strings in the language might be *recognized.* In a translator-writing system it is necessary to specify only how to recognize the source language. It thus becomes possible to extend the notation to include commands that direct the recognition process even though they would not

ARE YOU WELL
? NO
IS IT SERIOUS
? YES
IS IT FATAL
? YES
I MUST RUSH. GOODBYE.

Figure 12. A dialogue generating the specification of Fig. 10.

be readily meaningful with respect to the generation of strings. In our system, as noted above, an **if–then–else** command is included. Semantic rules, i.e. the specification of output to be generated, may be inserted into the specification using a language similar to that of Foxley and King (1968).

An important aspect of the system is the possibility of using clearly defined errors to guide the dialogue. As before, a technique that is an extension of that of Burgess (1972) is used. James (1975) has proposed a similar approach in a more limited context.

4 SOURCE-LANGUAGE SPECIFICATION

BNF-like languages have two kinds of object, terminals and nonterminals, which yield *terminal nodes* and *nonterminal nodes* in syntax trees. In BNF the nonterminals are distinguished by being enclosed thus: ‹ ›. For example, in:

‹*term*› ::= ‹*variable*› * ‹*term*›

‹*term*› and ‹*variable*› are nonterminals and the asterisk is a terminal. This rule states that the component shown in Fig. 13 may occur in a syntax tree (see also Fig. 14).

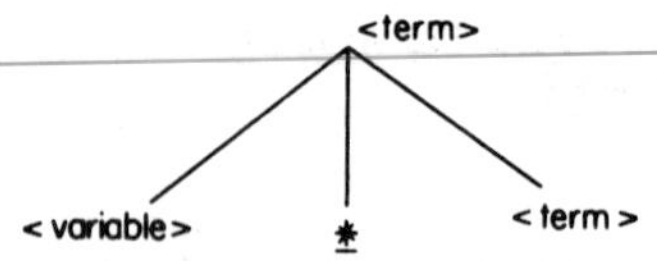

Figure 13. A component of a syntax tree corresponding to a BNF alternative.

In our notation the *terminals* are distinguished by enclosing them in single quotes. The names of *nonterminals* are restricted to a single letter or a single letter followed by up to four digits.

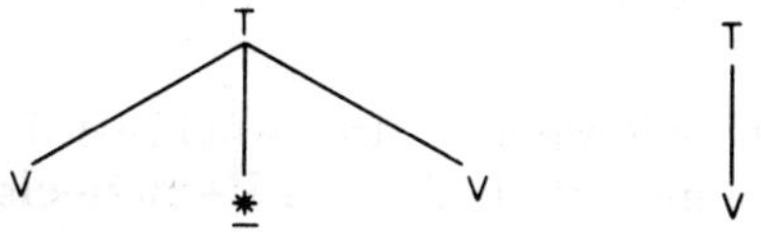

Figure 14. Syntax-tree components corresponding to rules in the notation of Edmonds and Guest.

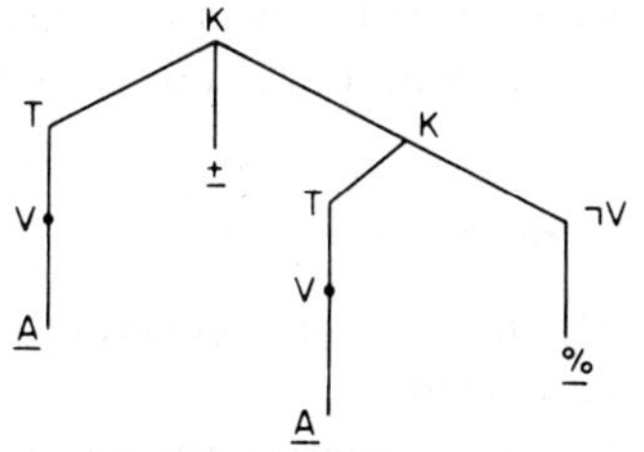

Figure 15. A subtree including a **not** operator.

The BNF rule given above could then be expressed (apart from termination, see below) by

T = V '*' T

Other examples of terminal strings are '3', '**' and of nonterminals T3, K1234. As in BNF, it is possible to specify *alternatives* in one statement, e.g.

T = V '*' T / V /.

which simply states that both the components shown in Fig. 14 are allowed. All statements must terminate with '/.', as shown.

If we also had the rule

V = 'A' / 'B' / 'C' /.

an example of a legal 'T' would be

A * B * C

In order to make the language more readable, *comment* is allowed to immediately precede the equals sign, e.g.

T TERM = V '*' T / V /.
V VARIABLE = 'A' / 'B' / 'C' /.

The **not** symbol '¬' may also be employed, but must apply only to a terminal or to a nonterminal which can only generate one terminal. Any terminal apart from the set specified is then taken to be acceptable. Thus if the rule

K = T‘+’K / T¬V /.

is introduced, then one allowable subtree would be that in Fig. 15.

In the place of a simple alternative, an **if–then–else** statement can be used. The statement may be of the form:

if alternative 1 **then** alternative 2 /
    else alternative 3 /.

with the meaning that, if alternative 1 is matched then alternative 2 is used for the analysis and transformation, and if not then alternative 3 is used.

Thus in, for example,

C = **if** ‘AAB’ **then** ‘A’ / **else** ‘AA’ /.

(1) AAB would match the first ‘A’ and generate the subtree in Fig. 16, leaving AB still to be incorporated;
(2) AA would match ‘AA’ and generate the subtree in Fig. 17;
(3) AB would fail.

Figure 16. The result of a parse using an **if** operator.

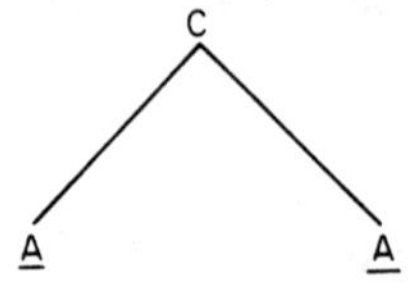

Figure 17. A second example using the same **if** rule as used in Fig. 16.

Figure 18. The result of a parse using a rule in which the alternatives were in an inappropriate order.

The first rule listed at a node is taken to refer to the root, i.e. the nonterminal left of the equals sign in the first rule will be used as the root of all trees built.

Two *restrictions* are placed upon the rules that may be provided:

(1) left recursion is not allowed (see for example, Foster, 1970), e.g.

T = T '*' V /.

would be illegal, as would

T = S '*' V /.
S = V / T /.

(2) alternatives should be presented so that the first match is the correct one, e.g.

T = V / V '*' T /.

would cause, when considering A*B, the subtree in Fig. 18 to be built, and the second alternative (the correct one) would never be tried.

In order to speed up the recognition process it is advisable to *place alternatives with common first parts next to one another*, e.g. in

T = V '*' T / V /.

if, in the first alternative, the V is matched but the '*' is not found then the second alternative will be accepted without further searching and, on the other hand, if the first alternative fails because the V cannot be matched then the second alternative will be failed without further consideration.

5 OUTPUT SPECIFICATION

Corresponding to any specified alternative an output rule may be provided. Its function is to indicate the action that must be taken when a given alternative occurs in a syntax tree that has been constructed. Following analysis the tree is scanned under the direction of the output rules and the object strings are generated.

The object string is passed to the main program for its attention. Characters are inserted in it from left to right as the rules are obeyed. An output rule consists of a string of output commands. There are three commands that can generate output directly:

(1) '$n_1\ n_2\ \ldots\ n_m$' outputs the strings of literal characters $n_1\ n_2\ \ldots\ n_m$ into the next m locations, e.g. '+', 'WORD'.

(2) "ddd . . . d" outputs the single integer terminal dd . . . d into the next location, e.g. "7", "54". Integer and character terminals may be mixed.

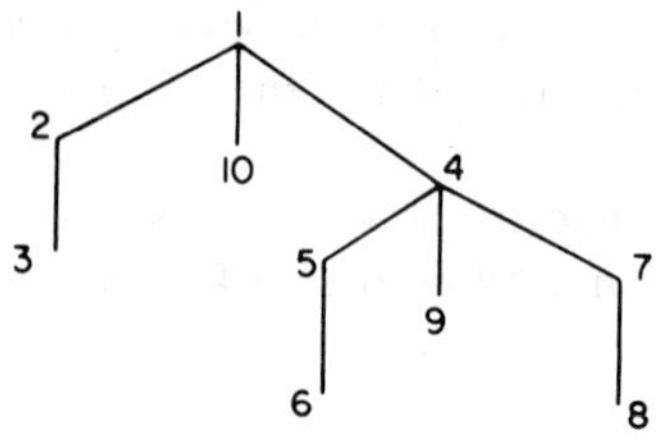

Figure 19. The order in which the nodes of Fig. 15 are visited during the generation of output.

(3) L(n) outputs the nth node in the syntax alternative, *counting from the right*, if it is a terminal, or the string of terminals that it generates if it is a nonterminal, e.g. L(2) applied to V*T would cause * to be output and L(1) applied to the uppermost K in Fig. 15 would cause A+A% to be output. L(n_1,n_2, . . . ,n_m) is equivalent to L(n_1)L(n_2), . . . ,L(n_m).

A fourth command directs the order in which the rules are obeyed, by specifying the way in which the syntax tree should be scanned:

(4) C_n causes the rule to be obeyed that corresponds to the alternative used to generate the next level of the tree from the nonterminal, that is the nth node in the syntax alternative *counting from the right*, e.g. C3 applied to the uppermost K in Fig. 15 would cause SYNICS to obey the semantic rule associated with the alternative T = V.

Output rules are enclosed thus: '[ ]' and placed directly after the syntax alternative to which they apply, e.g.

T TERM = V '*' T [C3C1 '*'] / V [C1] /.
V VARIABLE = 'A' ['1'] / 'B' ['2'] / 'C' ['3'] /.

would cause an input of A*B*C to generate 123**. The order in which the nodes are visited to do this is shown in Fig. 19. The output is generated at nodes 3, 6, 8, 9, 10, in that order.

REFERENCES

Anderson, R. H. and Sibley, W. L. (1972). A new approach to programming man–machine interfaces. *Report No. 876*. Advanced Research projects Agency, Santa Monica.

Arbib, M. A. (1969). *Theories of Abstract Automata*. New Jersey. Prentice-Hall.

Burgess, C. J. (1972). Compile-time error diagnostics in syntax-directed computers. *Computer J.*, 15, 302–307.

Conway, M. E. (1963). Design of a separate transition-diagram compiler. *Communications of the ACM*, 6, 396–408.

Denert, E. (1977). Specification and design of dialogue systems with state diagrams.

Proceedings of the International Computing Symposium. Liege.
Edmonds, E. A. and Guest, S. P. (1978). SYNICS — a FORTRAN subroutine package for translation, *Report No. 6*, Man–Computer Interaction Research Group, Leicester Polytechnic.
Edmonds, E. A. and Guest, S. P. (1979). A man–computer dialogue system. *Report No. 27*, Man–Computer Interaction Research Group, Leicester Polytechnic.
Foster, J. M. (1970). *Automatic Syntactic Analysis*. London: Macdonald.
Foxley, E. and King, P. (1968). A meta-semantic language for use with a top-down syntax analyser. *Proceedings of the IFIP Conference*, 366–372.
Hall, P. A. V. (1977). Man–computer dialogues for many levels of competence. Internal Report, Scicon, London.
James, E. B. (1975). Adaptive analysis: a model for perception. *Report No. 74/45*, Dept. of Computing and Control, Imperial College, London.
Losbichler, B. and Mühlbacher, J. (1974). Entwicklung eines Mensch-Maschine-Kommunikationssystems durch top-down Entwurf. *Angewandte Informatik*, 16, 453–463.
Maher, P. K. C. and Bell, H. V. (1977). The man–machine interface — a new approach. *Proceedings of the International Conference on Displays for Man/Machine Systems*, Lancaster, 122–125.
Parnas, D. L. (1969). On the use of transition diagrams in the design of a user interface for an interactive computer system. *Proceedings of the National ACM Conference*, 379–385.

[illegible]

Modelling User Interface–Application Interactions

William D. Hurley and John L. Sibert

Reprinted from: *IEEE Software*, pp 71–77, 1989

This paper introduces an explicit method for modelling the functional code that can be applied to the problem of defining the user interface/application boundary precisely. It represents, therefore, a very detailed look at the mechanisms for separability. An object-oriented approach is followed in which a number of extensions are proposed in order to meet the particular needs identified. The method is illustrated in the example of a spreadsheet.

Modelling User Interface–Application Interactions

W. D. HURLEY AND J. L. SIBERT

George Washington University

1 INTRODUCTION

Two reasons to separate user interface software from other software are to enhance reuse and to provide high-quality user interfaces. To promote reuse, it is necessary to minimize how much the user interface knows about application internals. On the other hand, researchers generally agree that high-quality user interfaces do not hide the application semantics from the user (Rhyne *et al.*, 1987). This implies that the user interface must have sufficient access to application internals to keep the user aware of application semantics (the application objects and operations).

Unfortunately, these motivations often conflict. This conflict is particularly important when the user interface — not the application — controls the human–computer dialogue, as is true in most user-interface management systems (UIMSs) (UIMSs may be defined in several ways; we define a UIMS as a system that has run-time control over the interactive dialogue).

The UIMS developer must create a logical separation between the application and the user interface. Separation lets specialists develop the user interface and the application independently, promotes interface consistency across applications, and allows application functions to be added or combined in new ways.

The earliest approach to separation was to maintain a strict division of responsibility between the user interface and the application: the application did the work and the user interface communicated with the user. However, the user interface must often assume some responsibility for functions that involve application semantics. For example, a good user interface protects the user from invoking an operation that cannot be executed successfully. On the other hand, if the user interface has too much

THE SEPARABLE USER INTERFACE
ISBN 0–12–232150–2

knowledge of the application, the distinction between user interface and application blurs.

Clearly, a good user interface has some knowledge of application semantics. The questions concern how much knowledge is necessary, and how it should be captured. We answer these questions with a methodology to model the requirements for interaction between the user interface and application. The methodology addresses the UI–application interface, the component that handles the interaction between the user interface (UI) and the application.

The model is sufficiently robust to model both the information flow through the UI–application interface and the knowledge of the application domain that it requires. The descriptive power of the model lets us determine if an interface component can be reused. The model itself becomes a template for implementing the UI–application interface.

2 INTERACTION MODEL

The interaction between a user and the application that occurs at the user interface drives the requirements for the UI–application interface. We define the semantics of this interaction to include knowledge about actions and their effects, and about the associated communication elements. Our model of these interaction semantics is object-centred and is influenced strongly by Anson's device model (Anson, 1980, 1982).

An object-centred model describes a domain in terms of two primitives: objects and operations performed by these objects. Objects have a structure, which is described by state variables. Our object-centred model also uses classes to organize the information about objects and operations. An object's class determines its state variables and its operations.

To capture our view of interaction semantics efficiently, we extended the object-centred model in several ways. A detailed description of the extensions is beyond the scope of this article, but has been presented elsewhere (Hurley, 1989). Briefly, the extended model must:

separate explicitly communication from action;

distinguish explicitly between state variables that describe internal structure and those that establish relationships with other objects;

define mutually independent primitives, so that the model can be modified easily;

support implementation-independent descriptions;

describe clearly patterns of interaction;

support descriptions of different kinds of relationships among and between objects;

support detailed descriptions of the properties of objects, operations and communication elements;

support the addition of arbitrary properties; and

distinguish explicitly intrinsic properties from properties that describe only the impact of interaction semantics on the UI–application interface.

Our model for satisfying these requirements contains five modelling primitives: *conceptual relation*, *entity*, *action*, *state* and *event*. Hence the name CREASE.

2.1 Primitives

In the CREASE model, an entity describes an object, an action describes an operation, and a state describes an object's structure in terms of its properties. An entity has a state and performs actions. The CREASE primitives that extend the object-centred model are as follows.

(1) A *conceptual relation* describes a property that establishes a relationship to other entities, such as an association, a connection or a link.

(2) An *action* is a response to an event; the action may receive data from the event that triggers it. Both the state of the entity performing an action and the triggering event's data influence an action's results. An action typically alters the state of the performing entity, generates other events, returns something and terminates.

(3) An *event* is a discrete unit of communication between two entities. An event is generated by an action performed by the entity sending the event, may trigger an action performed by the entity receiving the event, and may provide data.

Figure 1 illustrates how these primitives are used to model a data type, String, and two operations, CopyFromFor, which copies a designated portion of a string, and AllAfterFirst, which copies all but the first character in a string.

String is an entity with three state characteristics: *length*, *maximum length* and *value*. Characteristics are intrinsic to entities. If the entity is a string, then it must have a length, a maximum length and a value. Whether the value of maximum length is the same for all strings depends on the implementation. The characteristics of length and maximum length describe internal structure: the characteristic value describes a relationship between a string and a character array.

The value characteristic is one example of how to establish a conceptual relation. We could also have an entity contain other entities; an entity composed of interacting parts; and roles that relate entities to actions, such as agent, instrument or target, and influence relationships such as the binding between a graphical representation and the value of a characteristic.

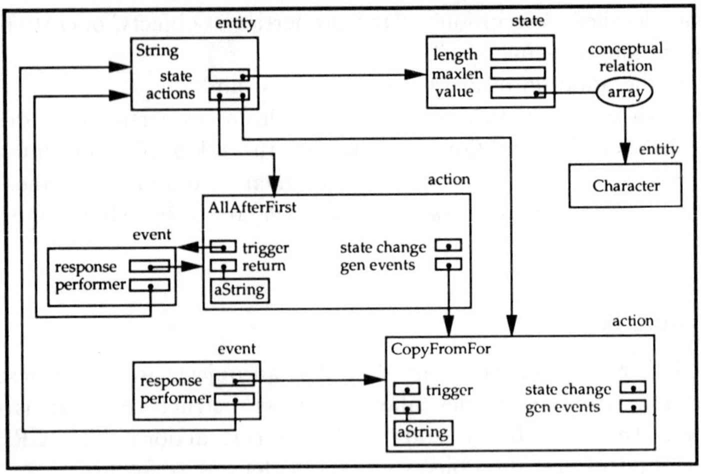

Figure 1. A model of String and some of its actions.

In Fig. 1, the actions AllAfterFirst and CopyFromFor are modelled separately from their associated events. In addition, the binding between actions and events is represented as part of the static structure of events and actions. The binding between AllAfterFirst and its triggering event is represented by the properties *trigger* and *response*, and the binding between AllAfterFirst and the events it generates is represented by the property *gen events*.

Representing actions and events in this way has two advantages. First, it gives greater clarity to the interaction patterns — it is clear that invoking AllAfterFirst results in a generated event that triggers CopyFromFor. Second, it is implementation independent.

In addition to describing interaction patterns clearly, the CREASE model distinguishes the direct effects of an action from side effects and supports modelling of arbitrary levels of indirection.

An action's direct effects are the final state of the performing entity, the events generated by the action, and the return. In Fig. 1, the direct effects of AllAfterFirst are no change to the performing entity's state, one generated event sent to the performer String to trigger CopyFromFor, and the return of a new string.

An action's side effects are determined by tracing its generated events and include the state changes and generated events produced by each directly or indirectly triggered action. Figure 1 shows that AllAfterFirst has no side effects because CopyFromFor produces no state changes and no generated events.

Mutual independence among modelling primitives makes it easy to revise individual primitives without affecting others. Suppose that it is decided to redefine the modelling primitive state to include both characteristics and other properties. This revision would also require revisions to all the existing state constructs, such as String's state description in Fig. 1, but would have no effect on String itself. Mutual independence also means that the binding between actions and their triggering events is external to the entities.

The CREASE model supports descriptions that are implementation independent. This means, for example, that the binding between actions and events assumes no specific run-time mechanism. It also means that there is no fixed correspondence between entities and actions. An action may apply uniquely to one type or class of entity, as in Smalltalk-80, or an action may be shared by several entity types.

2.2 Modelling system

The modelling system defines a formal methodology for generating descriptions of applications based on the CREASE model. The modelling system supports descriptions that reflect a logical view (logical views are independent of user interface and application), expose the impact of both the user interface and the application on the UI–application interface design (while explicitly separating each impact), and facilitate testing for completeness and consistency.

The modelling system has two fundamental modelling constructs: type and property. In general, a type describes the properties a collection of things share. In our system, a type is a logical description of structure and behaviour. Types may be specialized incrementally or composed to create new types. For example, the String in Fig. 1 could be specialized by adding a font, a font size and a font style to produce the type Text. In general, a property is any trait or quality that belongs naturally to or is peculiar to a thing. A thing is described completely by its properties' values at a given moment. In our system, all constructs based on the CREASE primitives consist entirely of properties.

The modelling system allows the definition of different kinds of properties and the association of arbitrary kinds of information with each property. Each kind of information is called a facet. Typical facets of a property include its name, its value and constraints on its value, such as type of value and range of value. The relationship between facets, properties and CREASE primitives is similar to the relationship between facets, slots and frames in a knowledge-representation language. In fact, an advantage of our approach is that the modelling constructs can be represented by a simple frame system.

The modelling system organizes types into a type structure. For example, the Text we created is a subtype of String, appearing below String in the type structure. Each type may have only one immediate supertype (or parent) and is distinguished from all other types by its properties. The type structure is formalized by rules that govern the inheritance of each kind of property from a type to its subtypes and by rules that define how each kind of property may differ between types. Because these rules are strictly enforced, our type relations support inferences about the properties of types based on their position in the type structure.

This formalized type structure differs from the class structures in most frame-based systems and object-oriented programming systems. In these systems, inherited properties may be cancelled or overridden, so that every type or class must be treated as a primitive (Brachman, 1985).

Our type structure has a single root, type, with two immediate subtypes: conceptual relation and concept. Concept has four immediate subtypes, i.e. the modelling primitives entity, action, state and event. Subtypes of conceptual relation support a variety of relationships among entities, as already described.

The type structure represents a logical evolution of types, for example, the evolution from bit-mapped images in paint programs, to object-based images in drawing programs, to the latest generation of images that can be treated both as objects and as bit-maps. This logical evolution differs from the evolution represented in class hierarchies based on implementation efficiency, such as the class hierarchy in Smalltalk-80.

Our modelling system defines two mechanisms to generate an application description. Tailoring operators produce new types by applying abstraction mechanisms, such as specialization and composition, to existing types. Tailoring rules govern the use of tailoring operators according to the formalization rules. Tailoring rules dictate conditions for applying individual operators, define allowable ways to use operators in combination, and invoke operators automatically under certain conditions.

Each tailoring operator is formally defined for a specific property and abstraction mechanism. Specialization operators create new types in one of three ways: by adding a new property, by adding a new constraint to an existing property, or by restricting an existing constraint. Composition operators create types describing interacting instances that have a mutual existence dependency. When a composite entity is created or destroyed, all the component entities are created or destroyed with it. Association operators create types that describe instances associated by conceptual relations that do not involve existence dependencies. Revision operators make changes and extensions to the CREASE primitives and their subtypes without generating new types.

3 SPREADSHEET EXAMPLE

We have implemented the modelling system as a tool we call the Tailor. The Tailor is implemented in Smalltalk-80 and Humble. The current version includes 107 tailoring operators, 326 tailoring rules and 767 Smalltalk methods (a Smalltalk method is roughly equivalent to a procedure or function definition in a procedural language). Our type structure includes 26 generic entity types, including the modelling primitives.

To illustrate our modelling methodology, we will use the Tailor to model the interaction semantics of a spreadsheet. Because space is limited, we will build only part of the spreadsheet model and describe only two major steps in the modelling process: defining the application's logical model, and defining an application's external boundary.

To start, we assume that the Tailor's knowledge base already contains the five CREASE primitives, basic conceptual relations (such as ordered collection, set and array), and generic entities and actions (such as Integer, Real, Character, and String).

The Tailor provides mechanisms to keep the model consistent and complete, but the model designer decides what to model. We have developed a set of guidelines to help the designer make design decisions. These guidelines are based on our overall goals and assumptions and help us make consistent modelling decisions. They are less formal than the rules built into the Tailor. For example, the goal of maximum separation between the application and the user interface leads to three modelling guidelines:

(1) place entities that the user uses directly to transfer information, such as clipboard or scrapbook buffers, in the user interface;

(2) whenever possible, reduce the information the user interface and application need about each other; and

(3) minimize the amount of data and data structure transfer across the UI–application interface.

Using the modelling primitives in the context of object-centred development leads to additional guidelines, such as:

(4) in general, entities do not know how to manipulate higher-order structures, such as structures that contain them; and

(5) actions are performed by entities that have the knowledge to perform them.

Given the Tailor's existing knowledge base and the modelling guidelines, we are ready to begin building a logical model of interaction semantics for our application domain.

3.1 Logical model

Our first task is to create our spreadsheet's entities and actions by applying tailoring operators to existing entities and actions. For each entity, we specify its characteristics and the actions it performs. For each action, we specify the event that triggers it, the preconditions for successful execution, the resulting state changes, the events generated by it and the data returned.

We ignore application structure and behaviour when they have no effect upon the UI–application interface. In practice, we can model entities and actions in any order, and we may have several incomplete types at any moment. However, to keep things simple we will describe an ordered modelling process: first we define some basic entities of a typical spreadsheet program, next we use the Tailor to model one of them, and then we do the same for the actions.

Our spreadsheet has six basic entities:

(1) *spreadsheet*: a matrix of rows and columns, with groups of cells identifiable by name, and groups of cells linked either to or from other spreadsheets;

(2) *matrix*: an array of rows and an array of columns ordered so that the keys used by a row or column for access to its elements range over the set of keys used by a spreadsheet to access its columns or rows;

(3) *rows*: an array of cells;

(4) *column*: an array of cells;

(5) *cell*: the basic element of a spreadsheet, may contain either an independent value such as a literal string or number, or a formula and a computed value; and

(6) *formula*: an expression consisting of literal strings, numbers, names of cell groups, operators (such as arithmetic operators and string concatenation), functions (such as logical, mathematical and statistical), cell identifiers and formulae.

Figure 2 shows the Tailor in use. The Tailor browser has three scrollable menus across the top, and a text window below. The three menus contain the existing entities, actions and conceptual relations. Associated with each menu is a hierarchical pop-up menu that contains the applicable tailoring operators: Fig. 2 shows the menu of entity tailoring operators. Invoking an operator initiates a series of dialogue boxes, menus and prompts that lead the user through the tailoring operation.

The user requests information from the knowledge base by selecting items from a hierarchical pop-up menu associated with the text window. The Tailor displays text information in the window of the Tailor browser and graphical information in pop-up windows. The window in Fig. 2 contains the text description of a spreadsheet. The text description contains

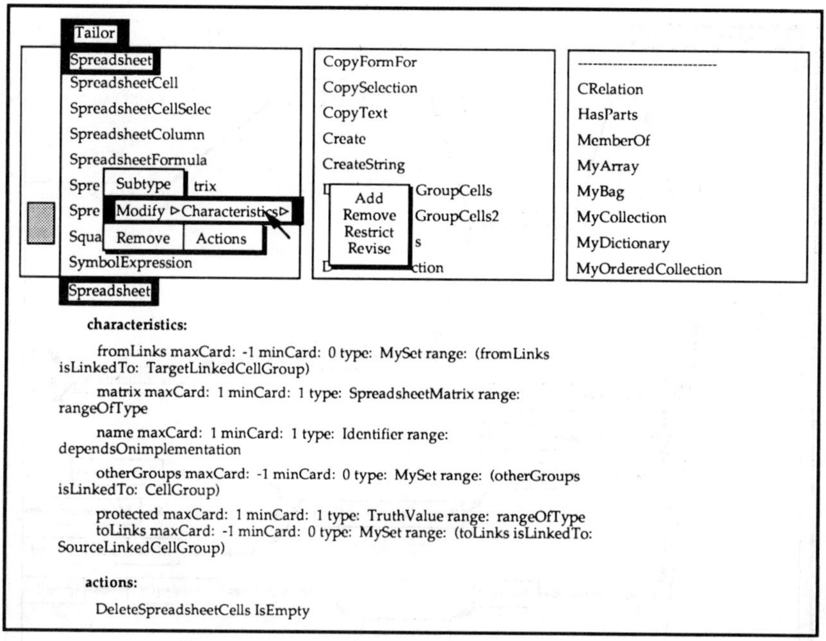

Figure 2. The Tailor browser showing spreadsheet descriptions.

information about the spreadsheet's characteristics and the names of actions performed by a spreadsheet.

For example, the characteristic *protected* is a boolean flag that indicates if a user can modify the spreadsheet. The description of *protected* includes four facets that describe its value: the maximum cardinality, minimum cardinality, value type and range of legal values. Figure 2 shows that protected must have exactly one value, of type TruthValue, and the value may be any value in the range of TruthValue.

Spreadsheet has six characteristics: fromLinks and toLinks are sets of cell groups linked from and to other spreadsheets, otherGroups is a set of named cell groups, matrix is a matrix of spreadsheet cells, and name is a unique identifier for a spreadsheet.

Figure 3 shows a graphical representation of the spreadsheet's composition. Entities are boxed with bold borders, conceptual relations are boxed with light borders, and characteristics have no boxes. The graphical representation is equivalent to the textual description in Fig. 2, except that it does not show actions.

To complete our logical model of spreadsheet interaction semantics, we must define and model the actions. To illustrate this process, we will apply

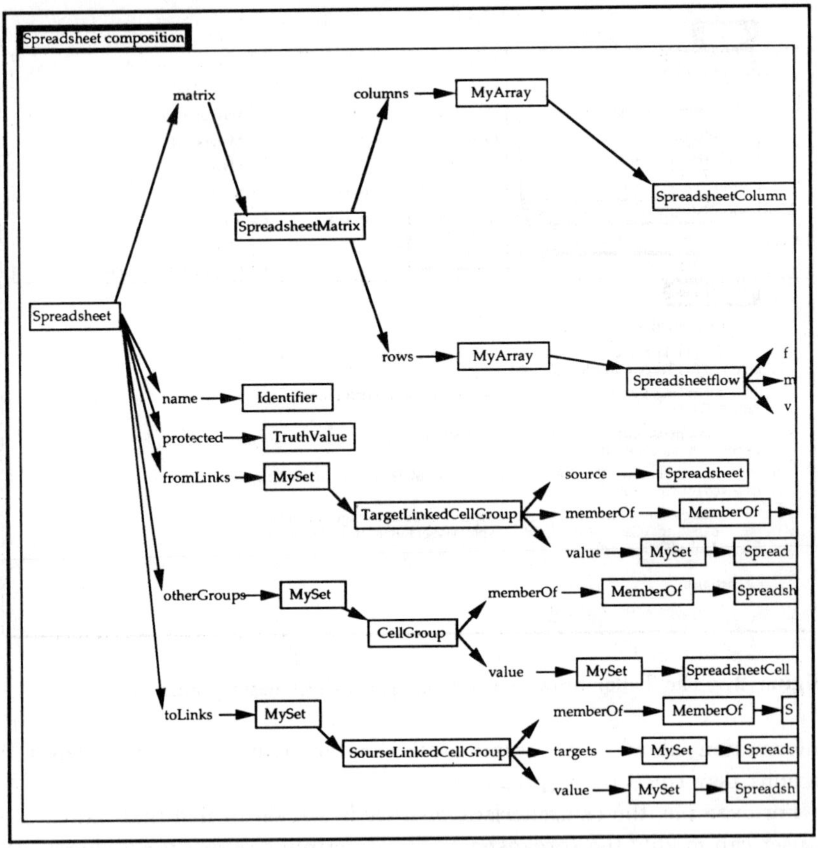

Figure 3. A graphical representation of the spreadsheet.

our guidelines to define the logical view of one command from an actual program, and then use the Tailor to model the action.

3.2 Interaction semantics

The command we choose cuts a rectangular block of cells from a spreadsheet. The cells are removed permanently from the spreadsheet and placed in a buffer where they are accessible for the user to put them back into the same spreadsheet or into another spreadsheet. Our five modelling guidelines help us develop our logical view.

First, because the user uses the buffer directly to transfer information, it belongs to the interface.

Second, to reduce the amount of information the interface needs about the application, our logical view is that the interface does not delete the cells directly but requests some application entity to delete them. If the interface deleted the cells directly, it would have to know several things about the application, such as how to shift the remaining spreadsheet cells into the positions vacated by the deleted cells.

Third, to minimize data transfer across the UI–application interface, we model with interaction types whenever possible. In this example we use the interaction type RectCellSel (rectangular cell group selection). Interaction types describe the kinds of information communicated across the UI–application interface without specifying what data structures represent the information. They allow information transfer to be described independently of implementation.

The fourth and fifth modelling guidelines state that entities generally do not know how to manipulate structures that contain them, and that actions are performed by entities that have sufficient knowledge to perform them. These guidelines support three assertions:

(1) a cell cannot delete itself from anything;

(2) rows and columns can delete any of their cells, but with unpredictable consequences to the integrity of the spreadsheet; and

(3) only the spreadsheet can safely delete cells from itself.

For example, cell deletion must not affect linked cell groups, and only a spreadsheet can determine if linked cells groups would be affected.

Figure 4 illustrates the logical view of interactions for the Cut command. Events and returns are numbered according to the order in which they occur. The user selects a rectangular block of cells and invokes the cut command. The UI–application interface converts the command into a form understood by the spreadsheet and sends a triggering event to the spreadsheet, requesting it to delete the group of cells. The spreadsheet asks the interface software to specify the direction in which to shift the remaining spreadsheet cells and, after receiving this information, the spreadsheet performs the cell deletion and returns a rectangular cell group (RectCellGrp), which the interface places on its clipboard.

Figure 5 shows the menu of action tailoring operators and the text description of this action. The triggering event has one associated data item (*input*, the interaction type for a rectangular cell selection). The action has three preconditions, no state changes, one return (a rectangular cell group), and three generated events. The first event describes the request for a shift direction from the interface, the second event describes a request to delete cells from cell groups, and the third event describes a request to delete cells from the spreadsheet's matrix.

Figure 6 is a graphical view of the action. The trigger's associated data item, *input*, and the returned rectangular cell group are on the left. The

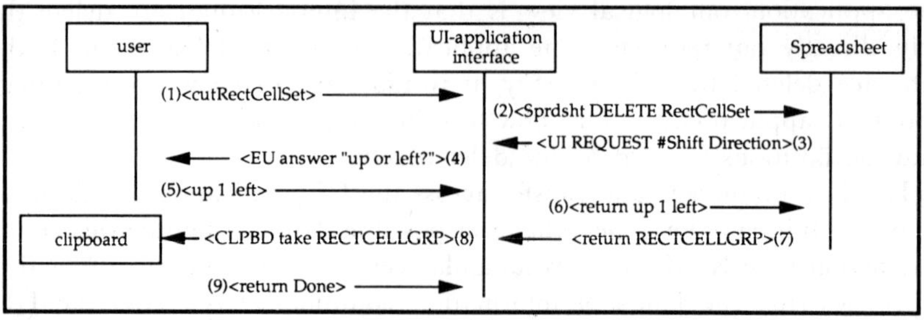

Figure 4. A logical view of the Cut command.

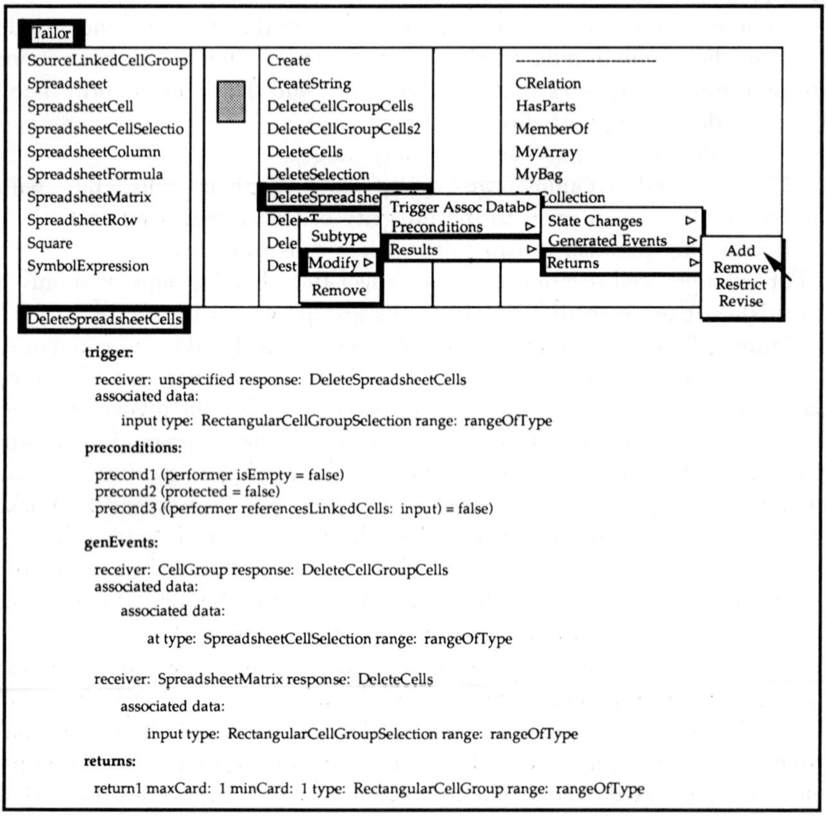

Figure 5. The action to delete cells.

three generated events are on the right.

This example illustrates several things about the model.

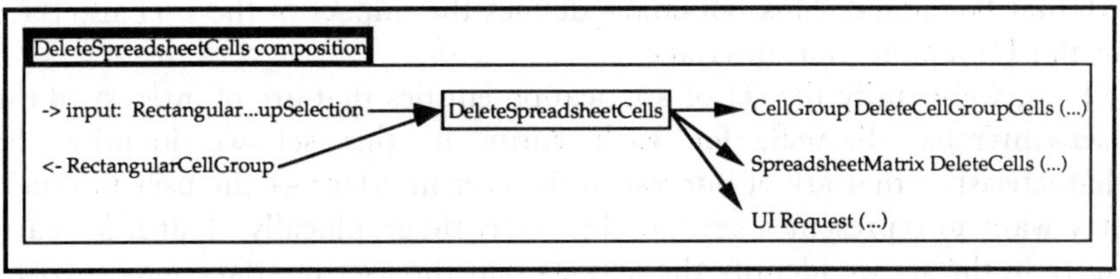

Figure 6. A graphical representation of delete action.

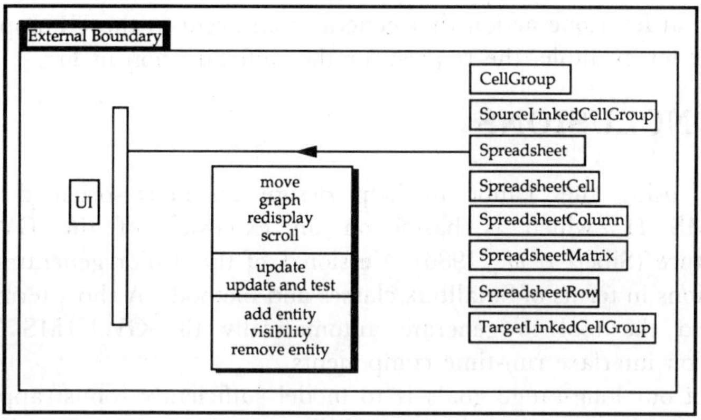

Figure 7. The external boundary.

(1) An action type may be shared by many entity types. Shared actions increase the efficiency of the knowledge base representation and suggest potential efficiency in software implementation. Each entity type must have sufficient common structure to support the shared action description. In Fig. 5, the precondition *precond2* refers to a specific characteristic, *protected*, which all entity types performing this action must have.

(2) To support sharing, action descriptions are parameterized to refer to any performer rather than to a specific entity type. In Fig. 5, preconditions *precond1* and *precond3* refer to the performing entity type as performer.

(3) The model lets us distinguish explicitly between the direct and indirect effects of an action. For example, although deleting cells obviously changes the application state, Fig. 5 describes no state changes. This is because the state changes are indirect; they are modelled in and may be computed from the actions triggered by the generated events.

3.3 External boundary

After testing the knowledge base for completeness and consistency and correcting any discrepancies, we proceed to establish the application's external boundary. This boundary defines the impact of the user interface on the UI–application interface.

First, we identify the set of application entities that are of interest to the user interface. Second, for each entity in this set we identify the characteristics that are of interest to the user interface — the user interface may want to represent a certain characteristic graphically. Third, for each entity in the set we identify the actions that the user interface may invoke.

Figure 7 shows the external boundary window. The arrow from spreadsheet to the UI–application interface tells us that a spreadsheet performs at least one action that generates an event to the UI–application interface: for example, the request for the shift direction in Fig. 4.

4 CONCLUSIONS

We are using the Tailor to help design an object-oriented UIMS, GWUIMS II, which is based on an extension of the GWUIMS architecture (Sibert *et al.*, 1986). Version I of the Tailor generates model descriptions in terms of Smalltalk classes and methods. A short-term goal is to extend the tool to generate automatically the GWUIMS II UI–application interface run-time components.

One of our long-range goals is to model sufficiently robust application domains so that we can tailor a UIMS to a wide range of applications. Other long-term goals include using the tool to generate a taxonomy of models of application domain interaction semantics, generating models of individual application-program interaction semantics, adding metarules to incorporate conceptual modelling guidelines, and using the tool to investigate conceptual relations further.

Finally, we believe that these modelling primitives have potential for more general use as a language to specify object-centred designs. We also believe that our tool has potential for more general use to generate and verify object-centred design specifications. We are in the early stages of investigating these extensions and cannot predict where our investigation will lead. Ultimately, we intend the tool to be the cornerstone of a system for designing object-oriented software.

REFERENCES

Anson, E. (1980). The semantics of graphical input. In: *Methodology of Interaction*. R. Guedj *et al.* (eds). Amsterdam: North-Holland, 115–126.

Anson, E. (1982). The device model of interaction. *Computer Graphics*, 107–114.

Brachman, R. (1985). I lied about the trees. *AI Magazine*, Fall, 80–93.

Hurley, W. (1989). A generative taxonomy of application domains. Doctoral Dissertation, George Washington University, Washington, DC.

Rhyne, J. *et al.* (1987). Tools and methodology for user interface development. *Computer Graphics*, April, 78–87.

Sibert, J., Hurley, W. and Bleser, T. (1986). An object-oriented user interface management system. *Computer Graphics*, August, 259–268.

Propositional Production Systems for Dialogue Description

Dan R. Olsen Jr.

Reprinted from: *Proceedings of CHI '90*, pp 57–63, 1990.

This paper proposes an approach that unifies the most common earlier approaches to user interface specification, although the recursive state diagrams used by Denert and others are not explicitly covered. As in many approaches, semantic actions are subservient to the user interface code. In the implementation of the approach described, the semantic actions are evoked by sending messages to appropriate objects. Thus the common strategy of embedding or calling conventional code is added to in a way that clarifies the separability.

Propositional Production Systems for Dialogue Description

D. R. OLSEN, JR

Computer Science Department, Brigham Young University, Provo, UT 84602, USA

1 INTRODUCTION

As the field of user interface management systems (UIMSs) has matured, a variety of models have been proposed for the handling of interactive inputs. The early models were state machines (Newman, 1968) which were augmented to provide hierarchies of machines and to provide for semantic control over the transitions of the machine (Jacob, 1983; Olsen, 1984). Most state machine models were constrained by the notion that there be a single current state, or stack of states, for the entire user interface.

As direct manipulation interfaces were developed this single-state model was found to be too confining. As such interfaces came to be built around windows, the notion of event translation tables was proposed (Rosenthal, 1983) where each window has a table associated with it which can be searched using the current input event to select a semantic action to perform. This model allows every visible window to behave independently rather than relying upon a single global state. However, each such window is expected to behave the same regardless of the context. If, for example, a window should draw either circles or lines in response to mouse input, the logic for deciding which should be done must be buried in the semantic actions.

Event response (Hill, 1986) systems have been proposed as a model for removing the single-event, single-action limits of translation tables as well as the single-state limits of state machines. The state of the user interface is characterized by events that have been asserted. Rules are written which cause actions to occur when specific combinations of events are active. Such actions may be semantic behaviours or may assert other events. Events can be used like states or may operate independently. The single-event

THE SEPARABLE USER INTERFACE
ISBN 0-12-232150-2

restriction is lifted by allowing rules to be based on combinations of events. Event response systems do not, however, provide for semantic control over the dialogue or for extracting information from the system about what inputs are acceptable at a particular point in the dialogue.

This paper describes propositional production systems (PPSs) which are a superset of state machines, translation tables and event response systems. The name is derived from the fact that the reasoning involved is equivalent to propositional logic. In addition, a PPS is formally equivalent to finite-state machines and regular grammars. A PPS can easily and directly support each of the three previously mentioned event-handling models as degenerate cases. The primary advantage of a PPS is its ability succinctly to describe systems which it would be very tedious to represent in other models of the same power.

There are three attributes of a PPS which are particularly applicable to the problem of handling graphical dialogues. A PPS can:

(1) report exactly what inputs are permissible at any point in the user interface;

(2) support semantic conditions such as not allowing a Save command to be performed when there is no file open; and

(3) inherit behaviour from one or more other PPS definitions, which is not possible in state machines or event response systems.

The discussion begins with a definition of PPSs and certain operations that can be performed on them. This is followed by a discussion of the dialogue-processing algorithms. Relationships are then shown for three of the other models of input handling. Lastly, a set of automatic optimizations are described which increase evaluation speed.

2 BASIC DEFINITION OF A PPS

A Propositional Production System consists of a state space definition and a set of rules. A state space is characterized by a set of conditions much like the events in event response systems or states and inputs in state machines. Conditions are grouped in fields, with all conditions in a given field being mutually exclusive. Take the example of a simple drawing application illustrated in Fig. 1. The state space for such an application might be represented as follows:

Field ActiveCmnd (NoCmnd, LineCmnd, CircleCmnd, RectCmnd)
Semantic Field SelectedObj (NoSelection, LineSel, CircleSel, RectSel)
Field DragMode (RubberLine, RubberCircle, RubberRect, DragSelect,
    NotDragging)
Query Field ConfirmDel (OKDelete, CancelDelete)

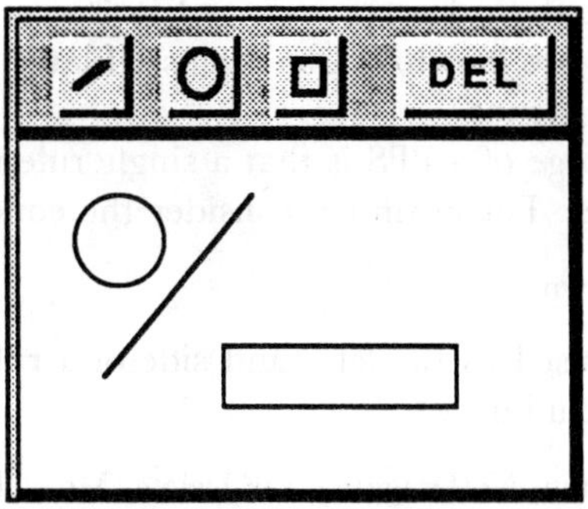

Figure 1. A simple drawing application.

Input Field Input (NullEvent, MouseDown, MouseUp, LineMenu,
CircleMenu, RectMenu, DelMenu)
Field Action (DrawLine, DrawRect, DrawCircle, SaveMousePoint, DelLine,
DelRect, DelCircle)

The fields each contain two or more conditions. Condition names must be unique across the PPS. Note that interface status information (ActiveCmnd, DragMode and Action), inputs (Input), semantic conditions (SelectedObj) and query fields (ConfirmDel) are all uniformly represented as fields in the state space. The only difference between these types of fields is the way in which their conditions are obtained. The conditions in a field are defined to be mutually exclusive. For example, NoCmnd and LineCmnd cannot be asserted at the same time.

Rules are defined on this state space which will transform one state into another. The following are possible rules that might be used in the drawing application. A rule consists of a left-hand side or condition, and a right-hand side or consequence. The left-hand side is a list of conditions which must be present in the current state, and the right-hand side is a list of conditions which will be asserted in the next state:

(1) NoCmnd, LineMenu → LineCmnd, NotDragging
(2) NoCmnd, CircleMenu → CircleCmnd, NotDragging
(3) NoCmnd, RectMenu → RectCmnd, NotDragging
(4) LineCmnd, MouseDown → RubberLine, SaveMousePoint
(5) RubberLine, NullEvent → RubberLine
(6) RubberLine, MouseUp → NotDragging, DrawLine
(7) DelMenu, LineSel, OKDelete → DelLine, NoCmnd
(8) DelMenu, RectSel, OKDelete → DelRect, NoCmnd
(9) DelMenu, CircleSel, OKDelete → DelCircle, NoCmnd

The above set of rules is not sufficient to implement the example application but is sufficient to illustrate the points that follow. It is also important to note that the rules are arranged in lowest to highest priority order. When two rules are in conflict, as discussed later, the higher priority rule always takes precedence.

The expressive leverage of a PPS is that a single rule may actually apply to a multitude of states. For example, consider the condition list:

LineCmnd, MouseDown

This condition list, if used as the left-hand side of a rule, would match to 280 different states including:

(LineCmnd, NoSelection, NotDragging, OKDelete, MouseDown, DrawLine)

It is this ability to define behaviour on a large number of states with the ability to be as precise as necessary that gives a PPS a significant expressive advantage over the other event-handling models.

2.1 Semantic actions

Simply transforming states does not accomplish much. We must attach semantic actions to the PPS so that it will do something. Semantic actions are attached to conditions. When a condition is asserted the corresponding action will be performed. Some fields, such as Action, are created purely for defining semantic behaviour. Others, such as DragMode, define semantic behaviour as well as exerting control over the dialogue. By arranging semantic actions in mutually exclusive fields we can reason about which actions might conflict with each other and which would not. It is assumed that actions attached to conditions which belong to different fields are independent of each other and will not conflict. This notion of action conflict is important to the inheritance capability of a PPS.

Semantic actions can take a variety of forms, such as addresses of C routines or Lisp list expressions. Our current implementation attaches an object to each PPS and defines the semantic actions in terms of messages to that object. The exact nature of the semantic actions is not important to this discussion. Descriptive strings are used here for exposition purposes. Example condition actions might be:

NoCmnd: 'Remove all menu highlights'
LineCmnd: 'Highlight line menu item'
NotDragging: 'Terminate any drag echoes'
DrawLine: 'Draw a line from the saved point to the current point'
SaveMousePoint: 'Save the current mouse location'
DelLine: 'Delete the selected line'

Note that in the example rule set the behaviour of ActiveCmnd is semi-independent of the DragMode. Using condition actions, each field can be

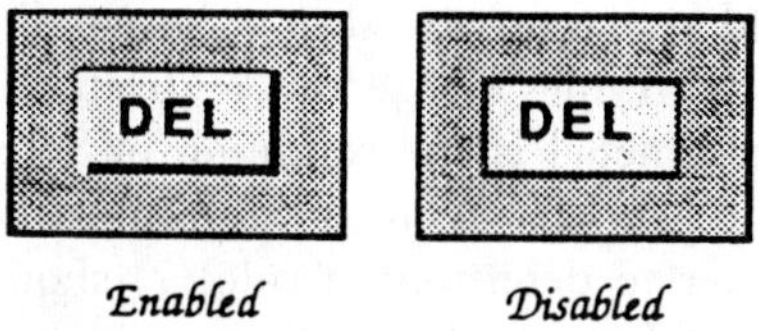

Figure 2. The DelMenu item.

viewed as an independent process which takes care of itself. By combining conditions from various fields, more refined interrelated actions can be created. Providing such flexibility in a state machine diagram would lead to a rat's nest of state transition arcs.

2.2 Input processes

It is assumed that the PPS is executed once for each new input. Whatever system is using the PPS would set the input conditions according to whatever inputs have been received and then evaluate the PPS. One facility that is required, however, is to extract information about what logical inputs are acceptable. Many logical input devices, such as menu items, will change their visual appearance when their input is not acceptable. The DelMenu item is an example of such behaviour, as shown in Fig. 2.

In the example PPS, only rules (7), (8) and (9) contain the DelMenu input condition. If, however, the SelectedObj field has the NoSelection condition, none of these rules can be activated. In such a case, DelMenu should be disabled. Each input field must have a semantic Disable action associated with it which can be called for each condition of the field that is not acceptable as input. The use of these Disable actions will be discussed in the section on PPS evaluation.

2.3 Semantic and query fields

Semantic fields (such as SelectedObj) are set by the application code. Their initial conditions are set before starting the PPS. Routines are provided which allow the application to set these conditions at any time. Other than the fact that a semantic field cannot appear on the right-hand side or consequence of a rule, semantic fields are treated just like any other field.

Query fields are also set by the application, but only on demand. Each query field has an associated query action which is executed whenever the field's condition is needed by a rule. The special nature of a query field is that if there are no rules that can be activated which are dependent on the value of that field, then the field's condition is never requested. In the example PPS we would not want to ask for the condition of ConfirmDel unless we were actually trying to execute a delete. If DelMenu is the condition of Input and LineSel is the condition of SelectedObj, then rule (7) could possibly apply. At this point a value must be obtained for the ConfirmDel field in order to determine if rule (7) should be activated. If, however, the condition of Input is MouseDown, there is a rule which can fire which uses a condition from ConfirmDel. The query action, therefore, need not be executed.

2.4 Inheritance

The major goal of having one PPS inherit behaviour from another is to be able to reuse portions of that behaviour without needing to understand it completely. PPS inheritance is additive, in that it allows the existing fields and rules of the inherited PPS to be reused without change and allows new fields to be defined and new rules to be added. There is one restriction: none of the inherited conditions may appear on the right-hand side of a new rule. Using inherited conditions in tests, or left-hand sides, allows the inherited rules to interact with the new rules. Forbidding inherited conditions from appearing in the consequence of a new rule prevents the new rules from interfering with the actions of the inherited PPS.

Take as an example the PPS described previously, and assume that we want to extend this system to show the dimensions of an object whenever it is selected (Fig. 3). We would inherit the previously defined fields and rules and add the following new fields:

Field DimDraw
  (LineLength: 'Draw the length of the selected line',
  CircleRad: 'Draw the radius of the selected circle',
  RectDim: 'Draw the dimensions of the selected rectangle')
Field Redraw (NoDimDraw, DimRedraw)

and the following rules:

(A1) LineMenu → DimRedraw
(A2) CircleMenu → DimRedraw
(A3) RectMenu – DimRedraw
(A4) DelMenu → DimRedraw
(A5) MouseDown → DimRedraw
(A6) LineSel, DimReDraw → LineLength, NoDimDraw
(A7) CircleSel, DimReDraw → CircleRad, NoDimDraw
(A8) RectSel, DimReDraw → RectDim, NoDimDraw

The inherited rules always have a lower priority than the new rules. Note that the old functionality is not changed, since the condition actions of

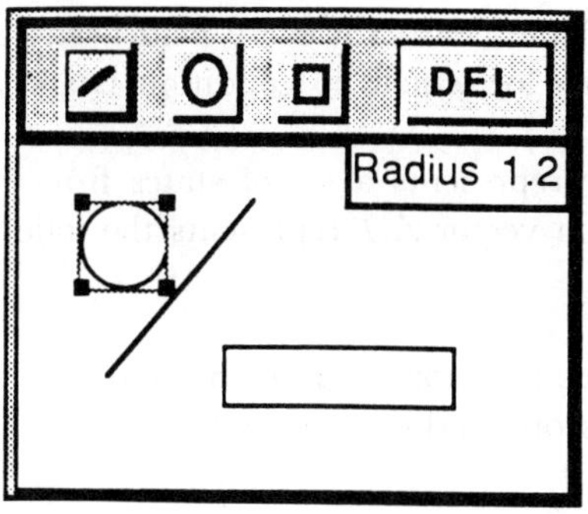

Figure 3. The application of Fig. 1 with display of dimensions.

DimDraw do not in any way affect the other field actions. The inherited rules still activate under the same circumstances, since they cannot conflict with the new rules. The Redraw field is used to make sure that the drawing of the radius happens only once.

Rules and fields can be inherited from more than one PPS. The only modification that must be made is that condition and field names may require some qualification to prevent multiple definitions with the same name.

With this inheritance model, existing functionality can be reused and added to as needed. The new fields can provide additional actions and state information without interfering with the inherited fields and rules. This is possible because of the inherent parallelism in the multiple fields. Similar inheritance mechanisms have been provided in translation table systems by simply appending additional callbacks to a particular input event in a translation table.

3 FORMAL DEFINITIONS

There are a number of definitions which are required before proceeding with the PPS execution algorithms. These definitions are better illustrated by the following simple PPS state space definition:

Field $X(A,B,C)$
Field $Y(P,Q)$
Field $Z(T,U,V)$

3.1 Condition vectors and state sets

The primary expressive vehicle in a PPS is the condition vector. A condition vector consists of a list of conditions where no pair of conditions are members of the same field. Not every field needs to be represented in the vector: those fields for which no condition is specified are marked as don't cares.

A condition vector represents a set of states from the state space. For example, the condition vector A,T represents the following set of states:

$\{ (A,P,T), (A,Q,T) \}$

By treating a condition vector as a set of states it is possible to define several set operations on condition vectors.

3.2 Subset

CVa is a subset of *CVb* iff every condition appearing in *CVb* also appears in *CVa*. For example:

(B,T) is a subset of (B)
(B,T) is not a subset of (B,Q)

3.3 Intersection

CVr = *CVa* intersect *CVb* iff every condition in *CVa* or in *CVb* appears in *CVr* and *CVr* does not have more than one condition for any field. For example:

(B,T) intersect (Q,T) = (B,Q,T)
(B,T) intersect (Q,U) = empty because (B,T) cannot contain any state with the condition U

3.4 Overlay

CVr = *CVa* overlay *CVb* iff,
for each field *F*,
if *CVa.F* is a don't care then
CVr.F = *CVb.F*
else *CVr.F* = *CVa.F*.

The result (*CVr*) is *CVb* with sufficient fields changed to match *CVa*. This is the basic operation used when applying the consequence of a rule.

3.5 Independence and conflict

Two conditions vectors *CVa* and *CVb* are said to be independent iff

CVa overlay *CVb* = *CVb* overlay *CVa*

This means that the conditions asserted by the two vectors are either the same or are not from the same fields. Two independent condition vectors will not force a field to have two different conditions.

Two rules *R1* and *R2* are in conflict iff *R1.lhs* intersects *R2.lhs* (there exists a state where they both apply) and *R1.rhs* is not independent of *R2.rhs* (they attempt to set one or more fields to conflicting conditions). The priority order defined on rules is intended to resolve rule conflicts. Algorithms have been defined which will remove all conflicts but these algorithms can cause an explosion of generated rules. In the strategies shown below we use the evaluation algorithm to resolve conflicts rather than modifying the rule list.

4 EVALUATION OF A PPS

Having defined a PPS as well as a number of operations on condition vectors, it is now possible to describe the evaluation of a PPS. At run time we can create instances of a PPS. Each instance contains a pointer to the PPS definition and a current state (*CS*). In order to resolve conflicts at run time we augment the current state with a condition vector (*KC*) to represent the known conditions. Each time we obtain an input from the event queue we set the appropriate input fields of the current state as dictated by our logical event structure, set *KC* to contain only the input conditions and then evaluate the PPS. The algorithm for a single input event is as follows:

```
CS = whatever value resulted from the application of this algorithm to the
       previous input
KC = the input conditions as dictated by the last input event; all other fields
       are don't cares
CS = KC overlay CS

For each rule R in highest to lowest order
    { If CS is a subset of R.lhs and
          R.rhs is independent of KC then
      {KC = R.rhs overlay KC
      Perform the semantic actions
          associated with the conditions in
          R.rhs
      }
    }
Cs = KC overlay CS
```

The use of *KC* will prevent any condition from being changed more than once. *KC* is only initialized to the input conditions, so that any conditions in the current state other than the inputs can be changed at least once. By working in highest to lowest order any conflicts are resolved, because *KC* will block any conflicting lower-priority rule from activating. *KC* will also accumulate the new field settings dictated by the triggered rules without changing *CS*. Not changing *CS* until the end is very important in preventing race conditions in the machine.

4.1 Input field enable/disable

Because we are concerned with interactive behaviours rather than general event handling, it is important to enable and disable input fields. Before accepting any inputs we check the current state (*CS*) of the machine and the rule set to determine which inputs might be acceptable. We first create the known state (*KS*), which is all fields from *CS* with any input or query fields marked as don't cares, since we will not know what the conditions of either of these kinds of fields will be after all of the inputs have been received. The algorithm for finding the inputs to enable is as follows:

```
KS = CS with all input and query fields marked as don't cares

Disable all input conditions
For each rule R
    {INT = CS intersect R.lhs
    If INT is not empty then
        For each input field F
            {If INT.F is not a don't care then
                {Enable INT.F}
            }
    }
```

Any input condition which is not enabled explicitly by this method will be disabled. Any rule *R* which cannot possibly be activated, given the current value of *CS*, will have an empty intersection between *KS* and *R.lhs*. Of the rules that can be activated we will enable any input condition which is mentioned explicitly.

As an example, suppose that the current state before inputs are received is:

(NoCmnd, NoSelection, NotDragging, _, _, DrawCircle)

The only rules which have nonempty intersections with the current state are (1), (2) and (3). This would cause LineMenu, CircleMenu and RectMenu to be enabled while disabling MouseDown, NullEvent, MouseUp and DelMenu. If, however, the SelectedObj field was set to LineSel, the DelMenu input would also be enabled because rule (7) would then have a nonempty intersection with the current state.

The above enabling algorithm is performed once before actually getting the next input from the user. After getting an input, the PPS evaluation algorithm described earlier is executed.

4.2 Query field evaluation

The evaluation of query fields is performed while processing each rule of the PPS. Each query field in *CS* is marked initially as a don't care, since its condition is unknown. As each rule is checked to see if it should apply, the rule is also checked to see if it depends on a query field. If such a dependency exists then the query is evaluated and then marked as known. The modified algorithm including semantic queries is shown below:

PPS Evaluation Algorithm with Semantic Queries

```
KC = the input conditions as dictated by the last input event; all other
        fields are don't cares
CS = KC overlay CS
Mark all query fields in CS as don't cares
For each rule R in highest to lowest order
    {INT = CS intersect R.lhs
    If INT is not empty and
        R.rhs is independent of KC then
      {For each query field Q which has a condition in INT
        {KC.Q = CS.Q = evaluation of Q.Action}
      If CS is a subset of R.lhs then
        {KC = R.rhs overlay KC
        Perform the semantic actions associated with the conditions in R.rhs
        }
      }
    }
CS = KC overlay CS
```

As an example, suppose that the SelectedObj has the condition LineSel and the input received is DelMenu. As the rules are being evaluated, rule (7) will intersect the current state but the field ConfirmDel will be unknown. The intersection of the current state with the left-hand side of rule (7) would contain OKDclctc, which is a condition of the unknown field ConfirmDel. ConfirmDel would be evaluated (which might consist of asking the user if deletion was OK). After evaluation, ConfirmDel is now known and rule (7) may or may not be activated depending on the result. Note that if the input had not been DelMenu, none of rules (7)–(9) would intersect the current state and therefore would never cause ConfirmDel's action to be evaluated.

5 PPS AND OTHER EVENT-HANDLING MODELS

The PPS model is formally equivalent to finite-state machines and regular languages. Its expressive model (the way in which the machine is specified) is a direct superset of a variety of other UIMS models.

5.1 State machines

A state machine is simply a PPS which has:

(1) a state field with conditions for all of the states;
(2) an input field with conditions for all of the logical inputs; and
(3) an action field with conditions for all of the semantic actions.

Each rule has a state and an input on the left-hand side with the action and next state on the right-hand side.

5.2 Event dispatchers

Event dispatchers are used in windowing systems to map events to actions. Such systems could be modelled as PPSs with multiple input fields (a main input field plus other fields for input modifiers such as meta-keys or control keys) and an action field. Each rule would map an input combination to an action.

5.3 Event response systems

Hill's event response systems are simply PPSs where all fields have exactly two conditions.

6. OPTIMIZATIONS

Two major optimizations have been defined which improve the run-time performance of a PPS, rule elimination and rule indexing.

6.1 Rule elimination

There are two cases in which a rule can be eliminated from a PPS: by removing rules that cannot activate, and by removing redundant rules.

6.1.1 Removing rules that cannot activate

If

(1) *R1* has lower priority than *R2*;
(2) *R1.lhs* is a subset of *R2.lhs*; and
(3) *R1.rhs* is not independent of *R2.rhs*

then

R1 can be eliminated because it will never be activated.

6.1.2 Removing rules that are redundant

If

(1) *R1* has **higher** priority than *R2*;
(2) *R1.lhs* is a subset of *R2.lhs*;
(3) *R1.rhs* is a subset of *R2.rhs*; and
(4) there is no rule *R3* between *R1* and *R2* such that *R3.lhs* intersects *R1.lhs*

then

R1 can be eliminated because all of its function is subsumed by *R2*.

6.2 Rule indexing

This optimization by rule indexing indexes the rule list based on one or more fields. Indexing partitions the rule list according to the conditions of the indexed field or fields. Rules with don't cares for the indexed fields will appear in multiple partitions. Rule indexing on the input field and state field, for example, would produce the normal two-dimensional state transition table. Partitioning the rule list serves to reduce the number of rules which must be matched for each cycle through the machine. Indexing, however, consumes additional space. Algorithms have been defined which, given a maximum size, will select automatically an indexing scheme which fits the PPS machine within that space while minimizing the size of the largest rule list partition.

An unindexed PPS executes in time proportional to the number of rules. An indexed PPS (given a good indexing choice) can reach or closely approach constant-time execution.

7 CONCLUSIONS

A Propositional Production System for defining interactive dialogues has been described. This system subsumes the major event-handling models with each of them appearing as a special case of a PPS. The issues of semantic control of dialogues, conditional semantic queries, inheritance and logical device enabling have all been addressed. Algorithms have been described for handling interactive dialogues. Optimizations have been briefly outlined which yield acceptable run-time performance for a PPS. The issue of extending PPSs to hierarchies of communicating machines has not been addressed, since the mechanisms provided for state machines (Jacob, 1983) and for event response systems (Hill, 1986) can readily be applied.

REFERENCES

Hill, R. D. (1986). Supporting concurrency, communication, and synchronization in human–computer interaction — the Sassafras UIMS. *ACM Transactions on Graphics*, 5, 3.

Jacob, R. J. K. (1983). Using formal specifications in the design of a human–computer interface. *Communications of the ACM*, April.

Newman, W. M. (1968). A system for interactive graphical programming. In: *Spring Joint Computer Conference*. AFIPS Press.

Olsen, D. R. (1984). Push-down automata for user interface management. *ACM Transactions on Graphics*, 3, 3.

Rosenthal, D. S. H. (1983). Managing graphical resources. *Computer Graphics*, Jan.

5. Architectures

The Man–Computer Interface: A Note on Concepts and Design

Ernest Edmonds

Reprinted from: *International Journal Man–Machine Studies*
No. 16, pp 231–236, 1982

This paper introduces the notion of an architecture for the user interface, in the sense of a classification of a set of components, as well as briefly reviewing design issues. The interface model proposed fed directly into the 'Seeheim model' described in the following paper.

The Man–Computer Interface: A Note on Concepts and Design

E. A. EDMONDS

The School of Mathematics, Computing and Statistics, Leicester Polytechnic, Leicester, UK

1 INTRODUCTION

If one draws meaningful boundaries round systems that include computers, at least one human being will normally be included within each boundary. In this paper we concentrate on the simple case in which we may consider a system to include just one human being, the user. Even in this case we argue that consideration of the design function leads us to consider a system that also includes the designer (Edmonds, 1981). The extra complicating factor that must be considered when several human beings are involved is the relationships that exist between them. Whilst we do not discuss this factor here, the general point needs to be made that proper consideration of the man–computer interface needs to be made in the light of the context and situation.

Once we try to go beyond the notion of the man–computer interface as the physical component of the system with which the user comes into direct contact, such as a keyboard or VDU screen, we are faced with choices that are not easily resolved. Perhaps the most attractive definition is that the interface is the part of the system that represents the user's model of it. Thus, actions by the computer that are simple conceptually, such as the generation of a representation of the edges that exist in an image, are represented in the interface very simply, despite the fact that they might be quite difficult to achieve. A problem with this view is that different users may have different models of the system. We are thus forced to take a flexible position with regard to the user's view. As we will see, it is nevertheless possible to identify a part of the system that may be considered to be the interface.

Maher and Bell (1977) proposed that the interface be seen as a virtual

THE SEPARABLE USER INTERFACE
ISBN 0–12–232150–2

machine. Krammer (1980) termed this the *attention processor*, whilst referring to the remaining computer system as a set of virtual *background processors*. He also pointed out that the human and these various processors may operate in parallel. Following Krammer, Fig. 1 is a modified version of the corresponding figure in Edmonds (1978). The whole system is seen as three major cooperating processors. Any of the three, including the human, might usefully be seen as more than one processor. In the next section we will look in more detail at the interface.

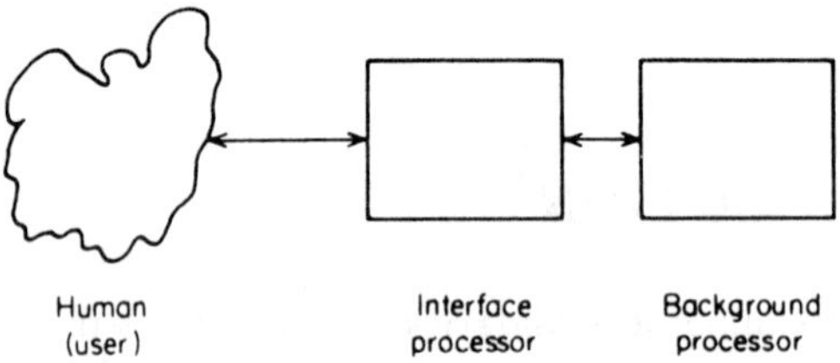

Figure 1. Cooperating processors in the man–computer interface.

The need to consider the design of man–computer interfaces as an adaptive process has been argued in Edmonds (1981). The more interactive a system is, and the more inventive or unpredictable the human's part in it is, the less we can discover from task analysis, etc. and the more we must rely on evaluation of the performance of the system in use. We will touch on these problems in section 3.

2 A MODEL OF THE MAN–COMPUTER INTERFACE

Moran (1980) considers the construction of interfaces that match the user's mental model of the system. He sees the interface in terms of three components: the physical, communication and conceptual ones. We may consider the interface processor in a similar manner as in Fig. 2. Corresponding to the physical, communications and conceptual components we have I/O processors, a dynamics processor and a description of the background processor in terms of a set of tasks that may be performed on its objects. As above, we are considering virtual machines that may or may not correspond to physically distinct processors.

The *I/O processors* perform conceptually simple transformation tasks, taking physical input acts and generating corresponding internal representations of them or vice versa. An obvious example of such a processor is

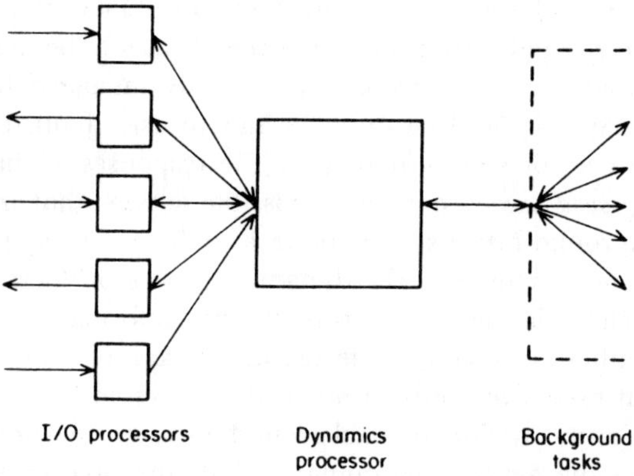

Figure 2. A virtual interface processor corresponding to the user's mental model.

a keyboard unit, which generates strings of coded characters. They may, however, be very much more complex: for example, speech input or speech output systems. The main characteristic of an I/O processor is that the transformation that it performs do not, for the most part, change with time, so that they do not need to be specified in terms of an internal state. An exception to this might be a speech input system changing its expected speaker. Thus the input processors that, in the figure, have communication paths into them from the dynamics processor, would not expect to receive information along such paths very often.

The *dynamics processor* determines the action or actions that the computer system should take at any given moment. This processor may also be seen as performing transformations. They are of three basic kinds (Edmonds, 1978):

input processor action → output processor action
input processor action → background processor action
background processor action → output processor action

More complex activities, where one or more actions generate one or more actions, frequently occur. In some instances a background processor action might transform to another background action. An important distinction between the dynamics processor and an I/O processor is that the transformations performed by the former are very dependent on the context in which they occur. Thus the dynamics processor is constantly changing its internal state and, hence, its behaviour. A very simple example of this would be a search in Prestel where the result of entering a given digit leads to a different displayed page of information at each step. This component in the system will then contain a description of how the dynamics of the interaction are to be managed from the point of view of the computer. It is important to recognize that the use of the phrase 'to be managed' here does not imply that the *whole system* is necessarily managed by this processor. Indeed, it may very well be that the human user manages the system, the dynamics processor simply managing the responses of the computer.

The *background tasks* are a set of possible actions that may be performed by the background processor. Some tasks will be entirely passive but others will yield some response to the dynamics processor. Certain tasks may be, in effect, self-initiating, so that they pass information to the dynamics processor without it having requested it. An example of the last form of task might be an excessive temperature warning system in an industrial plant.

Implicit in the notion of background tasks is the notion of *background objects* which the actions manipulate. Both the objects and the tasks are intended to be abstract descriptions that correspond to simple conceptual notions. An object might be a database whilst a task might be to retrieve an item from it.

With the above model of the interface in mind we may return to the notion of the representation of the user's model of the system in the interface. For a single known user we could clearly arrive at a set of I/O processors, a set of background tasks and a description of the computer system that were both understood by the user and implemented in the system according to our model. Thus we could arrange that the user's model matched the construction of the interface.

However, as mentioned above, different users may have, or need, different models of the system. Typically, users of the same system will include both novices and experts. We may handle this in two ways. Firstly, the dynamics processor might handle paths that need not be known to the novice, for example, a 'type-ahead' facility in a menu-driven system. Secondly, the full set of available background tasks, or the possible parameters associated with them, may not need to be known by all users. Thus, the novice user might simply think in terms of retrieving an item from the database, whilst an expert might understand the notion of retrieval by a particular, user-defined, search path. In such an example the novice would simply and unknowingly be using default parameter values. Obviously, the use of a larger repertoire of background tasks may well involve the use of extra paths in the dynamics processor.

3 DESIGNING THE INTERFACE

It is clear that human factors considerations apply at each of the three levels of the interface. They correspond approximately to hardware ergonomics, software ergonomics and cognitive ergonomics. The design of the purely physical components of the I/O processors and their physical relationship to one another forms part of *workstation* design. It is quite clear that the more knowledge that ergonomics at all levels can provide, the better design can be. We may thus make a general plea for more work on human factors before considering certain particular issues.

Before considering the design of interfaces themselves we ought to briefly note ten Hagen's view that the interface should be the first part of the system to be designed (ten Hagen, 1980). In a batch processing environment it is often thought desirable to determine the inputs and outputs of a program first and then design it so as to achieve those ends. In an interactive system the equivalent, but much more complex, procedure would be to design the interface first. The specification of background tasks would then provide first-level descriptions of the background processor. It is suggested that the isolation of the dynamics processor leads to a clarification of the design.

In reality, the designer (or design/implementation team) of a man–computer interface has their own interface to the system (Fig. 3). To obtain good systems we need to do more than extol the designer to follow good guidelines (Maguire, 1981). We also need to consider his interface so that he is encouraged and assisted in the production of good systems. The most complex part of the system, from the point of view of the designer, will often be the dynamics processor.

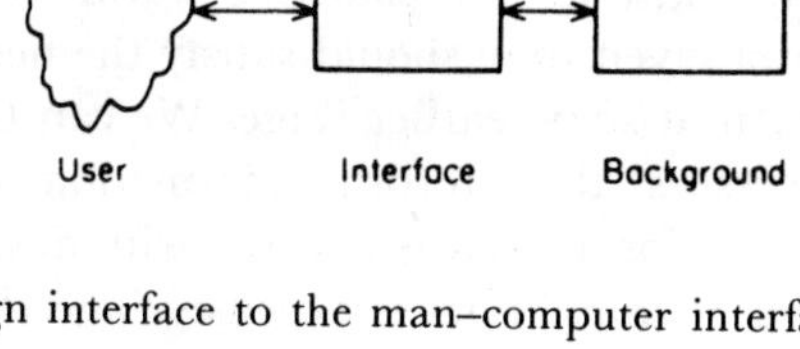

Figure 3. Design interface to the man–computer interface.

The need is for a specification notation that can also be used as an implementation language, as discussed and reviewed by Edmonds (1981). In that review, as in other papers, the basis of the specification of the dynamics is recursive transition networks. Hopgood and Duce (1980) have shown how, particularly when dealing with multistream input, a produc-

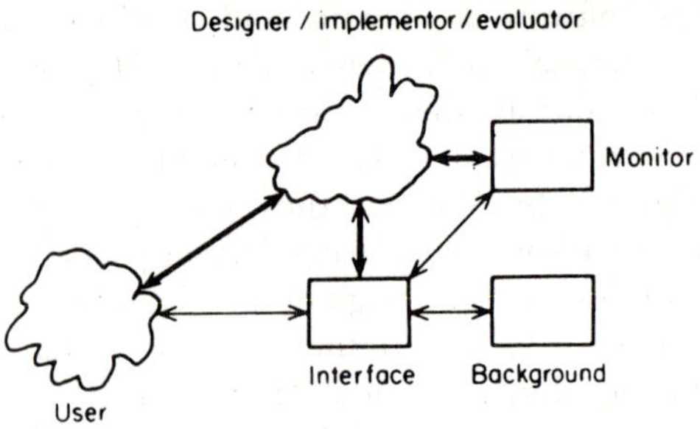

Figure 4. Monitoring of the man–computer interface.

tion system approach is more viable. A particular problem that needs to be faced here is that production systems seem to be found to be harder to use in certain respects than transition networks (Guest, 1982; Fitter and Green, 1981). As, in the work of Edmonds and Guest, a production system is used to implement recursive transition networks and some of the features of the production system are available at the transition network level, it would seem valuable to pursue the blending of the two approaches and so allow for various levels of competence in designers.

Whilst, from the point of view of the designer, the I/O processors are more likely to be selected, and possibly tailored, than specially designed, considerable problems still exist. Techniques for the handling of images and sound, particularly speech, are not yet advanced enough to provide all of the I/O processor for which we can identify a need. The possibilities are, however, sufficiently rich for human factors work to be undertaken on multichannel man–computer interfaces with the goal of providing more advice to designers on this topic.

The argument for adaptive design of man–computer interfaces is, in essence, that our knowledge about human behaviour is inadequate for us to proceed in any other way and that in a changing world we need to ensure that a system working at a given time should satisfy the needs of that time rather than those identified at some earlier stage. We can thus identify the need for monitor processors that record information concerning the activities of the interface and for interfaces to assist with evaluation (Fig. 4). Making use of a human–human interface is expensive and thus unattractive as a long-term method (Rosenburg, 1973). We need to develop sophisticated monitors and, if possible, make particular use of the possibility of providing intelligent monitors than can modify the interface without very much human intervention (Innocent, 1982).

4 CONCLUSIONS

A model of the man–computer interface has been presented and discussed and a number of problems for research briefly identified in relation to it. These problems are:

(1) the specification notations for the dynamics of interaction;

(2) the development of efficient methods for monitoring and evaluating interface behaviour;

(3) the study of self-adaptive interfaces; and

(4) the human factors aspects of multistream input/output systems.

It is important that work on these problems does not isolate them one from another or from other issues. A central research problem might be identified as the integration of work on these various aspects, i.e. the study of all of the communication channels identified in Fig. 4.

REFERENCES

Edmonds, E. A. (1978). Adaptable man/machine interfaces for complex dialogues. In: *Proceedings of the European Computing Congress*, London, 639–646.

Edmonds, E. A. (1981). Adaptive man–computer interfaces. In: *Computing Skills and the User Interface.* M. J. Coombs and J. L. Alty (eds). London: Academic Press, 389–426.

Fitter, M. J. and Green, T. R. G. (1981). When do diagrams make good computer languages? In: *Computing Skills and the User Interface.* M. J. Coombs and J. L. Alty (eds). London: Academic Press, 253–287.

Guest, S. P. (1982). The use of software tools for dialogue design. *International Journal of Man–Machine Studies*, 16, 263–285.

Hopgood, F. R. A. and Duce, D. A. (1980). A production system approach to interactive program design. In: *Methodology of Interaction.* R. A. Guedi, P. J. W. ten Hagen, F. R. A. Hopgood, H. A. Tucker and D. A. Duce (eds). Amsterdam: North-Holland, 247–264.

Innocent, P. R. (1982). Towards self-adaptive interface systems. *International Journal of Man–Machine Studies*, 16, 287–299.

Krammer, G. (1980). On computer problem-solving interaction. In: *Methodology of Interaction.* R. A. Guedi, P. J. W. ten Hagen, F. R. A. Hopgood, H. A. Tucker and D. A. Duce (eds). Amsterdam: North-Holland, 279–292.

Maguire, M. (1981). A study of the problems of man–computer dialogues for naive users. Ph.D. thesis, Leicester Polytechnic.

Maher, P. K. C. and Bell, H. V. (1977). The man–machine interface — a new approach. In: *Proceedings of the International Conference on Displays for Man/Machine Systems, Lancaster*, 122–125.

Moran, T. (1980). A framework for studying human–computer interaction. In: *Methodology of Interaction*. R. A. Guedi, P. J. W. ten Hagen, F. R. A. Hopgood, H. A. Tucker and D. A. Duce (eds). Amsterdam: North-Holland, 293–302.
Rosenburg, V. (1973). A technique for monitoring user behaviour at the computer terminal interface. *Journal of the American Society of Information Science*, 24, 1, 71.
ten Hagen, P. J. W. (1980). A conceptual basis for graphical input and interaction. In: *Methodology of Interaction*. R. A. Guedi, P. J. W. ten Hagen, F. R. A. Hopgood, H. A. Tucker and D. A. Duce (eds). Amsterdam: North-Holland, 239–246.

Report on Dialogue Specification Tools

Mark Green

Reprinted from: *User Interface Management Systems*, Pfaff (editor), Springer Verlag, pp 9–20, 1985.

This paper is the report from the working group that proposed the well-known 'Seeheim model'. A key contribution of the 1980s. The unlabelled lower path in Figure 1 is often missed out, or referred to as in some way a mystery, and yet it was explained in the body of the paper. One must presume that more people have looked at the diagram than have read the paper. The members of the working group were: Jon Derksen, Ernest Edmonds, Mark Green, Dan Olsen, and Robert Spence.

Report on Dialogue Specification Tools

M. GREEN

Department of Computing Science, University of Alberta, Edmonton, Alberta, Canada

1 INTRODUCTION

One of the goals of User Interface Management Systems (UIMSs) is the automatic (or semiautomatic) construction of user interfaces. In order to accomplish this, a description of the user interface to be implemented must be available. This report addresses three questions related to user interface descriptions. These questions are: what user interface descriptions are required to produce a user interface automatically, how do these descriptions relate to the human factors of user interfaces, and how can the existing user interface description techniques be classified? In order to address these questions an abstract model of a UIMS has been developed. This model does not represent how a UIMS should be structured or implemented; instead, it presents the logical components that must appear in a UIMS. Each of these components has a different function, and different description techniques are required for each one. The logical model of a UIMS is shown in Fig. 1. This model is similar to ones proposed by Edmonds (1982), Green (1984) and Olsen (1984). Each of the components of this model will now be discussed.

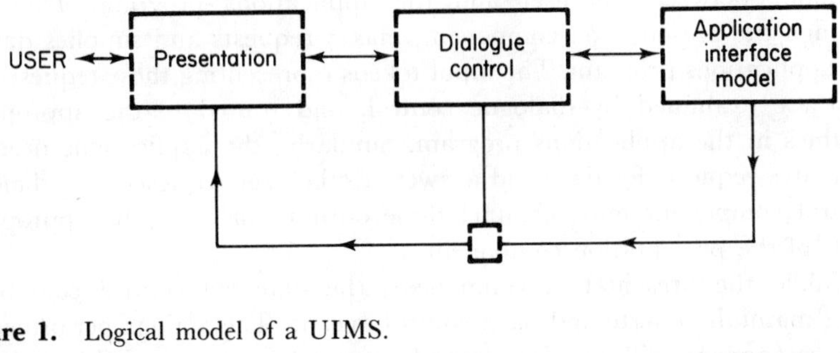

Figure 1. Logical model of a UIMS.

THE SEPARABLE USER INTERFACE
ISBN 0-12-232150-2

The *presentation* component is responsible for the external presentation of the user interface. This component generates the images that appear on the display screen, and reads the physical input devices, converting the raw input data into the form required by the other components in the user interface. The user interface employs an abstract representation for the input and output data. This representation consists of a type or name that identifies the kind of data, and the collection of values that define the data item. This representation is similar to that used to represent tokens in a compiler (Aho and Ullman, 1977). For this reason the term token is used for the chunks of information handled by the UIMS. The main purpose of the presentation component is to translate between the external physical representation of the tokens, and their internal abstract representation. In most cases this translation is a simple one-to-one mapping.

The external–internal mapping can be viewed as a dictionary, with one entry for each of the external and internal data items. This entry indicates how the token is to be translated. The presentation component has no control over the contents of the dictionary; it cannot change the external–internal mapping. The dictionary can only be changed by the dialogue control component. The dictionary is a generalization of the physical/logical device bindings that appear in some graphics packages. In terms of Foley's language model (Foley and Van Dam, 1982), the presentation component deals with the lexical aspects of the user interface.

The *dialogue control* component defines the structure of the dialogue between the user and the application program. This component receives a linear sequence of input tokens from the presentation component, and a linear sequence of output tokens from the application. Based on these two sequences of tokens, the dialogue control component determines the structure of the interaction, and routes the tokens to their appropriate destinations. The dialogue control component can be viewed as the mediator between the user and the applications program. The user, through the presentation component, makes requests and supplies data to the applications program. The input tokens representing these requests and data are examined by dialogue control, and routed to the appropriate routines in the applications program. Similarly, the applications program generates requests for data and answers to the user requests. The dialogue control component must channel these output tokens to the appropriate parts of the presentation component.

Unlike the presentation component, the dialogue control component must maintain a state and have control over it. The actions performed by this component will usually depend upon the context of the dialogue; therefore, any notations for it must be able to handle dialogue states and state changes. This component can also control the state of the presentation component; thus, a means of specifying these state changes is also required.

The *application interface model* is a representation of the application from the viewpoint of the user interface. This component defines the interface between the UIMS and the rest of the applications program. The application interface model defines the semantics of the application. This representation includes the data objects that are maintained by the application, and the routines the user interface can use to communicate with the application. This component contains the information required by dialogue control for routing tokens to the appropriate place within the application. It also contains constraints on the use of the application routines. This allows the user interface to check the semantic validity of the user input before the application routines are invoked. This information can also be used in error recovery and undoing user actions. This component of a user interface has not appeared explicitly in any of the existing UIMSs. However, most of them have some mechanism for performing some of the functions we have assigned to this component. The exact nature of this component will evolve as it is incorporated into UIMSs and used in practice.

2 HUMAN FACTORS

In this section the relationship between the human factors of user interfaces, and the three user-interface components is explored. There are two aspects to this relationship. First, how can human factors experts help us to design the three user-interface components? By dividing the user interface into three logical components it may be possible to develop better design guidelines, than by considering the user interface as a whole. Second, given descriptions of each component, is it possible to evaluate these descriptions from a human factors point of view?

Starting with the first aspect and the presentation component of the user interface, it appears that name spaces are a key issue. The presentation component is responsible for mapping between the user's symbolism and the internal representation of the user interface. When the user approaches an application he has a certain set of symbols he uses to name the physical and conceptual objects in the application. In order to have a smooth dialogue, the presentation component must deal with the user in terms of these symbols. The design of this set of symbols is where human factors enter the design of the presentation component. We need advice on how the symbols should be designed, how the symbol space should be structured, and the effects of interactions between symbols. Should the symbol space be designed in such a way that all the symbols are obviously disjoint, or is there something to be gained from interaction between symbols? In order to address these questions, advice from experts in human factors and cognitive psychology is needed.

In the dialogue control component the key human factors issue is command and dialogue structure. It is fairly well known that certain command formats and dialogue structures are superior to others, and numerous sets of guidelines have been produced for command language design. It has also been shown that interaction between commands can have an effect on the usability of a user interface. There is more readily available information on the design of this component than the other two components. However, there are still a large number of human factors issues to be addressed. One of the key issues is the effect of chunking and closure on dialogue design. How can we design a dialogue to take advantage of the user's natural chunking ability? Also, how can we design a dialogue so the closures occur at natural places, and the dialogue does not overload the user's processing abilities?

There is very little we can say about the human factors of the application interface model. The design of this component should be based on the user's model of the application. In many ways this component reflects the user's view of the semantics of the application. It must provide the operations that the user wants to perform in the application. If a particular operator is missing the user must construct a sequence of operators which has the same effect, and this may not always be possible. This imposes a greater cognitive load on the user than invoking a single command.

The design of both the presentation component and the application interface model requires a user's model of the application. In this context a user's model is the model the user has of the application. This model exists in the user's mind and he is usually not aware of it. There are two problems with user's models. The first is, how do we determine the model the user has of the application? Since the user is usually not aware of this model, he cannot produce a written version of it. It may be possible to interview the user, and then construct an approximate model from the results of the interview. However, we currently have no way of knowing if this model is correct. The second problem is, given that it is hard to extract the user's model from the user, is it possible to design a user's model, and then transfer it to the user? If this were possible the first problem disappears, and we are left with the problems of designing good user's models and transferring them to the user. The problems of user's modelling are beyond the scope of this paper, but these problems must be addressed in order to design good user interfaces.

The second human factors issue, the evaluation of user interface descriptions, is motivated by the precise descriptions of the user interface that are produced when a UIMS is used. The main purpose of these descriptions is to facilitate the automatic or semiautomatic production of a user interface. However, when such descriptions exist there is a great potential to use them for other purposes. Some techniques have already been developed for user interface evaluation. The best known of these are the grammar-based techniques of Reisner, and the keystroke model of Card, Moran and Newell. Both of these techniques require a complete description of the user interface. A UIMS should produce a human factors evaluation of a user interface at the same time it is producing the implementation of it. This would give the user interface designer a feel for how the user interface will perform, and where it could be improved. This could lead to a process of user interface debugging similar to the programming language debugging that is currently done with compiler generators.

3 NOTATIONS

Over the past few years a number of UIMSs have been designed and implemented. All of these systems have, in some form or another, the three user-interface components identified in section 1. The designers of these systems have developed notations for these components, largely without knowledge of what other UIMS designers were doing. One of the major goals of this working group was to analyze and attempt to classify the notations that have been used in UIMSs. The classification scheme presented here is by no means complete, but it does cover most of the existing UIMSs. It is interesting to note that most of the members of this working group already had a classification scheme in mind before the workshop. The classification scheme that resulted from our discussions does not differ radically from any of these preconceived schemes.

Our classification scheme is based on the three user-interface components. Each component has its own set of notations. The notations for dialogue control are further divided into three groups.

3.1 Presentation component

For the presentation component the notation must deal with both input and output. At the present time output notations deal mainly with graphical output. The range of these notations should be extended to cover sound, touch and movement (as in robotics). Most of the notations for graphical output are based on the routines provided by standard graphics packages. Calls to these routines are combined to form the symbols presented to the user. This form of notation is very similar to a programming language, and in most cases the target language of the UIMS is used as the basis for the notation.

This is not an acceptable form of notation, for the following two reasons. First, a textual language is used to describe something that is graphical in nature. As a result, the notation is hard both to use and to read. Given a collection of subroutine calls it is not an easy task to determine the image they produce on the display screen. What is really required is a graphical notation for the output symbols. One attempt at this can be found in the MENULAY system (Buxton *et al.*, 1983). Second, by using a programming language notation, the user interface designer is forced to do the work of the UIMS. The user interface designer should produce a high-level description of the symbol, and let the UIMS convert it into a program.

A similar situation exists on the input side of presentation component notation. In most cases the input primitives provided by a graphics package are used as the input symbols generated by the user. Most of the UIMSs do not provide a mechanism for combining the input primitives into more complex symbols at the presentation level. Currently this function is performed by the dialogue control component. The range of input primitives should be extended to cover video, voice and more complicated body gestures (such as character recognition). As yet, no really useful input notations have appeared.

The last issue to be dealt with in presentation component notation is the external–internal mapping. This mapping is controlled by the dialogue control component, but it resides in the presentation component. There are several issues associated with this mapping. The first is whether the mapping is a simple table lookup, or whether some form of simple decision making can be involved. These decisions could be based on the values of the token. For example, the presentation of an output token may depend upon the magnitude of its values. A detailed presentation would be given for small values, and an overview for large values. If decision making is included in the mapping what form should it take, and how would it be expressed? The presentation component contains the definitions of internal and external tokens. The dialogue control component must be able to reference these tokens in order to establish the mapping between them. How does the presentation component assign a name to the tokens, and how are these names passed to the dialogue control component? These issues must be addressed in any notation for the presentation component.

3.2 Dialogue control component

The dialogue control component has the most highly developed notation.

Since most of the existing UIMSs have concentrated on this component, it has more notations and there is considerably more experience with their use. The notations that have been used for this component fall mainly into three groups. The major difference between these groups is the model the notations have of the user interface. The transition network notations view the user interface as a collection of states, and the user's actions cause transitions between these states. The grammar group views the dialogue between the user and the computer as a language, and uses grammar-based techniques to describe this interaction. The event group views the user interface as a collection of events and event handlers. When the user interacts with the computer, one or more events are generated which are processed by the event handlers, possibly generating more events. This is not a complete classification scheme for dialogue control notations, since at least one well-known system does not fit (the Tiger system of Kasik (1982)).

The transition network group is the oldest group of notations for dialogue control. This approach to user interface management dates back to at least 1968 with the work of Newman (1968). This style of notation has been used in a number of systems since that time, and considerable experience has been gained in its use. A pure transition network, consisting solely of states and transitions between these states, is not powerful enough to handle a wide range of user interfaces, and tends to be hard to use. This is due to the fact that most user interfaces have a large number of states, with a large number of possible transitions between them. As a result, several schemes have been developed for partitioning the network. One approach is the use of subnetworks. A subnetwork is an independent transition network having its own set of states and transitions. A subnetwork can be used to replace any of the states or transitions in another network. Once a subnetwork has been entered it retains control of the dialogue until one of its terminal states is reached. When this happens control returns to the point, in the calling network, where the subnetwork was invoked. Thus, compound dialogues can be built up from smaller dialogues, each represented by a subnetwork. An extension of this approach is recursive transition networks (RTNs), where the subnetworks are capable of invoking themselves recursively. Experience with transition networks indicates that RTNs are necessary to handle the types of user interfaces that arise in practice. An example of a notation based on RTNs is SYNICS (Edmonds, 1981).

Experience with transition network-based systems indicated that a multithreaded implementation is desirable. This allows the user to interact with several networks at the same time. This can be used in help processing, where there is a separate network for the help command. The user can invoke the help network without fear of losing his place in the original dialogue.

The grammar-based notations use techniques from programming languages for both the description and implementation of the dialogue control component. These notations are based on using context-free grammar to describe the dialogue between the user and the program. As with transition diagrams, pure context-free grammars do not form an ideal notation for the dialogue control component, so numerous extensions have been made. Most of these extensions give the dialogue designer more control over the order in which the user's input is parsed. For example, it may be possible to specify that the ordering of the symbols in a production is arbitrary. This allows the user to enter these symbols in any order. Other extensions deal with error detection, error recovery and the ability to undo parts of the dialogue. It should be noted that the descriptive power of RTNs and context-free grammars is the same. There is some indication that RTNs may be easier to use than context-free grammars. Two examples of grammar-based notations are SYNGRAPH (Olsen and Dempsey, 1983) and DIALOG (Derksen, 1983; Borufka *et al.*, 1982). Closely related to this approach is the work of van den Bos (1980).

The event model is not as well known, or as highly developed as the other two groups of dialogue control notations, so a brief description of it is presented here. The event notations are based on the concept of events, and special procedures called event handlers. In many ways events are similar to the input and output tokens discussed in section 1. Each event has a name and a collection of data values. An event is generated each time the user interacts with an input device. These events are processed by one or more of the event handlers associated with the input or display device involved in the interaction. An event handler is a procedure that performs a set of actions based on the name of the event it receives. These actions include passing output tokens to the presentation component, passing input tokens to the application interface model, performing some calculation, or generating new events. The collection of events processed by an event handler can be viewed as a state. The set of event handlers active (able to receive events) at any one time defines the legal user actions at that point in the dialogue. This set can be changed by disassociating an event handler with a particular device, or associating a new event handler with a device. An event may be sent to more than one event handler. In this case each event handler is responsible for one aspect of the event's processing, such as the different levels of feedback, error checking and routing to high levels of the user interface. The event model is in many ways similar to object-oriented programming as in Smalltalk (Goldberg and Robson, 1983).

Most of the event-based notations have the appearance of programming languages. This is due mainly to the procedural nature of event handlers. These notations need some way of describing both the events and how they are processed. In most notations these two components are combined into one description, that of the event handler. That is, each event handler defines all the events it can receive, even if these events are used in several event handlers. This results in self-contained event handlers, at the price of increasing the redundancy of the descriptions, and possibly introducing inconsistencies. The description of an event handler contains one section for each of the events it can process. The section for an event starts with a description of the event itself, followed by the sequence of actions required to process the event.

3.3 Application interface model

Since the application interface model has not appeared explicitly in any existing UIMS, there have been no notations developed for it. In most UIMSs the application procedures called by the user interface form an implicit application interface model. While this identifies the application procedure used by the user interface, it tells us very little about the application, and these calls are usually embedded in other descriptions, making them hard to find. The application interface model must contain certain information about the application. To be useful the application interface model must cover at least the following three areas. First, it must contain a description of the application data structures that are of interest to the user and the user interface. The description of these data structures is at an abstract level, and implementation details are usually not important. The UIMS needs to know only the information that is stored in the data structures, and how it can find it. Second, there must be a description of the application procedures available to the user interface. This description must include the name of the procedure, and the operands it expects. This part of the description defines the interface between the user interface and the application. Third, constraints on the application of the operators must be outlined. These constraints include any preconditions for the operators, and any ordering restrictions on them. This allows the user interface to filter out some of the semantically illegal operations before they reach the application. While this is the minimum amount of information that must be included in the application interface model, there are several other things that would be useful. One of these would be the effects, or postconditions, of the operators. This would allow the user interface to anticipate the effects of commands, provide automatic help and perform automatically some undo processing. Another useful component of an application interface model would be procedures for performing standard tasks in the application. These procedures could be used by the user interface to guide naive users, and to provide sophisticated help facilities.

Since notations for the application interface model have not been developed, a classification scheme for them cannot be presented. Instead, several possible notations are presented, along with several of the issues that arose in our discussions. One possible notation is that of objects and operators. The objects correspond to the data structures in the application program, and the operators correspond to the application procedure available to the user interface. A notation of this kind, called UML, has been described by Green (1981, 1984). In order to handle a wide range of user interfaces this type of notation must treat object descriptions as type definitions, and allow the creation of arbitrary numbers of object instances. In a number of applications a network of objects is required, so notations that support only object hierarchies are not desirable. Another issue related to this type of notation concerns the parameters to the operators. An operator definition will contain a number of implicit parameters, but should these be the only objects available to the operator? Should there be global objects that represent the context of the interaction? If there are, how are these global objects to be defined and referenced?

Another possible notation for the application interface model is based on relations (as in relational databases (Date, 1981)) and first-order logic. This idea was prompted by the work done by Garret and Foley (1982) in graphical databases. The relations are used to represent the data structures in the application, while statements in first-order logic model the effect of the application procedures.

Two issues that must be addressed by any notation for this component are invariants, and sequential relationships between application procedures. Invariants state properties of the application that are always true. There are two reasons why they are a useful part of the application interface model. First, they form a concise description of general properties of the application. In most cases these properties can be described by other means, but this will usually entail a large amount of redundant material. Second, the UIMS can use them to detect errors in user input, and as the basis for guiding the user through interaction sequences. One issue related to invariants is whether they should be passive or active. A passive invariant describes some property of the application, while an active invariant takes an active part in the computation. That is, either the application or the UIMS will perform whatever actions are required to maintain the truth of an active invariant.

Some of the procedures in the application cannot be performed in arbitrary sequences. For example, a file cannot be processed until it is open; therefore, an open call must always precede any read or writes on the file. This is an example of a sequencing constraint.

4 INTERRELATIONS BETWEEN COMPONENTS

Figure 1 shows the interfaces between the components in our model of a user interface. These interfaces represent the flow of information or control between the components. In order to describe the user interface completely, the nature of these interfaces must be understood.

There are two issues related to the interface between the presentation component and dialogue control component that affect user interface notations. One of these issues is the form of the tokens flowing between these components. There are a number of ways in which this flow can be viewed. In one view, dialogue control treats the presentation component as a collection of logical devices. In this view there are problems related to the definition of device classes and device characteristics. One device characteristic is the type of the value produced by the device. Most graphics packages have a fixed set of types that can be used for device values. In the case of the presentation component, a fixed type structure may be too restrictive. On the other hand, the full type definition facilities of modern programming languages may be more than is required here, and would needlessly complicate the interface between these components. Work needs to be done on the set of types required to support communications between these two components. A related issue is the handling of picks. In existing graphics packages there is one type for all pickable objects. This type usually refers to the display file segment containing the object selected, and not the object itself. With the presentation component, each pickable object type could have its own device type, and the pick would contain a pointer into the application data structure identifying the object selected. This would relieve the dialogue control component of determining the object selected by the user. Another important device characteristic is its mode (as in the GKS model of graphical input; Rosenthal *et al.*, 1982). What are the interpretations of event, sample and request modes at the level of the presentation component? If the logical device view is not taken, some of these issues disappear. Another view of this interface is to treat the output of the presentation component as a simple stream of tokens, without any information concerning the devices that produced them (either logical or physical). In this view, the problem of device modes does not occur but the type problems remain.

Another important feature of this interface is the manner in which dialogue control exerts its control over the presentation component. Dialogue control is responsible for the state of the presentation component: it controls the external–internal mapping. How much information does dialogue control need in order to perform this function adequately? It must at least know the names of all the internal and external tokens, otherwise it will not be able to define the mapping. However, does it need more detailed information about these tokens? For example, should the physical devices associated with the external tokens be available to dialogue control? Or, is there a set of general device properties that would serve its needs? Another issue is whether dialogue control or the presentation component is responsible for enabling or initializing devices. The presentation component deals directly with the devices, so there is some argument for having it responsible for device initialization and control. On the other hand, dialogue control is responsible for the state of the presentation component, so it knows when the devices should be enabled. It may be necessary to share this responsibility between these two components.

At present there are far more issues associated with this interface than there are answers. More experience with UIMS implementations is required before a more detailed description of this interface can be produced.

The major issue associated with the interface between dialogue control and the application interface model, concerns the access dialogue control has to the application data structure. In particular, can dialogue control directly access the application data structure without informing the application? An argument can be made that dialogue control must always call an application routine whenever it wants to change the application data structure. This isolates the user interface from the implementation of the application data structure, and ensures that all modifications to the data structure are legal. On the other hand, this approach can be too inefficient for some applications, and places the burden of error recovery and undo processing on the application. This was an issue at the previous workshop in Seattle, and still appears to be unresolved. One possible, but inefficient, solution is to give the UIMS its own copy of the application data structure. The UIMS is free to modify this data structure without informing the application routines. At key points in the dialogue (determined by dialogue control) the UIMS copy of the data structure is used to update the application copy. In this approach error recovery and undo processing can easily be accomplished by restoring the UIMS copy of the data structure from the application's version.

There are two issues associated with the interface between the presentation component and the application interface model. The first issue deals with picking. The result of a picking operation should be some object in the application data structure that is currently displayed on the screen. The presentation component is responsible for the allocation of screen space, and the appearance of everything on the screen. However, it does not know about the application data structure. When a pick occurs, the presentation component knows the coordinates of the pick, but it doesn't know how to relate these coordinates to the contents of the application data structure. Some form of cooperation between the two components is required to determine the object the user selected. There needs to be some correlation mechanism between the coordinates in the presentation component, and the data structure maintained by the application.

The other issue involves the flow of output data from the application to the presentation component. In theory, all the information from the application that is to be displayed, must go through dialogue control. In most cases dialogue control is not interested in the actual data; it assigns the data a format or template, and passes it on to the presentation component. Since dialogue control does not need to process these data, it could be transferred directly to the presentation component, saving some processing time. This flow of data is represented by the arc flowing from the application interface model to the presentation component in Fig. 1. Dialogue control has control over this flow of information; it assigns the formats to the output data, and establishes the pipeline between the application and the presentation component. Once the pipeline has been established, dialogue control does not take part in information transfer. This approach is particularly effective when large amounts of data must be transferred from the application to the screen.

5 CONCLUSIONS

In this report we have presented some of the issues pertaining to the notations used in UIMSs. At present there are a small number of implemented UIMSs, so there is some experience to draw upon. This is the first workshop of this nature where there has been a significant number of participants with implementation experience. This experience seemed to raise more issues than it resolved. The conclusion that can be drawn from this, is that there is still a considerable amount of work to be done in notations for UIMSs.

One of the major problems encountered by this working group was the inability to compare different UIMSs. The systems discussed in this group have been used to produce user interfaces for different application areas, with different interaction styles and requirements. This makes it very difficult to compare the ease of use (for the user interface designer), and the quality of the resulting user interface. This problem could be partly solved by constructing a standard set of user interface problems. Each of the UIMSs could be used to solve these problems, and the results used as a means of comparison. This set of problems could be viewed as a benchmark test for user interface management systems. Along with developing the problems, techniques for measuring ease of use and the quality of the user interface must also be developed.

REFERENCES

Aho, A. V. and Ullman, J. D. (1977). *Principles of Compiler Design.* Reading, MA: Addison-Wesley.

Borufka, H. G., Kuhlmann, H. W. and ten Hagen, P. J. W. (1982). Dialogue cells: a method for defining interactions, *IEEE Computer Graphics Applications,* 2, 5, 25.

Buxton, W., Lamb, M. R., Sherman, D. and Smith, K. C. (1983). Towards a comprehensive user interface management system. *SIGGRAPH '83,* 35.

Date, C. J. (1981). *An Introduction to Database Systems.* Reading, MA: Addison-Wesley.

Derksen, J. (1983). *Een ontwerp van programmeergereedschap voer dialoogsystemen gebaseerd op dialoogoellen (Tools for dialogue systems based on dialogue cells).* TNO-IBBC Rapport Nr. B1-83-62/68.0.0004.

Edmonds, E. A. (1981). Adaptive man–computer interfaces. In: *Computing Skills and the User Interface.* M. J. Coombs and J. L. Alty (eds). London: Academic Press.

Edmonds, E. A. (1982). The man–computer interface — a note on concepts and design. *International Journal of Man–Machine Studies,* 16, 231.

Foley, J. and Van Dam, A. (1982). *Fundamentals of Interactive Computer Graphics.* Reading, MA: Addison-Wesley.

Garret, M. T. and Foley, J. D. (1982). Graphics programming using a database system with dependency declarations. *ACM Transactions on Graphics,* 1, 2, 109.

Goldberg, A. and Robson, D. (1983). *Smalltalk-80: The Language and its Implementation.* Reading, MA: Addison-Wesley.

Green, M. (1981). A methodology for the specification of graphical user interfaces. *SIGGRAPH '81, 99.*

Green, M. (1984). Design notations and user interface management systems. In *User Interface Management Systems,* G. A Pfaff (ed), Berlin: Springer Verlag, 9–20.

Kasik, D. J. (1982). A user interface management system. *SIGGRAPH '82.*

Newman, W. M. (1968). A system for interactive graphical programming. In: *Spring Joint Computer Conference 1968.* Washington, DC: Thompson Books.

Olsen, D. (1984). Presentational syntactic and semantic components of interactive dialogue specification. In *User Interface Management Systems,* G. A. Pfaff (ed), Berlin Springer Verlag.

Olsen, D. and Dempsey, E. (1983). SYNGRAPH: a graphic user interface generator. *SIGGRAPH '83.*

Rosenthal, D. S. H., Michener, J. C., Pfaff, G., Kessener, R. and Sabin, M. (1982). The detailed semantics of graphics input devices. *SIGGRAPH '82,* 33.

van den Bos, J. (1980). High-level graphics input tools and their semantics. In: *Methodology of Interaction.* R. A. Guedi *et al.* (eds). Amsterdam: North-Holland, 159.

The Run-Time Structure of UIMS-Supported Applications

John R. Dance, Tamar E. Granor, Ralph D. Hill, Scott E. Hudson, Jon Meads, Brad A. Myers and Andrew Schulert

Reprinted from: *Computer Graphics*. Volume 21. Number 2, pp 97–101, 1987.

This paper is another report from a working group discussing user interface systems. It addressed the problem of providing high levels of semantic feedback, as is often required in direct manipulation interfaces. A possible approach and outstanding problems are identified.

The Run-Time Structure of UIMS-Supported Applications

J. R. DANCE, T. E. GRANOR, R. D. HILL, S. E. HUDSON, J. MEADS, B. A. MYERS AND A. SCHULERT

1 INTRODUCTION

This group was concerned with the run-time support provided by a user interface management system (UIMS), as opposed to design, analysis, evaluation or other support. In particular, we were concerned with the demands placed on a dialogue manager by user interfaces that require a high level of semantic feedback.

Traditionally, dialogue managers have attempted a strong separation of the semantic component and the user interface component. The assumption was that these were relatively independent, and that separating them would lead to the benefits of modular programming: each component could be developed and changed independently of the other, multiple interfaces could be provided to the same application, consistent interface styles could be developed, and so on.

Unfortunately, this has not worked in practice. One important reason is that many user interfaces, especially direct-manipulation interfaces (Hutchins *et al.*, 1986; Shneiderman, 1983), require that semantic information be used extensively for controlling feedback, generating default values and error checking and recovery. For example, when using the Apple Macintosh, an icon may be dragged around with the mouse. When it is over other icons that can operate on it, such as the trash can, the operator icons are displayed in reverse video. This requires that semantic feedback (derived from the types of the icons) be provided while the mouse is tracking.

In general, the traditional breakdown of feedback into lexical, syntactic and semantic feedback does not adequately describe the variety of types of feedback currently in use. In fact, feedback is best classified as a continuum based on the amount of application semantic knowledge that is required. Myers gives the example of mouse tracking to illustrate this. From less

THE SEPARABLE USER INTERFACE
ISBN 0-12-232150-2

knowledge required to more knowledge required, the cursor can do the following: (1) directly follow the mouse; (2) follow the mouse, but move more per increment when the mouse is moving faster; (3) echo only at fixed grid points, where the application sets the grid spacing; (4) echo only at legal character positions in a text editor with a fixed-width font; (5) echo only at legal character positions in a text editor with a variable-width font; and (6) echo only at legal and 'good' moves in a game (such as Go or chess).

In general, semantic information is needed frequently to support feedback. It is also needed to provide meaningful default values for parameters to commands and to allow error checking and appropriate responses. Clearly, all dialogue managers have had to allow the user interface to change in response to semantic processing. However, because of the previous emphasis on separation of the application and the user interface, the communication between the two components has been too narrow and too slow to support rapid feedback. What is needed is 'fine-grain control' (Myers, 1987) rather than the 'coarse-grain control' provided by most existing dialogue managers. The problem is how to provide this without giving up the advantages that were realized in separating these components in the first place.

2 FRAMEWORK FOR RUN-TIME SUPPORT

There are three areas of concern in providing semantic information to the interface: the *dialogue manager*, the *application* and what we term the *semantic support component*, a subcomponent of the dialogue manager that contains information of concern to both dialogue manager and application. (When we use the term 'dialogue manager' in this report we often mean that part of the dialogue manager which is not the semantic support component. Unfortunately, we did not assign a name to that part of the system.) The relationship of these components is shown in Fig. 1.

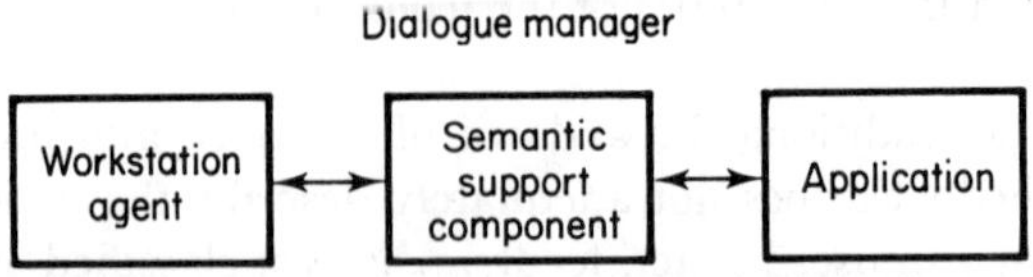

Figure 1. Relationship among system components.

This decomposition is similar to that proposed in the 'Report on dialogue specification tools' from the Seeheim conference on user interface management systems (Green, 1985a). We suggest that the *presentation component* of that model corresponds to the workstation agent, as described elsewhere (Lantz *et al.*, 1987), and possibly to part of the dialogue manager, as described below in Section 3.1.2. Their *dialogue control* and *application interface model* components are similar to our dialogue manager and semantic support components, respectively. The following sections discuss the purpose, responsibilities and contents of each component.

2.1 The dialogue manager

The primary purpose of the dialogue manager is to provide a higher level of abstraction for interaction services. The dialogue manager contains those parts of the system that:

are consistent across all applications, such as support for the presentation of help;

are device-dependent, such as the interaction technique library;

are in a generic user profile of interest to many interfaces and systems, such as whether the user is right- or left-handed; and

vary across different interfaces to the same application, such as facilities for supporting multiple command names for a given function.

2.2 The semantic support component

The purpose of the semantic support component is to provide information for semantic operations such as feedback, default values and error checking and recovery, to provide application-specific help information and to support modification of dialogue (such as changing menu contents) based on the application state. The semantic support component contains those parts of the system that:

are in an application-specific user profile, such as the preferred method for stereo viewing in Grip-75 (Lipscomb *et al.*, 1981);

define what is being displayed, such as the percentage shown of a file in a file browser; and

are unique to a specific application, such as the user's conceptual model.

The semantic support component is similar to the application interface model proposed at the Seeheim conference. However, while that was proposed as a passive interface definition, we view the semantic support component as an active component of the dialogue manager. The specification of the semantic support component implicitly specifies the interface to the application, but also defines how the semantics of the application are incorporated into the user interface.

2.3 The application

The application, in addition to processing and analysis, is responsible for the integrity of the data, although the other components may be responsible for error-checking. The application contains those parts of the system that:

do not need to know about the user interface, and about which the user interface does not need to know, such as procedures that perform finite-element analysis in a structural design system; and

are consistent across all interfaces to the application, such as the basic functions of the application.

3 POTENTIAL ARCHITECTURES

This section presents some models for how the dialogue manager and the semantic support component might be structured to support rapid feedback. We do not propose a single architecture, but instead simply discuss alternatives that have been proposed in other research.

3.1 Structure of the dialogue manager

The two primary options for the structure of the dialogue manager discussed in our group were: (1) having no structure imposed within the dialogue manager; and (2) splitting the dialogue manager into lexical and syntactic components. Since there is sometimes no sharp or well-understood division between the lexical and syntactic levels, the division is often made for convenience rather than because of strongly held beliefs in a layered structure.

3.1.1 Homogeneous object space

The first option proposes a homogeneous object space where the only differentiation among the objects is conceptual. The dialogue manager makes no distinction in its handling of an object based on the function of the object. The value of this type of dialogue manager is that it allows a fairly flexible definition of the components constituting an interface. It is assumed that objects will be provided with timely messages informing them of relevant input data, such as mouse movement, keyboard strokes, button clicks and clock ticks. Objects may also send and receive messages from other objects.

Objects may produce geometry for display in any of a number of ways. A message may be sent to a presentation server or workstation agent requesting that a previously displayed entity be replaced or updated. New display entities may also be created and old entities may be deleted as needed. The nature of the presentation server and its interface to objects may be considered to be implementation dependent. However, the specification of an object and its use of presentation server facilities must be available to the application in a standard manner.

By means of passing and acknowledging messages in turn, it should be possible to specify any needed syntax for a given interaction. In addition, instantiating several objects — each of which is capable of receiving input independently — allows for multiple concurrent interactions.

Using a homogeneous object space may involve a tradeoff of power and flexibility against ease of use and structure. A purely homogeneous system, which makes no distinctions between different levels or components of the system, provides a great deal of flexibility and power. However, it may also reduce the level of structure placed on the system and consequently make such systems harder to create, debug and maintain. Nonetheless, it is conceivable that a system supporting a homogeneous object space could be developed that would allow creative user interfaces to be specified more easily than with a highly structured support system.

There are several questions that need to be investigated and answered in order to develop an interface using this approach. One question is how to define the mechanisms and filtering needed for passing device input data to appropriate objects. Second, the mechanisms for instantiating and linking an object, particularly generic objects available from the dialogue manager's library, to one of several independent applications needs to be resolved. Third, there is the major issue of determining how an application will be able to define an object, instantiate an object and communicate with various objects through the dialogue manager. Finally, a dialogue manager is expected to provide a number of servers for purposes such as providing help, tracking history and accessing user profiles (as well as generating displays). Mechanisms need to be developed that will allow such servers to instantiate application-specific objects as needed in support of a given application.

3.1.2 Lexical/syntactic structure

The second option for structuring the run-time portion of a dialogue manager is to decompose it into lexical and syntactic components. The internal structure of a user interface is often expressed as having lexical, syntactic and semantic components. In the structure we developed, the semantic component is provided by the application and the semantic support component.

The lexical component is normally treated as a collection of low-level building blocks with built-in feedback. We call these building blocks *interaction modules*. Each interaction module typically implements an *interaction technique* — a simple, self-contained interaction with the user. Examples of possible interaction modules are tools to support pop-up menus, text string input and simple graphical input techniques like rubber-band line drawing. These typically do not change from interface to interface (although they may be customized by changing parameters), and can be collected into a library. It is important to be able to add new interaction modules that are needed by specific user interfaces.

The syntactic level is typically written for each user interface. It accepts input from the lexical level. Then it maps input sequences into commands that can be applied to the data in the semantic support component, or that can be sent to the application. Historically the syntactic level has been specified with grammars, such as finite-state machines. Other possibilities include event-based specifications, such as in the University of Alberta UIMS (Green, 1985b), Sassafras (Hill, 1987) and GUIDE (Granor, 1968), and object-oriented techniques, such as in the GWUIMS (Sibert *et al.*, 1986). Other techniques are possible, and in some cases the syntax may not be declared explicitly.

In the case of multithreaded, or concurrent, user interfaces, the syntactic level is responsible for mapping (sequences of) concurrent input into semantic-level commands. This implies that the syntactic-level specification technique will probably require simple concurrency control constructs. Examples of dialogue managers with a lexical/syntactic division follow.

In *Sassafras* (Hill, 1987), the lexical level consists of an extensible library of interaction modules. These are coded in a systems programming language, and provide a high-level interface to the input devices. The syntactic level is specified in event response language. This is an event-based language designed specifically to support implementation of concurrent or multithreaded interfaces.

In *GUIDE* (Granor, 1968), as in Sassafras, the lexical level consists of interaction modules called tools. These are coded in Pascal, using CORE graphics (Graphics Standards Planning Committee, 1979), and reside in an extensible library. The syntactic level is composed of tasks, each of which may contain several tools. Tasks are created by the user interface designer and provide the user with alternative methods of providing input.

The *GWUIMS* (Sibert *et al.*, 1986) is based on an object-oriented approach. While it does not require or enforce a distinction between lexical, syntactic and semantic objects, the authors suggest that such a categorization could be layered on top of the underlying system. The technique and graphical objects deal primarily with lexical level issues, while the interaction and representation objects provide the syntactic level, and part of the semantics (primarily parts of the semantic support component).

3.2 Structure of the semantic support component

Give the decomposition of an interactive application into dialogue manager, semantic support component and application, the layout of the data structures in the semantic support component (SSC) can depend on the application (APPL), the dialogue manager (DM), or both the application and the dialogue manager. Alternatively, the data structures can be independent of both the dialogue manager and the application. These alternatives can be represented as (DM) (SSC APPL), (DM SSC) (APPL), (DM SSC APPL) and (DM) (SSC) (APPL).

In the *(DM) (SSC APPL)* approach, the application determines the structure of the information in the semantic support component. This allows the structure of the shared information to reflect the specific needs of the application. However, it may make it more difficult for the user interface implementor to use this information (or may even render it inaccessible to the user interface).

The *(DM SSC) (APPL)* approach limits the structuring of the shared information to using structuring techniques specified explicitly by the dialogue manager. Although this may restrict the generality of the shared information, it makes it much easier to access from the user interface. It also allows the dialogue manager to provide standard display-update and dependency-analysis tools that have embedded knowledge of the structures. The availability of these tools may simplify the implementation of some user interfaces.

The *(DM SSC APPL)* approach is probably not possible. It would require that the user interface and the application both impose restrictions on the structuring of the information in the semantic support component. In some cases this may work well, but there is the risk of imposing too many constraints. This approach is likely to suffer from the limitations of both (DM) (SSC APPL) and (DM SSC) (APPL), without any of the benefits.

In the *(DM) (SSC) (APPL)* approach, the structuring of the information in the semantic support component is independent of the user interface and the application. There are therefore likely to be interface problems on both sides of the semantic support component and so this does not appear to be a viable alternative.

In practice, the (DM SSC) (APPL) approach will be preferred in dialogue managers that attempt to provide a lot of support for display update, or that are designed for applications with specific types of user-visible data. The (DM) (SSC APPL) approach is more flexible, but this flexibility requires extra effort from the user interface implementor.

The (DM) (SSC APPL) approach requires the application to export both data and procedures to the semantic support component. The procedures will be used by the user interface to update both the display and the data. In the (DM SSC) (APPL) approach, the structure of the data in the semantic support component is constrained by the design of the dialogue manager, so the dialogue manager can provide the standard routines to update the display and the data.

Examples of the (DM SSC) (APPL) approach include Cousin, DOMAIN and the work of Hudson (1986). *Cousin* (Hayes and Szekely, 1983), is one of the first examples of a system that makes the exchange and sharing of information between the application and the user interface explicit. It uses a form exchange paradigm, where the types of elements that may appear in the form are determined by the user interface. With *DOMAIN/Dialogue* (Schulert *et al.*, 1985), the connection between dialogue manager and application is based on shared data. Each datum is called a *task*. Each task is presented to the user by one or more *interaction techniques*. When the user modifies a task the application is notified. Similarly, when the application modifies a task, the technique is updated. There is a fixed set of task types, and it is managed by the dialogue manager. The information in the semantic support component in *Higgens* (Hudson, 1986) must be encoded in structures that are purposely limited by the designer of Higgens. This allows Higgens to provide tools to assist in display update, including dependency analysis, to ensure that these updates are done efficiently. This means that many user interfaces can be implemented quickly and easily. The cost is a lack of flexibility. This is not a major problem if the goal is to provide tools for developing specific types of user interfaces.

Examples of the (DM) (SSC APPL) approach include GUIDE and Sassafras. The interface designer provides *GUIDE* with declarations for all application objects that are visible to the interface. These may include constants, types, variables and headers for procedures and functions. This allows GUIDE to perform type checking on all references to application objects. The semantic support component for GUIDE also converts between the types of interaction technique values and the tasks that contain them. For example, it will convert from a character string to a real number or check to see that a string is a valid file name. The application is responsible for the display of application objects, while GUIDE controls the display of interaction techniques. This approach gives the interface designer a great deal of expressiveness in describing the interface. However, information passing is restricted to one direction, from the application to the interface; the interface must invoke application routines to modify application variables.

With *Sassafras* (Hill, 1987) the application programmer must supply procedures to do all updates and redisplays. Sassafras controls the interaction with the user, and maps user commands into invocations of procedures supplied with the application routines. This makes Sassafras very flexible. This flexibility costs in two ways: the application programmer (or perhaps the user interface implementor) must write routines in a traditional programming language for the semantic support component, and the functionality implemented in these routines may not be adequate to support some user interfaces, thus impeding their development.

4 RESEARCH ISSUES

This section discusses research questions that the working group felt were important. These are mostly orthogonal to the issues discussed above.

4.1 Concurrency

Concurrency is necessary to allow multiple input devices to be *operating* at the same time. This is different from allowing multiple input devices to be *available* at the same time, which just means that the user can choose which device to use. Dialogue managers that support multiple concurrent input devices include Sassafras (Hill, 1987), Adagio's Switchboard (Tanner *et al.*, 1986) and Peridot (Myers and Buxton, 1986).

The advantage of allowing concurrent access to multiple input devices is that it makes some interactions more natural and efficient. Experiments have demonstrated that users can easily and naturally use two hands at the same time and in doing so, will perform some tasks faster, more efficiently and with less learning time than with conventional one-handed interfaces (Buxton and Myers, 1986). Examples of this kind of concurrency are: (1) setting the position of a graphical object with one hand while controlling its size with the other hand; and (2) selecting words in a document with a mouse while using the other hand to control scrolling using a touch tablet. Although these interfaces can be implemented in systems without concurrency by sampling the two devices alternately, such systems make it more difficult to define a modular run-time structuring of the user interface.

A disadvantage to providing concurrency is the performance penalty that must be paid if there is inadequate operating system support. Also, concurrent programs are significantly more difficult to debug. This is especially true if the application program must also be concurrent and/or deal with the concurrency of the interface.

4.2 Multiprocessing and network issues

An important question is how a UIMS architecture is affected by the need to support distributed applications. For instance, one might identify four levels of interprocess communication, with progressively slower bandwidth: processes sharing address space, processes with disjoint address space, processes separated by a local area network, and processes separated by a wide area network.

Smooth feedback requires a responsiveness of the order of a tenth of a second. We therefore suspect that the dialogue manager and semantic support component must be connected by a local area network or reside on the same machine. The connection between the semantic support component and application is less critical in many (but not all) applications. However, a 'distant' application must have some way to export semantics to those dialogue manager facilities which are close to the user and able to support direct manipulation.

Predicting the performance requirements of these links, providing user interface design guidelines for reducing the dependencies on these links, and making the most of the available links are important research questions. Also, the capabilities required to export semantics from a 'distant' application to a dialogue manager supporting direct manipulation remain to be determined.

4.3 Role of object-oriented programming

A very promising model for how dialogue managers should be built is based on object-oriented programming. Systems using this new style include GWUIMS (Sibert *et al.*, 1986) and MacApp (Schmucker, 1986). The advantages of this approach are that the inheritance properties of objects make it easy to provide specialization and slight modifications of existing and supplied interaction techniques as well as higher-level structures. Whereas object-oriented programming makes it much easier to program user interfaces, it is still a programming technique, and dialogue managers can do more to help create user interfaces than just providing a programming framework. Therefore, research in this area is investigating how object-oriented programming fits into dialogue managers, how the objects should be structured to handle user interfaces (for example, the model–view–controller structure of Smalltalk), and how object-oriented programming affects the dialogue manager model.

4.4 Support for evaluation of user interfaces

Clearly, the run-time part of the dialogue manager should be saving information that the postprocessors can use to evaluate the interface. This information might also be used to enable UNDO and REDO facilities and macro construction.

The real challenge is not to record this information, but instead to aid in its evaluation. The manual process of reviewing and evaluating recorded user sessions can be quite tedious and time-consuming. The dialogue manager could help by adding semantic information to the recorded session, such as what tasks or application commands were being invoked by the lexical actions recorded. This would allow the user interface evaluator to look quickly at a cross-section of users performing a particular task and concentrate on trouble spots in the interface. The dialogue manager might also keep basic statistics on the number of times facilities such as HELP, CANCEL or UNDO were invoked before, during and after particular tasks or commands. This could provide a rough guide to isolating trouble spots in the interface quickly.

4.5 Support for sequencing

Direct-manipulation interfaces tend to have much less syntax and fewer ordering constraints than textual interfaces. However, there are still some situations where sequencing is important and necessary. For example, often one menu selection will cause a different menu to appear. It would be useful to have a tool to help with this kind of ordering.

Typically, transition diagrams have been used in this area. However, they do not handle concurrency and seem inappropriate for interfaces where semantics play a big part in determining what comes next. Hill's event-driven system (Hill, 1987) and GUIDE (Granor, 1968) are other approaches, but more work needs to be done.

5 CONCLUSIONS

We recognize the need to incorporate semantic information into a dialogue manager. We address this need by introducing a subcomponent of the dialogue manager, which we term the semantic support component. However, this raises questions about how the semantic support component is coupled with both the application and dialogue manager. More research needs to be done to learn how to structure this area better to support interactive applications.

REFERENCES

Buxton, W. and Myers, B. A. (1986). A study in two-handed input. In: *Proceedings CHI '86 Conference on Human Factors in Computing Systems (Boston, April 13–17, 1986)*. New York: Association for Computing Machinery, 321–326.

Granor, T. E (1968). *A user interface management system generator. Technical Report* MS–CIS–86–42. Graphics Lab. 12, Computer Science Dept., University of Pennsylvania.

Graphics Standards Planning Committee (1979). Status report of the Graphics Standards Planning Committee. *Computer Graphics*, 13, 3.

Green, M. (1985a). Report on dialogue specification tools. In: *User Interface Management Systems*. G. E. Pfaff (ed.). Springer-Verlag, 9–20.

Green, M. (1985b). The University of Alberta user interface management system. Proceedings of SIGGRAPH '85. *Computer Graphics*, 19, 3, 205–213.

Hayes, P. J. and Szekely, P. A. (1983). Graceful interaction through the COUSIN command interface. *International Journal of Man–Machine Studies*, 19, 3, 285–305.

Hill, R. D. (1987). Supporting concurrency, communication and synchronization in human–computer interaction — the Sassafras UIMS. *ACM Transactions on Graphics*.

Hudson, S. E. (1986). A user interface management system which supports direct manipulation. Ph.D. Thesis, University of Colorado, Boulder, CO.

Hutchins, E. L., Hollan, J. D. and Norman, D. A. (1986). Direct manipulation interfaces. In: *User Centered System Design*. D. A. Norman and S. W. Draper (eds). Hillsdale, NJ: Lawrence Erlbaum Associates, 87–124.

Lantz, K. A. *et al.* (1987). Reference models, window systems, and concurrency. *Computer Graphics*, 21, 2.

Lipscomb, J., Pique, M., Brooks, F. P. and Wright, W. V. (1981). The GRIP-75 man–machine interface [videotape]. *SIGGRAPH Video Review 4*. New York: ACM.

Myers, B. A. (1987). Creating dynamic interaction techniques by demonstration. *Proceedings of CHI + GI '87 (Toronto, April 5–9, 1987)*, New York, ACM.

Myers, B. A. The issue of feedback.

Myers, B. A. and Buxton, W. (1986). Creating highly interactive and graphical user interfaces by demonstration. *Proceedings of SIGGRAPH '86. Computer Graphics*, 20, 4, 249–258.

Schmucker, K. J. (1986). MacApp: an application framework. *Byte*, August, 189–192.

Schulert, A. J., Rogers, G. T. and Hamilton, J. A. (1985). ADM — a dialog manager. In: *Proceedings CHI '85 Human Factors in Computing Systems (San Francisco, April 14–18, 1985)*. New York: ACM.

Shneiderman, B. (1983). Direct manipulation: a step beyond programming languages. *IEEE Computer*, 16, 18, 57–69.

Sibert, J. L., Hurley, W. D. and Bleser, T. W. (1986). An object-oriented user interface management system. *Proceedings of SIGGRAPH '86. Computer Graphics*, 4, 20, 259–268.

Tanner, P. P., MacKay, S. A., Stewart, D. A. and Wein, M. (1986). A multitasking switchboard approach to user interface management. *Proceedings of SIGGRAPH '86. Computer Graphics*, 20, 4, 241–248.

Ru[illegible] structure [illegible] DBMS-[illegible] applications [illegible]

Tahiro, R. [illegible]

Localization of Application Knowledge in Incremental Development of User Interfaces

Philip D. Gray, Catherine A. Wood and Alistair C. Kilgour

Reprinted from: *Proceedings of INTERACT '90*.
D. Diaper *et al.* (Editors). Elsevier Science, pp 645–650, 1990.

This paper introduces an explicit 'linkage component' to deal with user interface/application communications. The functional components are separate processes from the user interface and each functional process has its own linkage component. Special 'linkage variables' constitute the shared data between the user interface and the application. This arrangement is one way of allowing clean and well defined links between the user interface and the application code.

Localization of Application Knowledge in Incremental Development of User Interfaces

P. D. GRAY*, C. A. WOOD* AND A. C. KILGOUR†

**Department of Computing Science, University of Glasgow, Glasgow G12 8QQ, UK*
†Department of Computer Science, Heriot-Watt University, 79 Grassmarket, Edinburgh EH1 2HJ, UK

1 INTRODUCTION

We may compare user interface management systems (UIMSs) with respect to a horizontal dimension along which UIMSs are ordered in terms of the number, and characteristics, of the actual components which mediate information flow between user and application. As Cockton (1987) has argued, separation of dialogue control from application functionality requires the existence of an actual component of the UIMS, the *linkage*, which handles communication between the user interface and application.

UIMSs may be compared along this horizontal dimension of separation with respect to whether:

there exists a distinct run-time component which handles communication between the dialogue control and the application;

such a component, if present, is specifiable independently of dialogue control and application; and

the component is reconfigurable at run time.

Additionally, we may identify a vertical dimension along which UIMSs may be compared with respect to the degree of modularization of their linkage. Task structures, and the dialogue control components which reflect them, often exhibit a hierarchical or graph-like organization. The application knowledge encapsulated in a linkage may be organized similarly, providing a number of advantages, including:

from the point of view of design, the structure of tasks in the conceptual description of the interface will be reflected in the semantics of the

THE SEPARABLE USER INTERFACE
ISBN 0-12-232150-2

application, as represented by the linkage's description of the application functionality; and

from the point of view of software engineering, the modularization of linkage brings attendant benefits such as information hiding and complexity control.

The Chimera UIMS, built as part of Project Druid at the University of Glasgow, has a user interface–application linkage which exhibits a high degree of localization of knowledge in both dimensions. In the remainder of this paper, we describe this component, its relationship with dialogue control and application, and how knowledge localization is achieved.

2 DIALOGUE CONTROL IN THE CHIMERA UIMS

Before looking in more detail at user interface–application communication in Chimera, it is necessary to examine briefly the dialogue control component, with which the application will communicate, as well as the overall system within which it resides. A fuller description of the system may be found in Wood and Gray (1990).

Chimera is a UIMS intended to provide rapid prototyping via run-time reconfigurability (Gray *et al.*, 1988). It consists of a specification language (Chisl) and an interpreter (Chip). Interfaces constructed in Chisl consist of three linked parts:

a presentation system defined in terms of interactive objects;

a dialogue control component defined as an acyclic directed graph of dialogue units; and

a user interface–application linkage which consists of a set of linkage units.

Of these, the presentation system is of no direct relevance to the present discussion, and the linkage component will be described in greater detail in later sections of this paper. The dialogue control component is discussed below.

The dialogue control component is composed from dialogue units (DUs) which form the nodes of the graph structure and define the flow of control of the interface. The DUs consist of definitions of presentation details such as windows, textpanes and fonts; declarations and definitions of interactive objects; declarations of local and global variables; options; and entry, exit and clean-up actions. The first two categories are actually part of the specification of the presentation system, which is itself modularized via the DUs but is implemented as a separately executing process. Interactive objects are presentation entities which have a visible representation and, in most cases, internal state and behaviour which can be changed as the result of user, dialogue control or application actions. Typical interactive objects include buttons, editable textfields and PostScript-defined images.

The heart of a DU is its options, which consist of condition–action pairs and which determine the flow of control. Conditions are tests over expressions referring to DU variables and the state of interactive objects. When an option condition is evaluated as true, the option's set of actions is executed. These actions include effecting changes to interactive objects, assigning values to DU variables, activating application processes and activating other DUs (subDUs).

Communication with application processes does not occur directly as a DU action but takes place via a separate component, the linkage component, described below. When a DU is activated via an option action, its set of options is added to the currently active options. Its parent's options are also still active unless disabled explicitly, thus allowing selection 'up' the DU activation path.

3 THE HORIZONTAL DIMENSION

In the Chimera architecture, application functionality resides in one or more Unix processes external to the user interface, which is itself a separate process. Communication with an application process is initiated by the dialogue control component. There is a predefined Chisl action which, given the name of an executable file; launches the associated process; assigns a Chisl identifier with the link (called the link identifier); establishes the pipes to and from the application process and creates and activates a component to handle user interface–application communication: this component is called a linkage unit (LU).

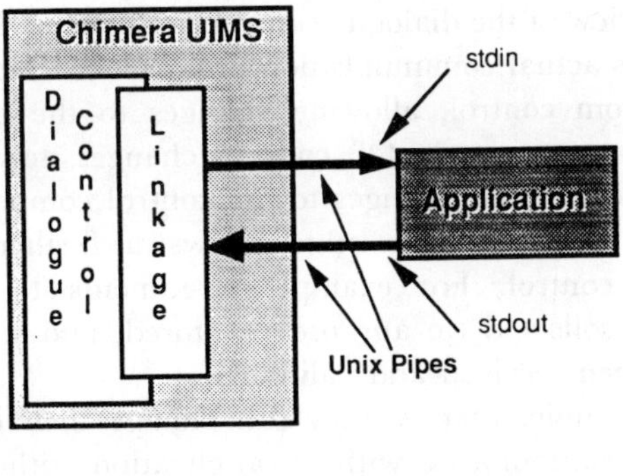

Figure 1. The dialogue–application communication process.

Once the application process has been launched and the linkage established, all communication between dialogue control and the application is mediated by the linkage. Subsequent Chisl actions may merge further LUs with the linkage, or replace it with a new one. Figure 1 illustrates the arrangement for one application process. In principle, a Chisl interface may communicate with any number of processes simultaneously, each with its own communication channels and linkage.

Like DUs, LUs contain declarations of local and global variables, as well as options. However, unlike DUs, LU option conditions may include tests over the contents of the input pipe from the application and a predefined LU action is available to place data on the output pipe. LUs may not include declarations of interactive objects.

Linkage and dialogue control communicate via special linkage variables, which constitute the only shared data between the two components. These variables may be used, changed or tested in the conditions of options in either component. Linkage variables are somewhat like active values, a communication and control mechanism used in some other UIMSs (Myers and Buxton, 1986), in that changing the value of a variable in one component may cause associated actions to be executed in the other component.

The options of both active DUs and active LUs are liable for firing. That is, input from the application is treated no differently from input from the user, allowing interleaving of user-generated and application-generated actions. In practice, DU conditions are given priority over LU conditions to enable user actions to be serviced with a minimum of delay.

We believe that this approach to horizontal application knowledge localization provides a number of advantages, the most important of which are listed below.

(1) The linkage variables provide an adequate model of the application from the point of view of the dialogue control component. The particularity of the application's actual communication protocol — lexical and syntactic — are isolated from control, allowing changes to the protocol without requiring changes to control. Of course, changes to the application semantics may well demand changes to the control component.

(2) The fact that LUs have state allows a further decoupling of application from control. For example, arguments to an application operation may be collected (in any order), stored, and sent when all the arguments have been received and validated.

(3) LUs are dynamic: that is, they can change their own state. This allows an LU to communicate with an application without causing any change to dialogue control state, for example when dealing with application messages of no relevance to the rest of the interface.

(4) The similarity of LU and DU structure simplifies the specification of an interface, in that a designer does not need to learn two entirely separate subsets of the specification language; a single computational model and, largely, a single syntax are applicable to both components.

4 THE VERTICAL DIMENSION

As mentioned above, when a link to an application process is created by a DU, the associated LU is 'attached' to the DU which created it. The LU's lifetime is thereafter coextensive with that of its parent DU; when the DU is deactivated, so is the LU.

Once a linkage is created, subDUs of the DU which created the linkage may add linkage units to that linkage. Typically, each subDU will add a corresponding LU which deals with the application-specific aspects of the task supported by the subDU. This vertical localization of application knowledge provides a powerful method of defining communication protocol incrementally. Each DU is thus responsible for adding to the protocol the content relevant to the 'task' which the DU represents.

This structure is similar to the approach of Coutaz's PAC model (Coutaz, 1987) in which each object in a PAC hierarchy may possess its own linkage to the application. The advantage of our architecture is that the overall linkage exists as a single (albeit compound) entity, thus allowing a designer to specify in terms of a single application model. Furthermore, global application actions can be handled at any level without having to pass information explicitly from one level to its predecessors. Figure 2 shows the combination of horizontal and vertical dimensions of modularity in the Chimera architecture.

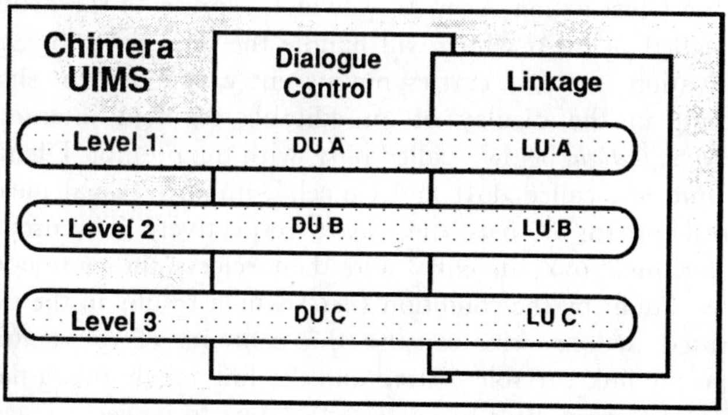

Figure 2. The horizontal and vertical modularization of application knowledge.

5 AN EXAMPLE

In order to illustrate the dynamics of UI–application communication, and the way horizontal and vertical separation are implemented, we present a simple example of an interaction in Chisl.

Consider the task of saving some prespecified data to a new file. We shall assume, for the purposes of this example, that the application can interpret the command 'Save as: ‹*filename*›'. If the filename refers to an existing file, the application will respond with 'File exists: ‹*filename*› Overwrite (y/n)?'. If 'y' is received by the application, the file will be overwritten with the specified data, otherwise the operation is cancelled. To save to another filename, the entire operation must begin again. Apart from the concrete syntax, this is not unlike the Macintosh's 'save as . . .' command.

Figure 3 shows the communication between the four components necessary to complete the task using a Chisl-specified interface. The presentation column describes the actions carried out by the user in terms of visible interaction objects, the dialogue column shows the dialogue unit options executed as a result of user actions and/or changes to DU or LU state (not all options are shown, only those which are in fact executed), the linking column indicates the LU options executed as a result of changes to link variables and/or application actions, and finally, the application column describes the actions carried out by the application as a consequence of data received from the linkage.

We assume that our example interaction begins partway through a larger interactive session. The user has already specified the data to be saved and is offered the choice of button interactive objects (referred to as *buttons* below) labelled Save, SaveAs and Delete. At the start of this task, the user selects the SaveAs button. The selection is tested in the dialogue control component via an option with the condition {*saveAs*}. On firing, the option executes the Chisl action *doSaveAs[ ]*, which represents the activation of a new DU called *doSaveAs* which will handle the required subtask.

On activation, the DU carries out its entry actions (not shown here), which result in the display of an editable textfield interactive object (referred to as *textfield* below), called *entry*, with the prompt 'Filename:', plus two new buttons, called doIt and cancel, with their usual meanings and with representations *Do Save* and *Cancel*, respectively. The user enters the desired filename, 'roo', in entry and then selects the button doIt. This selection is caught by the condition {*doIt*} which results in the execution of its associated actions, viz. causing the contents of the textfield to be assigned to the link variable *filename* and the link toggle (i.e. a flag which is automatically cleared after being tested) *doSave* to be set.

The linkage, as represented by the linkage unit associated with/activated

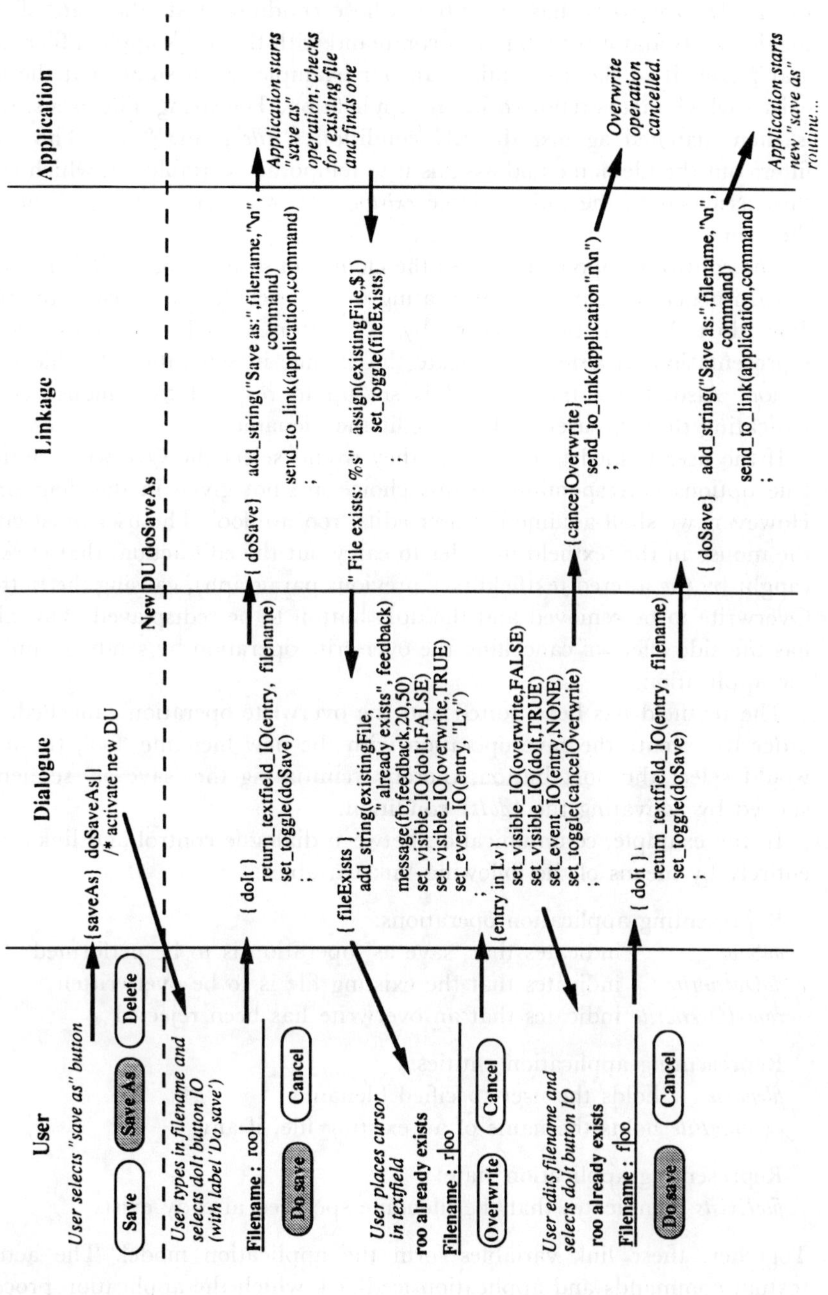

Figure 3. An example interaction.

by the DU *doSaveAs*, has an option whose condition tests the state of the toggle *saveAs* and if true, builds a command with the user-supplied filename and passes it to the application. In our example, we assume that the file exists, which fact is reported by the application. The string 'File exists: roo' is then matched against the LU condition {'*File exists: %s*'}. The '*%s*' filters out the file name and assigns it to temporary variable, *$1*, which is in turn assigned to the link variable *existingFile*. Another toggle, *fileExists*, is then set.

The control component catches the change of state of toggle *fileExists* and in turn generates a message indicating to the user the existence of the file. The doIt button is replaced by a button called Overwrite (with representation *overwrite*) to indicate the change in semantics of a file save action. Also, the entry textfield is set up to respond to a mouse click, indicating that the user wishes to edit the filename.

If the user wished to overwrite, they would select the Overwrite button (the options corresponding to this choice are not given in the diagram). However, we shall assume the user edits 'roo' to 'foo'. The user must click the mouse in the textfield in order to carry out the edit action; that click is caught by the altered textfield (see previous paragraph), causing the button Overwrite to be removed and the doIt button to be redisplayed. This also has the side effect of cancelling the overwrite operation by sending 'n\n' to the application.

The textfield has been edited and the overwrite operation cancelled. In order to execute the save operation with the new filename 'foo', the user would select the doIt button, thereby reinitiating the 'save as' sequence started by activating the {*doIt*} condition.

In the example, communication between dialogue control and linkage is entirely by means of the following link variables:

Representing application operations:

doSave	indicates that 'save as' operation is to be performed
doOverwrite	indicates that the existing file is to be overwritten
cancelOverwrite	indicates that an overwrite has been rejected

Representing application entities:

filename	holds the user-specified filename
existingFile	holds the name of an existing file, if any

Representing application state:

fileExists	indicates that the filename specified already exists

Together, these link variables form the application model. The actual textual commands and application feedback which the application process understands and can generate are isolated in the linkage component and could be changed without affecting either the dialogue component or the communication between dialogue and linkage. Furthermore, note the application operation to cancel an overwrite has now been embedded in the task of selecting the textfield for editing.

Although this example describes the horizontal dimension in some detail, it does not show the vertical modularity explicitly. However, each of the other options available in the parent DU (i.e. *save* and *delete*) would have their own LUs to handle communication for those tasks.

6 CONCLUSIONS

In its present form, the Chimera linkage component provides an explicitly specifiable, dynamically reconfigurable and active UIMS component which modularizes application functionality. We believe that it provides considerable flexibility for design and that the separability it provides between dialogue specification and application linkage specification is an indispensable aid to the designer in conceptualizing and prototyping the different aspects of an interface which must be combined to form an effective system.

Currently Chimera supports only string and toggle variables. More complex data structures will be necessary in order to handle sophisticated application models.

ACKNOWLEDGEMENTS

We would like to thank Kieran Clenaghan, David England and Kevin Waite for their helpful comments on an earlier version of this paper. The initial realization of the need for a Chimera linkage is the natural consequence of working near Gilbert Cockton. The work in this paper was supported by the UK Science and Engineering Research Council under Grant GR/D 80124. Their assistance is gratefully acknowledged.

REFERENCES

Cockton, G. (1987). A new model for separable interactive systems. In: *Proceedings of Interact'87*. Bullinger and Shackel (eds), 1033–1038.

Coutaz, J. (1987). PAC, an object oriented model for dialog design. In: *Proceedings of Interact'87*. Bullinger and Shackel (eds), 431–436.

Gray, P. D., Kilgour, A. C. and Wood, C. A. (1988). Dynamic reconfigurability for fast prototyping of user interfaces. *Software Engineering Journal*, November 1988, 257–262.

Myers, B. A. and Buxton, W. (1986). Creating highly interactive and graphical user interfaces by demonstration. *ACM SIGGRAPH*, 20, 4, 249–258.

Wood, C. A. and Gray, P. D. (1990). User interface–application communication in the Chimera UIMS. Glasgow University, Department of Computing Science, *Research, Report CSC/90/R1.*

The User Interface Management System DIAMANT

Bernhard Trefz and Jürgan Ziegler

Reprinted from: *Engineering for Human–Computer Interaction.* C. Cockton (Editor). Elsevier. pp 177–195, 1990.

This paper presents an object oriented user interface management system in which the separation between the user interface and the functional code is mediated by a 'representation manager'. The key issue addressed here is the support of a variety of external, user, representations for a single internal, functional, object and the maintenance of consistency that is then required. It is shown that the representation manager, in certain circumstances, can be implemented within the user interface system. The problems of achieving this in general are discussed and it is concluded that it is unlikely to always be possible. The argument supports the flexibility proposed in SLINKY, mentioned in Chapter 1.

The User Interface Management System DIAMANT

B. TREFZ AND J. ZIEGLER

Fraunhofer Institute IAO, Stuttgart, W. Germany

1 INTRODUCTION

Increasing interactivity, as well as graphical and multimedia features of user interfaces, has led to an increased effort and cost for user interface software in relation to the whole system. Furthermore, the quality of the user interface is gaining more and more significance for the acceptance and the success of a product. Software tools for the design and the implementation of user interfaces are important aids to tackle these problems. To build such tools, we need models for software architectures of interactive systems and control models to describe the dynamic aspects in the user interface.

Models for software architectures of interactive systems have to describe how the user interface component is separated from the rest of the system. A well-known model of this kind is the Seeheim model for the run-time architecture of user interface management systems (UIMSs) described in Pfaff (1985). Other models are described in Dance *et al.* (1987) and Cockton (1987). Often-used control models are state transition networks, context-free grammars and event-driven models. Much work has been done in this area (see for example, Green, 1986; Hill, 1987; Jacob, 1986; Olsen and Dempsey, 1983; Myers, 1988).

In the context of the ESPRIT project HUFIT (Human Factors in Information Technology), we are developing the object-oriented user interface management system DIAMANT (Dialogue Management Tool) which is designed to support the development of direct manipulation interfaces. An initial version of this system focused on presentation objects and on the dialogue control component, but lacked a clear architectural framework of how to organize an interactive system beyond simply separating the user interface from the rest of the system. In particular, there was no support to keep consistency among different external representa-

THE SEPARABLE USER INTERFACE
ISBN 0-12-232150-2

tions of one object. We therefore developed a software architecture which maintains a clear separation between user interface components and the rest of the system but also includes specific components responsible for consistent external representations of data objects. The architecture serves as a framework for DIAMANT applications but can also be used as a framework for any other interactive system. This paper introduces the software architecture and describes in its second part an implementation using the DIAMANT UIMS.

2 ARCHITECTURE

In this section we develop a software architecture for interactive systems which:

can be supported by UIMSs;

ensures consistency between different external representations; and

can be used for multimedia interfaces.

The architecture assumes that it is possible to separate an interactive system into two main parts, so that one part implements the underlying functionality of the system and the other part implements the user interface of the system. In the rest of the paper we will refer to these parts as 'the application' and 'the user interface'. By separating these two components, it is possible to develop software tools which are tailored to support the functionality of the user interface component in an efficient and transparent manner.

The advocated separation of a system leads to a separation of a data

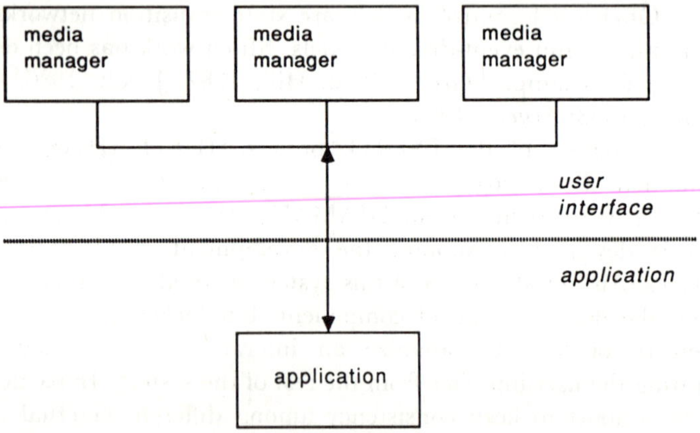

Figure 1. Initial separation of interface functions.

object into an internal object, used by the application to perform semantic processing, and its external representations presented to the user to give feedback about the state of the internal object. The external representations are also used for referencing the internal objects, for example by pointing. Each internal object, located in the application, may have zero or more external representations, located in the user interface. For example, a directory of the Macintosh's hierarchical file system may be represented on the screen as icon and additionally as a window. The external representations are not restricted to the same output medium; in fact, it may be quite reasonable to use different media for representing certain aspects of an object or certain relationships among objects. Figure 1 shows a first architecture according to this separation.

We see an application interacting with various components which manage the external representations for the user and which we call media managers. The media managers hide the low-level details of their underlying devices and provide a more abstract, device-independent interface towards the application, thus allowing the application to generate external representations in a convenient manner. Different media managers can use the same medium. One media manager may use the screen to display interaction objects like buttons or menus, and another one may use the same screen to display structured graphics objects. Other media managers may provide interfaces for speech input/output, animation or other presentation techniques.

External representations are stored by media managers so that some user references to an external representation, for example a reference by pointing, can be resolved by the media manager if no semantic or even conceptual knowledge is required. For example, a media manager can translate a mouse click on a button in a 'button pressed' event, whereas a mouse click on a door of a house displayed as a structured graphics element can refer to the rectangle representing the door, to the graphics of the whole house, to the internal object door for which the rectangle displayed on the screen is just a graphical representation, or to some other entity. The problem addressed in this paper is to keep consistency among the different representations of one internal object: we discuss this point later.

The architecture described so far has no specific component to implement the dialogue syntax. This component can be separated from the parts of the system implementing the functionality, and can therefore be located in the user interface. It can also be separated from the various components which display objects by means of output media. This corresponds to the definition of syntax for a graphical input language, as proposed by Foley *et al.* (1984). In this model the syntactical level is decomposed down to device-independent interaction tasks which can be

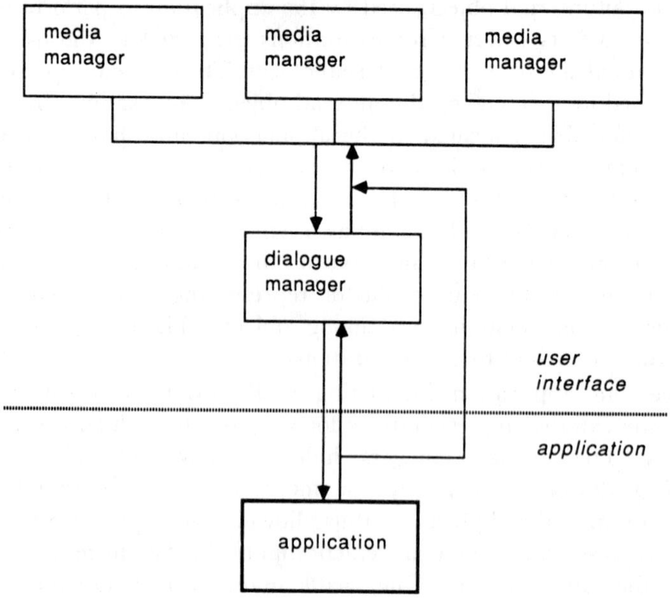

Figure 2. Interface including dialogue manager.

mapped to several device-dependent interaction techniques. Following these lines, we arrive at the architecture shown in Fig. 2.

The dialogue manager implements the syntax of the system. It interacts with the media managers to accept user input and to give syntactic feedback, such as highlighting a selected object or to displaying a command menu. It also interacts with the application, the operations of which are triggered by the dialogue manager.

As mentioned already, a major problem is to keep the different representations consistent. Inconsistencies can occur if the application changes the state of an internal object and no update on the corresponding external representations is done. Hence the application has to trigger update operations on external representations if it changes the state of internal objects. Another kind of inconsistency can occur among different external representations of one object if the dialogue manager changes one external representation to show a syntactic state of the user interface and does not change the other corresponding external representations. For example, if one external representation is selected by the user and the system gives feedback to show this selection, all external representations of this object should, say, be highlighted.

In order to free the application and the dialogue manager of the need to

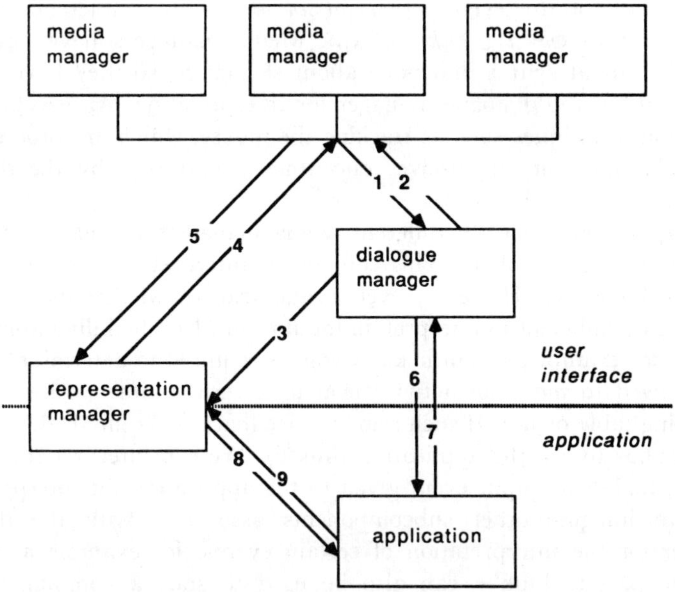

Figure 3. Final architecture including representation manager.

know every external representation in the media managers, a representation manager is introduced in the final architecture shown in Fig. 3. Its operations are triggered by the application and the dialogue manager and its data structures link together the different representations of internal objects. All update operations on external representations of internal objects will be done by the representation manager, hence relieving the dialogue manager and application from the burden of knowing the dependencies among external representations.

In Fig. 3 the representation manager is placed at the border between the user interface and application because its operations are triggered by both and it needs at least hooks into the data structures of both components. The architecture says nothing about how the representation manager should be implemented. Its data structures can be linked, if possible, with the internal representations of the application, thus using the given structure of internal representations and avoiding redundancy. They can, however, also be implemented as separate data structures in the user interface component.

The links in Fig. 3 explain the flow of events among managers. All user input is first processed by the media managers which try to interpret low-level input events within their scope of knowledge about external representations, producing higher-level input events. An example is the interpretation of the event ‹*mouse pressed at x,y*› as a reference and its translation into ‹*object z picked at x,y*›. Media managers have only little knowledge about syntax and none about semantics, so they have to pass most events to the dialogue manager for interpretation. An exception are interaction techniques such as tracking the mouse, which are processed by the media managers themselves once they are started by the dialogue manager.

All input events leaving different media managers are gathered in the dialogue manager (link 1). This component interprets the events in their syntactical context. However, even syntactical knowledge may in some cases not be sufficient to interpret an input event. In scheduling application systems, for example, semantic knowledge is required to determine whether it is allowed to move an activity icon to a certain time position on the scheduling table or not. If such semantic feedback is required, the dialogue manager has to ask the application (link 6). We can interpret this as just another, high-level input event given to the application for interpretation. One can imagine other subcomponents associated with the dialogue manager for the interpretation of certain events, for example a natural-language parser. Link 6 can also be used to start a command in the application, whereas the application can use link 7 to start commands in the user interface component.

All update operations for presentation objects are controlled by the representation manager (link 4), which keeps track of the different external representations. We can identify two kinds of update operations. The first is triggered by the dialogue manager and involves only external representations (link 3). Examples are highlighting an object or opening an object, i.e. asking for a more detailed view of an object. The second kind of update operation is triggered by the application and is caused by a change in the internal representations (link 9).

The representation manager may have not enough knowledge to produce a certain external representation of an object. In this case, it has to ask the application for more information. For example, if the dialogue manager orders the representation to show a directory as a window, the representation manager might have to ask the application for the subcomponents of the directory (links 8).

Interaction techniques, such as mouse tracking, are started by the dialogue manager using link 2. Some objects represented to the user, for example a command menu, do not correspond to a internal object, because they are used only by the dialogue manager for syntactical issues. The update of these objects can be done by the representation manager if the representation manager is located in the user interface component (links 3 and 4), or by the dialogue manager itself (link 2).

Link 5 is used if an object in a media manager asks for a different external representation without involving the dialogue manager. For example, if a object in a media manager shows the content of a directory either in iconic or in textual form and already provides buttons to allow a user to switch between different representations, it can use link 5 to ask for a different representation.

3 IMPLEMENTATION OF THE INTERFACE ARCHITECTURE: DIAMANT

This section describes the DIAMANT UIMS and shows by the use of examples how an interactive system can be built up using DIAMANT, according to the architecture proposed. DIAMANT is an object-oriented UIMS directed to the development of graphical user interfaces. Currently DIAMANT consists of a programming language (user interface description language, UIDL), a library of predefined classes, and an editor for the combination of graphical building blocks. The run-time kernel of DIAMANT also provides facilities for interprocess communication, allowing a user interface component written in UIDL to communicate with other processes. DIAMANT's run-time kernel establishes and manages the communication lines to other processes and translates requests or replies from other processes into UIDL events.

The user interface description language of DIAMANT is an object-oriented programming language, which was designed with the aim of supporting the implementation of user interfaces based on an event-driven model (Green, 1986; Hill, 1987). In an event-driven model, each action in the user interface is considered as a direct response to a recognized event. Other models, like transition networks or context-free grammars, can be mapped onto an event-driven model, as shown by Green (1986). Event-driven models are well suited to describe user interfaces which have few modes and require no complex command parsing but allow multiple command threads or even parallel input.

UIDL allows the construction, modification and combination of classes. Each class has rules which specify the behaviour of the class after an event has occurred. The response to events may include a change in the state of the receiver object, creating new instances or sending events to other objects. A UIDL class inherits rules from its superclass. By this means, predefined classes from a library, for example classes of a media manager, can easily be modified by the user of UIDL. UIDL programs are translated into C++ programs in order to achieve a high efficiency of the generated code.

UIDL was designed to implement interfaces following an event model. In an initial version, the semantics of sending an event were to insert a new event in a queue and to return control immediately to the sender. The advantage of this approach is that the UIMS provides the same model of an event queue as do the window system and graphical toolkit. Furthermore, an event can be sent to an external process without blocking the UIMS: it can continue processing user input without waiting for the external process to complete the event handling. A disadvantage of this nonblocking send is that race conditions between different threads of events may occur. For example, if one event thread creates a new window and makes it visible on the screen and a second thread inserts components into the window, it depends on the number of processing steps in each thread whether the components are inserted in the new window before making it visible, or whether the window is made visible and the components are inserted afterwards, which causes flickering on the screen.

This also conflicts with the concept of a class, also provided in UIDL, because a class promises a certain service to its clients independent of the class implementation. A change in the implementation of a UIDL class, using the nonblocking send, might change the behaviour of the class because new race conditions might be introduced by the change. Therefore UIDL currently provides two kinds of *send* functions, nonblocking send and a blocking send which behaves like message passing. The *send* function used in the following examples is the blocking send.

To implement an interactive system following the architecture developed above, a designer using DIAMANT has to write classes for the dialogue and the representation manager. The media managers are accessed from DIAMANT UIDL by means of libraries of predefined classes which are written in plain C++. A user of UIDL can adapt these classes by subclassing to his/her specific needs.

3.1 Media managers

Currently DIAMANT provides four different media managers, one for graphical interaction objects like buttons or menus, one for speech input, one for speech output and a media manager controlling a video recorder. The media manager handling graphical interaction objects is always present in each DIAMANT application. The other media managers are implemented as separate processes which can be added optionally to a DIAMANT application. Objects in the media manager are accessed by predefined UIDL classes.

The media manager for graphical interaction objects uses the graphical toolkit InterViews which sits on top of X-Windows. Almost all interaction

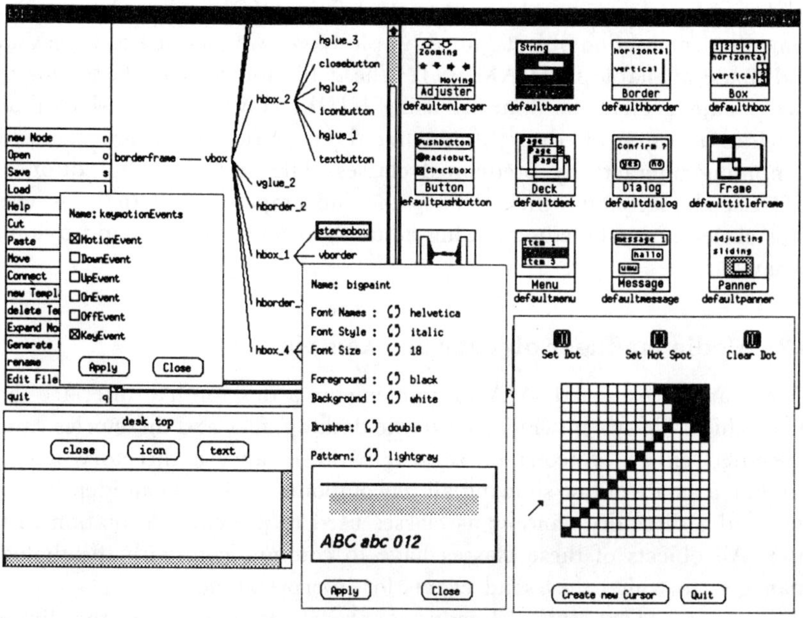

Figure 4. Editor to combine graphical building blocks.

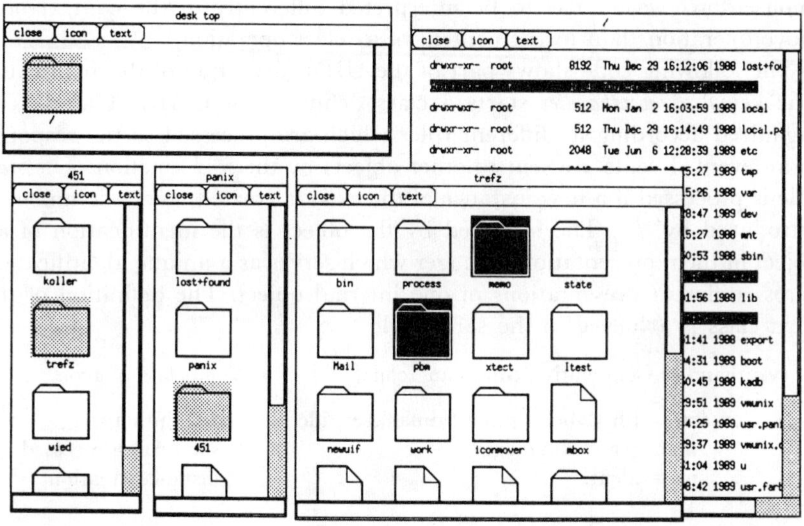

Figure 5. DIAMANT desktop interface.

objects of InterViews can be used as predefined UIDL classes. Furthermore some new interaction objects, for example Icons, were added to InterViews and made available in DIAMANT. The definition of new classes for this media manager can be done by using UIDL. However, DIAMANT also provides a graphical editor (Fig. 4) for the construction of new classes by combining interactively predefined classes. The output of the editor is a UIDL code skeleton which defines the subcomponents of the new class. This skeleton can be edited, using a standard text editor, to add dynamic behaviour.

3.2 Media manager objects: an example

One example using DIAMANT implements a desktop-like interface for a hierarchical file system (Fig. 5). On the desktop, files and directories can be presented either as icons or as text. Additionally, a directory may be presented as a window showing all its components. So we can identify icon, text and a directory window as classes used to present information to the user. All objects of these classes have to communicate with the dialogue manager, to which they send events for interpretation.

Icons and Text exist already as predefined classes of the library; therefore, we can build subclasses which just send all events originated by the user to the dialogue manager. This is because these objects cannot determine the syntactic context in which the event occurred. For example, a 'mouse-down' event has to be interpreted differently in the context of a move operation than in the context of a select operation.

The following code shows part of the UIDL definition of the Icon class. The keyword *eventhandler* starts a class definition in UIDL. The class is organized according to different rules which are processed as the response to an event. Events are sent to other objects by the *send* function. The *start* rule is processed if a new instance of the class is created, and a comment is introduced by '//'. The *id* stored by the object is the identification of an object in the representation manager which serves as a unique identification across different presentations of one internal object. The definition of the Text class is achieved in the same style:

```
eventhandler CooperativeIcon is an Icon {          // subclass of Icon

    on start with (label, bitmap, dmanager, ident) : (label, bitmap) {
        manager = dmanager;                        // start rule processed
        id = ident;                                // instance creation
        }
    on 'down' {                    // rule processed on mouse-down event
        send (manager, 'down', id);          // send to dialogue manager
```

```
        }
      .
      .
    }
```

The class DirectoryWindow allows a user to switch between an iconic and a textual presentation of its contents. Therefore it has to communicate with objects in the representation manager which are asked for a certain representation. The following UIDL code omits the details of the graphical representation but shows the parts which implement the communication to the representation manager objects:

```
eventhandler DirectoryWindow is a Border Frame {

    on start with (title, ident, comps, dmanager, . . .) {
        .
        .
        components = comps;            // components to display
        id = ident;                    // id of representation object
        manager = dmanager;            // dialogue manager
        state = 'icon';                // start with iconic presentations
        send (this, 'displayAll');     // send to itself
        }
    on 'displayAll' {
        for each key in components do {
            send (this, 'display', key);   // send to itself
            }
    on 'display' with (comp) {
        view = send (comp, 'activate',
                state);                // ask for presentation object
        components [comp] = view;      // store for later use
        send (box, 'insert', view)     // insert into an interior layout box
        }
    on 'switch' with (newState) and newState != state {
        send (this, 'removeAll');      // remove old presentation objects
        state = newState;
        send (this, 'displayAll');
        }
    .
}
```

The Directory Window class stores its components in the field components, The communication is done in the 'display' rule in which an 'activate' request for a certain presentation encoded by the variable state is sent to the representation object. The representation object will then create the requested presentation which can be either a CooperativeIcon or a CooperativeMessage.

3.3 Dialogue managers

The purpose of the dialogue manager is to concentrate the code dealing with syntactic issues. The following UIDL code shows part of a dialogue manager class which interprets a 'mouse-up' event with the right mouse button as an request to open this object. The identification sent with the up and down events is the identification of the object in the representation manager which manages the sending presentation object. Requests to highlight external representations or to create new external representations can therefore be send to this identification. It is the responsibility of the representation manager objects to highlight existing presentation objects and to activate new presentation objects:

```
eventhandler DialogueManager {

    on 'down' with (id) and RightDown( ) == 'true') {
        client = id;
        send (id, 'invert', 'true');              // highlight representations
        }
    on 'up' with (id) and WasRight( ) == 'true') {
        window = send (client, 'activate',
                  'window');                      // ask for window
        if (window) {
            send (client, 'gray', 'true');        // mark as open
            send (world, 'insert', window);       // make window visible
            }
        }
  .
  .
    }
```

Dialogue manager objects of different applications often show a similar pattern: for example, a typical move command is started by clicking into the selected object and moving the mouse outside the object. It is thus possible to implement a library of dialogue manager objects, freeing a developer from the task of implementing the dialogue manager from scratch. UIDL will then be used to modify and combine predefined objects of the dialogue manager in the same way it is used to modify and combine objects of the media managers.

3.4 Representation manager

Although UIDL can be used to implement a representation manager (RM), it is an open question whether it is preferable to implement the RM as a part of the UIMS, to place it in the application or to implement it as an independent component which can be accessed from both sides and has access to both sides (see also the discussions in Dance (1987) and Cockton (1987)). This is because the RM has to keep track of several structures or relationships between objects. First, it has to take into account the structures of the internal representations. However, it has also to take into account the relations between the external representations, which are used to represent the internal structure. In the example of a hierarchical file system, a command which deletes a directory and all its subcomponents will cause the application to traverse the directory tree and delete the corresponding entries. The application has to inform the RM that these objects are deleted. If the RM is not part of the application, this can be done by a 'delete tree' command given by the application to the RM. This requires that the RM has to maintain those parts of the tree for which external representations were created. Alternatively, it could be done by 'delete node' commands for every node deleted, which would not require rebuilding of the tree structure. If the RM is part of the application it can use data structures, like trees, provided by the application.

The following class definitions show how an RM can be implemented using UIDL. This solution assumes the RM to be part of the interface component. All objects in the RM managing external representations of application objects are instances of classes derived from class RepresentationObject. This class maintains collections of existing (created) and of active (created and used) presentation objects. If a certain presentation object is requested ('activate' rule) which does not exist, it sends a request to create this object to itself. Subclasses have to implement the rules to create specific presentation objects. The class also maintains a collection of attributes, such as invert, applied to presentation objects. If a presentation object is activated, all stored attributes are applied to it. By this means, it is possible for example to switch from an iconic to a textual representation of directory entries and the RepresentationObject class will invert the textual views if the corresponding iconic views were inverted:

```
eventhandler RepresentationObject {

    on 'activate' with (type) {
        if (viewList[type] == 0) {                  // create if it does not exist
            viewList[type] = send (this, type);     // responsibility of subclass
            }
        if (!viewList[type] || activeViews[type]) { // can't create view
            Result = 0;                             // or currently used
            }
        else {
            activeViews[type] = viewList[type];     // mark view as active
            for each key in attributes do {         // apply all attributes to
                                                       view
              send (view, key, attributes[key]);
```

```
                }
                Result = view;                      // Result stores return value
                }
            }
        on 'deactivate' with (type) {
            remove activeViews[type];
            }
        on 'apply' with (attribute, value) {        // apply an attribute
            attributes[attribute] = value;          // store attribute
            for each key in activeViews do {        // apply to all active views
                send (activeViews[key], attribute, value);
                }
        }
    .
    .
    }
```

Class IconText is capable of creating iconic or textual presentation objects. Its own identification is given to these presentation objects, which send this unique identification to the dialogue manager if a user event occurs. The predefined variable *Result* is used to store return values. Result is initialized to a default value before the body of a rule is processed:

```
eventhandler IconText is a RepresentationObject {

    on start with (labl, bitmp, longText, dmanager) :( ) {
        label = labl;                        // label for icon
        text = longText;                     // for textual presentation
        bitmap = bitmp;
        manager = dmanager;                  // dialogue manager
        }
    on 'icon' {
        Result = create (CooperativeIcon, label, bitmap, manager, this);
        }
    on 'text' {
        Result = create (CooperativeText, manager, this, text);
        }
    on 'invert' with (value) {           // apply to whatever views are active
        send (this, 'apply', 'invert', value);
        }
    .
    .
    }
```

UIDL is tailored to the purpose of modifying and combining predefined classes and for implementing dialogue managers following an event-response model. However, the language provides little support for the definition of complex data structures and their traversal. It is therefore still an issue for further investigation, whether UIDL is suitable for implementing a complex RM. As in the case of the dialogue manager, it is possible to offer a representation manager library for often-used data structures such as different kinds of trees, list or queues, and to use UIDL once again to modify and to combine these predefined classes.

4 EXPERIENCE AND FUTURE DEVELOPMENTS

DIAMANT is currently used internally at our Institute by a small group of users. The basic architecture of DIAMANT has been found to be sufficiently flexible, that it is quite easy to extend the system by other support components implemented as separate Unix processes. The user interface description language is well suited for smaller modifications and or combinations of predefined classes. UIDL provides good abstractions for user interfaces and dialogue implementation. The language, however, has not sufficient means to model complex data structures. This is caused by a trade-off in the design of UIDL between ease of use and functional power, where ease of use was judged to be more important than functional power for the design of complex data structures.

A number of smaller demonstration developments have been implemented using DIAMANT, including the desktop component mentioned in this paper, multimedia facilities for video and speech, and components for a production planning system. For these applications the architecture appears so far to be useful. Future work will address the issues of new media managers, of libraries for the dialogue- and the representation-manager objects, and mechanisms for easy adaptation of generic building blocks.

REFERENCES

Cockton, G. (1987). A new model for separable interactive systems. In: *Proceedings of Human–Computer Interaction – INTERACT'87*. Amsterdam: Elsevier, 1033–1038.

Dance, J., Granor, T., Hill, R., Hudson, S., Meads, J., Myers, B. and Schulert, A. (1987). Report on the run-time structure of UIMS-supported applications. *Computer Graphics*, 21, 2, 97–101.

Foley, J. D., Wallace, V. and Chan, P. (1984). The human factors of computer graphics interaction techniques. *IEEE Computer Graphics and Applications*, 4, 13–48.

Green, M. (1986). A survey of three dialogue models. *ACM Transactions on Graphics*, 5, 3, 244–275.

Hill, R. D. (1987). Event-response systems — a technique for specifying multi-threaded dialogues. *Proceedings SIGCHI+GI'87: Human Factors in Computing Systems, Toronto, Ontario, Canada, April 5–9, 1987*, 241–248.

Jacob, R. J. K. (1986). A specification language for direct manipulation interfaces. *ACM Transactions on Graphics*, 5, 4, 283–317.

Myers, B. A. (1988). *Tools for creating user interfaces: an introduction and survey.* Carnegie-Mellon University, Pittsburg, PA, CMU-CS-88-107.

Olsen, D. R., Jr. and Dempsey, E. P. (1983). SYNGRAPH: a graphical user interface generator. SIGGRAPH '83 Conference Proceedings. *Computer Graphics*, 17, 3, 43–50.

Pfaff, G. E. (ed.) (1985). *User Interface Management Systems.* Springer Verlag, Berlin.

Rosenberg, J. (1988). UIMSs: threat or menace? In: *Proceedings of CHI, 1988 (Washington, May 15–19)*. New York, ACM, 197–200.

DISCUSSION

MHe It's about consistency maintenance between the multiple views and its relation with dialogue control. It seems you assume that you interact with different views using the same protocol, i.e. the different views react to the same events. For example, what happens if I have the iconic editor on one side and a textual one on the other. Does this architecture work with this?

BT I hope so — why not?

MHe Could you explain how the architecture would let this be managed? On one side I only have icons, on the other side I only have keystrokes. The way the user interacts with these views is not the same [*CE* i.e. in that there are radically different edit operations].

BT I need different dialogue managers.

MHe It turns out taking PASTA-3 (EHCI Part I) as an example, you have one view of entities and relationships in the E-R schema, and the class hierarchy is another view, but what I see in each is conceptually the same thing. Still, they belong to completely different environments and they interact with end users differently.

BT The dialogue manager would call the application, this would change the underlying application data structure which would be propagated by the representation manager.

MHe In that case the abstract state of the views is kept in the application.

BT You have edited something in a view which causes a change in the underlying application structure. You have to propagate this change to the different views. There are two possibilities, either I store it in the application (but there are several views), or I just give notification of the change to the corresponding representation manager object. This object has to find out what changes are necessary on the different views.

GC Looking at Jöelle's PAC model (EHCI Part II), you could have different windows on the screen which, as interaction objects, have very different abstractions. Conceptually, the operations are not isomorphic to each other. Now in the underlying application they are the same underlying operation, but some people don't want the convergence to be this far back in the information processing. In DIAMANT there is a choice [on where to model the convergence], but it does not seem principled.

JZ It is principled. If you look at the [desktop] example, you have alternative views — the iconic and textual lists. They have the same underlying structure and operations [and the representation manager is used]. But where this isn't the case, say a forms interface to a database, you must go back to the underlying application where the data is stored.

CU Looking at your architecture, you have a fully connected graph. So it may be difficult for designers to separate the functionality of the dialogue manager and the representation manager. I don't see the need for having a direct link between the dialogue manager and the underlying application as well as between the dialogue manager and the representation manager. So two questions. Is it difficult for the DIAMANT user to decide where to put functionality in? If the underlying application changes slightly or the presentation changes slightly, could it be that the direct link between the underlying application and the dialogue manager cannot be used anymore because of these changes?

BT Yes, almost every link is present, but I think they are needed. If I have to call an application function, it has to be done from the dialogue manager to the underlying application.

CU Why not via the representation manager?

BT Because the representation manager only stores data objects. If I want to call a function or I need some kind of semantic feedback, I think I have to go via link 6 [Fig. 3 of paper] or via link 7 if I have an asynchronous event coming from the underlying application (e.g. per-cent done [Myers, *ACM Proc, CHI'85*]). But I fully agree, it is very difficult to specify which functionality belongs to the representation manager and so on. We have hypotheses for an architecture and we have to work on it and build generic objects and place them in a library. By that means we can assist a designer in structuring an interactive system. We can give guidelines too: the dialogue manager will do the syntactic things: don't send an invert message from the underlying application straight to a presentation object.

GC To be fair, this is a problem with most architectures. We just haven't seen an architecture yet where it's obvious which component does what. I think when we come to discuss open research issues [second panel], describing architectures unambiguously is something which, as far as I can see, we cannot do yet, as we do not want to describe components in terms of the underlying abstractions, because that's overcommitment. In SERPENT, you want to have different presentation abstractions and because you end up in this position of not being able to say exactly [what a component does], I was wondering if this is a Catch-22 of architectures which we have to live with?

KH It's actually a problem with whether you divide control communication between objects, from data communication. This is the principal thing. The designer of the architecture is saying fundamentally what control messages and what data messages are passed and the paths down which these messages flow. That determines the architecture.

CE Another aspect of judging this as an architecture is not only lines, but also the extent to which the modularization means that these lines don't need to be used much because things are lumped together rather well. So you take control and you split it between the dialogue manager (controlling dialogue) and the representation manager (controlling consistency of views). It remains to be seen how much that modularity means that we can actually separate our thinking about things.

KH But separation of thinking and separation of code into recognizable code objects are very different things.

CE Hopefully here we would be more concerned with the former. (KH That's right.)

PD Is the representation manager's object list fundamentally different from the dependencies list in Smalltalk? What benefits are you introducing here?

BT They are not fundamentally different. We are working with UNIX, C and C++. The functionality is similar, but our dependencies just concern views and are not as general as Smalltalk dependency lists. In our experience of building user interfaces at the Fraunhofer Institute, we have had to explicitly code views into the data model but this is just because the C language does not provide the facilities of a Smalltalk environment.

CB How much semantic behaviour does the representation manager have to perform? Are semantics only executed in the underlying application, or is part of it going on in the representation manager?

BT I'm not sure. We don't have enough implementation experience with this architecture. The example [desktop] I showed today is the main application we have built up to now. It doesn't have much semantics in the representation manager.

CB I'm asking because of performance issues. You may want to cache things in the representation manager and then get into all the issues of how much semantics you put where.

BT I think this is a general problem of what semantics you put in the user interface level.

Participants

MHe – Marc Herrmann
BT – Bernhard Trefz
GC – Gilbert Cockton
JZ – Jürgen Ziegler
CU – Claus Unger
KH – Keith Hopper
CE – Clarence Ellis
PD – Prasun Dewan
CB – Carl Binding

An Architecture for Knowledge-based Front Ends

Ernest A. Edmonds and Edward McDaid

Reprinted from: *Knowledge Based Systems.*
Volume 3. Number 4, pp 221–224, 1990

The paper draws upon the Seeheim model, but extends it in two significant respects. Firstly, knowledge-based modules are introduced to allow for the inclusion of intelligent support systems for the user. Secondly, the notion of a Back-end manager is introduced. This enables the use of existing systems for the functional elements and also provides facilities for the integration of a collection of systems to provide a single solution for the user. The concept of the Back-end manager is explored more fully in the next paper.

An Architecture for Knowledge-based Front Ends

E. A. EDMONDS* AND E. McDAID†

* *LUTCHI Research Centre, Loughborough University of Technology, Loughborough, Leicestershire, LE11 3TU, UK*

† *Department of Informatics, Magee College, University of Ulster, County Londonderry, Northern Ireland*

1 INTRODUCTION

There are many software systems for engineering and scientific applications in existence that were developed with great care in relation to accuracy and function and represent a significant investment. Their potential usefulness is considerable, and the cost of replacing them is often prohibitive. However, their benefits can be offset by the end user's difficulties in locating, selecting and employing the facilities that they offer. In addition, such software often suffers from badly designed or obsolete user interfaces that do not take advantage of modern user interface technology. Such software may be seen, therefore, as useful but not readily usable.

The FOCUS project (ESPRIT2 Project 2620: Front Ends for Open and Closed User Systems) addresses these problems. The prime goal of the project is to develop generic tools and techniques for constructing and maintaining knowledge-based front ends (KBFEs) to existing software systems, with a particular emphasis on libraries of routines and closed packages for scientific and engineering applications. The major objective is to enhance the usability of the systems by providing both improved user interfaces and knowledge-based support to the end user. In this paper, the software architecture which has been developed for KBFEs and a central component, known as the Harness, are described. The architecture provides a clear approach to the integration of diverse software systems and to the provision of support for their use. The Harness is responsible for the control and management of the user interface and all of the communications between the various front-end modules, the user and the back-end

THE SEPARABLE USER INTERFACE
ISBN 0–12–232150–2

software systems. A prototype Harness has been implemented, incorporating X-Windows (McCormack and Asente, 1988), and a number of prototype KBFEs have been implemented using it.

The development of KBFEs and their underlying software architectures derives from work done over the last quarter of a century in the field of human–computer interaction. The developments in interface architectures from which the FOCUS project's KBFE architecture evolved have been reviewed by Edmonds (1990). One of the extensions to that history is the use of a standard message-passing convention between all the KBFE components, and this is discussed below. An important component in the architecture that is closely related to the Harness, is called the back-end manager. This deals with the problem of front-end separability and is introduced briefly. It is described more fully by Pratt *et al.* (1990).

It has long been argued that separation of the user interface code from the functional code is of benefit (Edmonds, 1982, 1990). Software systems designed to support the separate development of user interfaces have become known as user-interface management systems (Pfaff, 1985). These systems exploit the concept of separation of concerns introduced earlier with database management systems. However, user-interface management systems have not normally contained knowledge-based user support systems and they have not specifically addressed the general problems of front-ending existing software.

2 KBFE ARCHITECTURE CONCEPT

The KBFE architecture developed within the FOCUS project is simple in concept. The system is seen as a set of concurrent processes. The different software processes communicate with one another, using a single message-passing convention, through the module known as the Harness (see Fig. 1). The most important players in the process are, of course, the end users and, although they do not use the same formal communication methods, they also communicate with the rest of the system through the Harness. In effect, the Harness is the KBFE's operating system.

Thus, the various modules which comprise the KBFE can be distinct software entities produced in quite different ways and in different languages. The modules need not be physically located on the same machine: they can communicate with one another over networks if appropriate. It is of general interest to note that the Harness is a demonstrable software system that can be used to integrate an unspecified number of facilities running on various machines with different environments, and that this integration takes place at the user interface.

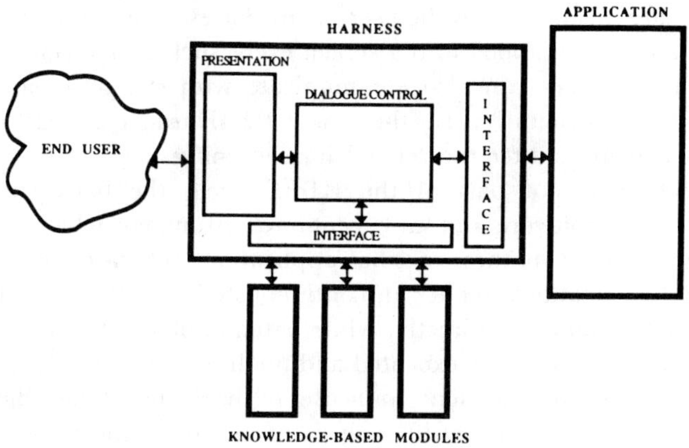

Figure 1. A KBFE architecture: the basic concept.

The architecture described here is an extension of the Seeheim model (Green, 1985). That consisted of a presentation layer, a dialogue control module and an application-interface model. The application interface contained an explicit model of the underlying application in order to provide a clear and clean interface between the front and back ends. Although this approach has been widely adopted in spirit, the key issue of specifying a complete and consistent notation in which a specific interface can be defined remains unsolved. The Seeheim model is, in effect, subsumed within the Harness in this architecture. The messages employed here are expressed in relation to abstract interaction objects and are introduced as an approach to the interface notation problem.

In addition to the three Seeheim user interface layers, the KBFE contains an unspecified number of knowledge-based modules, which provide the user with guidance and assistance. It is the knowledge-based modules that enable the KBFE to be a cooperative system. They can incorporate knowledge about the functions supplied in the application software as well as the ways in which they can and cannot be used in relation to particular problems, and so on. They can also contain information about the problem domain, the user's environment and the characteristics of the end users themselves. The choices rest with the KBFE developer. However, the key point is that, whatever facilities the developer is able and willing to supply, the architecture allows for them to be modularized appropriately and run as concurrent processes.

The knowledge-based modules communicate with the user through the Harness. In providing this facility, the Harness maps between the abstract interaction objects of interest to the modules and the physical realizations of them that are meaningful to the user. Thus, for example, the selection of an item from a list is mapped into a screen event such as a specific pull-down menu. The modules can also communicate with one another, using the same message structures. In this case, the Harness simply routes the messages and looks after the related housekeeping.

Although it is not part of the KBFE itself, the back end requires communication software and an execution environment which will depend upon the specific nature of the application software. For example, interactive applications might run continuously in parallel with the KBFE and might communicate directly, while batch applications might require a sequence of processes to be executed and might communicate through files.

The creation, management and use of back-end data objects is an important issue, particularly in such cases as subroutine libraries. As has been indicated above, these issues are handled by the special module in the architecture, known as the back-end manager (Edmonds, 1990). While the Harness and the knowledge-based modules are concerned with the 'whys' and 'wherefores' of the end user's task, it is the back-end manager that takes care of the 'how' in relation to the software systems available. Its prime responsibility, therefore, is that of mapping a software system-independent specification of the task into a form that can be used actually to execute the task using the particular software and of extracting the relevant results from that system's output. Thus, while the back-end manager communicates within the KBFE using the standard message conventions, it must communicate with the back-end software in whatever way that software can accept.

It is clear that there is no need to limit the back-end software to a single system. In a simple case, for example, the back-end manager might have to link some subroutines to user- or KBFE-supplied code, compile and run. Already, we have more than one back-end software element in use. Thus, in the architecture, no restriction is placed upon the number of back-end software systems that a given KBFE might have access to.

3 COMMUNICATION ISSUES

As we have seen, the KBFE consists of the Harness, the back-end manager and a number of knowledge-based modules and it will connect to one or more back-end software systems. These will often be separate processes and may well run on different machines connected by networks. Whereas it is important to allow any component in the KBFE to communicate with any other, it is not practical or helpful if each such link has to be set up specifically within the operating system(s) environment in use. Instead, each module simply has a link with the Harness and then the communications that it needs can be routed through that component. If, for example, a selection from a list is required, and the recipient of that request is a knowledge-based module, the Harness needs only to deliver the message to the correct location. If, on the other hand, the user is to be asked to make the selection, then the abstract selection interaction object will be transformed to some appropriate concrete form. However, both exchanges look exactly the same to the module that originated the request.

The basic form of a message is:

message (*identifier*, *content*, *route*)

The *content* parameter specifies an interaction object type, any required modifiers and the appropriate parameters. The modifiers specify such attributes as 'persistent' (lives on after a user response), 'modal' (must be responded to before any other object from this source is active), etc. Validation information is also provided in the *content* list.

The Harness is constructed so as to handle a core set of interaction object types, but provision is also made for a KBFE developer to introduce a new type and to provide an appropriate definition of it. In certain circumstances, these definitions can be handled automatically in real time, provided that the definitions can be generated by the knowledge-based modules. Complex, or multiple, interaction objects can be specified by giving *content* as a list of lists, to any required degree of complexity.

As was understood in Seeheim (Green, 1985), some communications are not able to be reduced to the bandwidth implied by the message type structure: for example, the data that describe the images seen in a flight simulator as the operator 'flies' overland. The Seeheim solution has been adopted in the KBFE architecture. Thus, a high-bandwidth route is provided from the back ends to the presentation layer of the interface. It passes through a 'switch' which directs the data, under the direction of dialogue control, without it having to pass through the various software components that together make up the full Harness.

The full KBFE architecture is as shown in Fig. 2. The final issue for consideration here is the extent to which knowledge must be exchanged between the knowledge-based modules and the back-end manager. It is clear that the latter requires a considerable amount of knowledge and that much of it is similar to that required by knowledge-based modules. There is, however, a significant distinguishing feature. When a task is given to the back-end manager, it should be fully specified, so that the knowledge available must be complete in the sense of being sufficient to execute the task. On the other hand, knowledge-based modules will typically be concerned with advising and helping the user to make decisions, so that

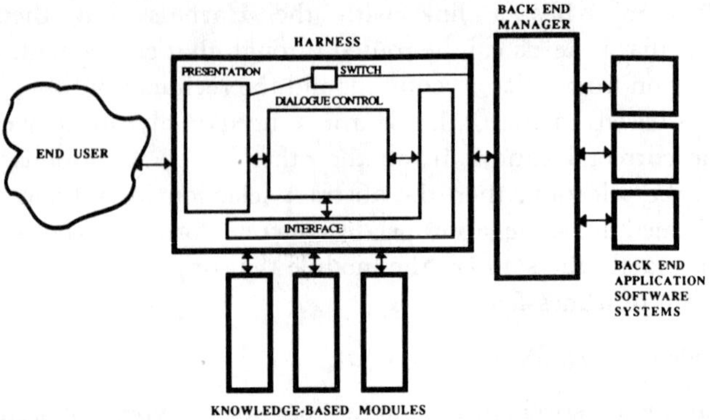

Figure 2. The full KBFE architecture.

they would normally operate in conjunction with the user. Thus, the knowledge available to the latter may be incomplete and tentative, while the knowledge available to the former should be complete and clear. In this sense, the knowledge available to the back-end manager is, strictly speaking, procedural information and associated facts about the operation of the back ends. Therefore it does not necessarily require knowledge-based formalisms for its representations.

4 ARCHITECTURE IN PRACTICE

The use of the Harness is central to applying the KBFE architecture described above. In its first implementation the Harness runs under Unix and employs X-Windows to realize the user interface. The developer sees the Harness as an independent process with which the other components must communicate using standard Unix facilities. The back-end manager is one of those processes but performs the special task of managing and operating the appropriate set of back-end software systems, which run unchanged on the same or other machines.

The key points about the Harness are, then:

it provides a single channel for all communications between KBFE modules;

those communications are made using a standard message structure;

the messages operate upon abstract interaction objects;

for interactions with the user, the Harness maps these abstract objects onto concrete ones;

any number of concurrent knowledge-based modules can be employed in the KBFE; and any number of existing software systems can be employed as back-ends.

Thus, in the KBFE architecture presented above, the Harness provides a facility for integrating diverse systems, both conventional and knowledge-based, in order to provide a single end-user service. The approach extends earlier work on architectures for interaction to provide a flexible and practical method for this provision, and has added to the facilities offered by user-interface management systems by the development of the front-end's Harness.

ACKNOWLEDGEMENTS

The work described in this paper was partly funded by the EEC through ESPRIT (Project 2620). The authors would like to thank the partners of the Project for many helpful discussions and comments: NAG Ltd, Imperial College of Science and Technology, Metek, Philips, Solvay, the Universitat Politecnia de Catalunya, and Westfalische Wilhems-Universitat. Particular thanks are due to Jenia Ghazikhanian and Bryan Murray for work on the Harness, and to Linda Candy for comments on an earlier draft of the paper.

REFERENCES

Edmonds, E. A. (1982). The man–computer interface: a note on concepts and design. *International Journal of Man–Machine Studies*, 16, 231–236.

Edmonds, E. A. (1990). The emergence of the separable user interface. *ICL Technical Journal*, 7, 1, 54–65.

Green, M. (1985). Report on dialogue specification tools. In: *User Interface Management Systems*. G. E. Pfaff (ed.). Berlin: Springer Verlag, 9–21.

McCormack, J. and Asente, P. (1988). An overview of the X toolkit. In: *Proceedings of the ACM SIGGraph Symposium User-Interface Software*. New York: ACM, 46–55.

Pfaff, G. E. (ed.) (1985). User interface management systems. In: *Proceedings of the Workshop on User Interface Management Systems, Seeheim, 1983*. Berlin: Springer Verlag.

Pratt, A., Lores, J., Fletcher, P. and Catot, J. M. (1990). The back-end manager: an interface between a knowledge-based front end and its application subsystems. *Knowledge Based Systems*, 3, 4, 225–229.

Back-End Manager: An Interface between a Knowledge-based Front End and its Application Subsystems

Albert Prat, Jesus Lores, Paul Fletcher and Josep M. Catot

Reprinted from: *Knowledge Based Systems*. Volume 3. Number 4, pp 225–229, 1990.

This paper elaborates the concept introduced in the previous section. An important assumption is that the 'application subsystems' may already exist and that source code may not be available for revision. A framework for constructing the separation component, as one might view it, is proposed.

Back-End Manager: An Interface between a Knowledge-based Front End and its Application Subsystems

A. PRAT, J. LORES, P. FLETCHER AND J. M. CATOT

Seccion de Tecnicas Cuantitativa de Gestión, Departmento de Estadística e Investigacion Operativa, ETSIIB, Universitat Politecnica de Catalunya, Avda Diagonal, 647 08028 Barcelona, Spain

1 INTRODUCTION

In the FOCUS project of ESPRIT2 (Project 2620), an architecture for knowledge-based front ends (KBFEs) has been proposed based on an extension to the Seeheim model (Pfaff, 1985; Green, 1985; Edmonds and McDaid, 1990). In order to maintain the concept of interface separability

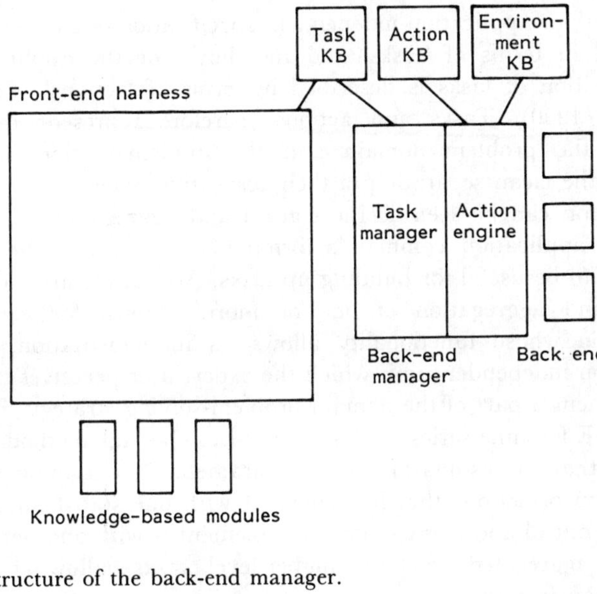

Figure 1. Structure of the back-end manager.

THE SEPARABLE USER INTERFACE
ISBN 0–12–232150–2

within this architecture, the front-end Harness and the knowledge-based modules concern themselves with the 'whys' and 'wherefores' of what the end user is or should be doing, while the back-end manager (BEM) takes care of the 'how'. The BEM's prime responsibility therefore is that of mapping an application-independent specification of the 'what' into an executable specification of the 'how' with respect to a particular application or package (i.e. mapping from a semantic to a syntactic specification), controlling the execution of the application, and passing the relevant information back to the appropriate KBFE component.

To carry out this role, the BEM must be 'programmed' by an appropriate expert user with knowledge about the syntax, semantics, functionality and environment of the application software. This is stored in the form of specification objects (tasks and actions), back-end I/O objects (templates and extractions) and an environment knowledge base. Figure 1 illustrates the structure of the BEM, showing its relationship to the rest of the proposed KBFE architecture.

2 LANGUAGE OF SPECIFICATION — TASKS AND ACTIONS

The 'what', or application-independent specification of back-end activity, is described in terms of 'tasks' and the 'how', or the application-specific decomposition of tasks is described in terms of 'actions' (Edmonds and McDaid, 1990). Tasks and actions therefore represent the boundary between the problem domain and the implementation domain, thus allowing the clean separation of their respective issues.

An action can be seen as the control and aggregation of one or more back-end application commands forming a unit which the expert user perceives to be useful for building up tasks. A task, in turn, consists of the control and aggregation of one or more actions, for each back-end application whose functionality allows its implementation, forming an application-independent unit which the expert user perceives as being able to implement a part of the domain problem-solving strategy. For example, in a KBFE for time-series analysis using Box–Jenkins methodology, a task may be that of 'estimating model parameters' containing control and aggregation of actions that implement it with one statistical package and different control and aggregation to implement it with another. Tasks may even be aggregated to form higher-level tasks, allowing a powerful specification facility.

A task may contain the following data structures:

name;

description;

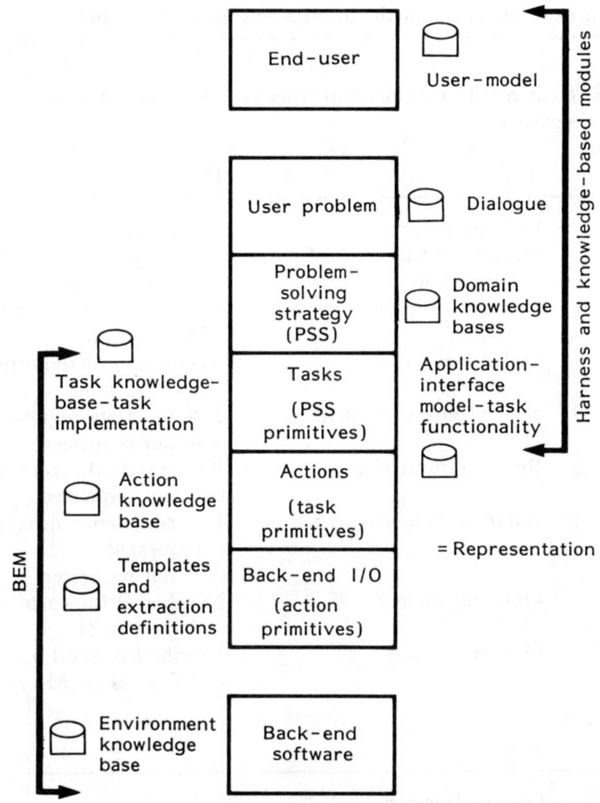

Figure 2. Concepts, their representations and 'managers' in a KBFE.

a set of input/output parameters; and
definition of control and aggregation of actions for each back end.

In terms of KBFE architecture, this information does not have to reside in one place. Figure 2 shows the relationships and means of representation of tasks and actions, together with their role in the communication between the end user and the back ends. The application interface model, providing information on back-end functionality for the rest of the KBFE, will most probably contain the name, description and parameters of the task, whereas the BEM's task knowledge base will contain the details of its definition of control and action aggregation. Table 1 shows an example entry in the application interface model for a task whose function is to perform univariate forecasting on a given time series with two possible back-end platforms — the Genstat and SCA statistical packages — available to it.

Table 1. An example entry in the application interface model.

Task: Forecast
Description: Given a model specification, this task forecasts X time periods ahead from a time series Y

Input parameters:

Name	Type	Description
Series	Obligatory/vector	Actual data to base forecast on
Model_spec	Optional/real vector of model parameters	Model specification parameters (d, D, p, P, q, Q, s)
Origin	Optional/integer	Origin of forecast, default is last observation
Output_spec	Obligatory/binary	Vector complete output specification
Output_spec(1)	Binary output element	1 = forecasts requested 0 = not requested
Output_spec(2)	Binary output element	1 = standard errors requested 0 = not requested
Output_spec(3)	Binary output element	1 = confidence intervals requested 0 = not requested
Steps_ahead	Optional/integer	Number of forecasts required, default is 24
Back_end	Optional/string	Specific back-end package to use, default is BEM chooses

Output parameters:

Name	Type
Forecast	Optional/vector
Standard_error	Optional/vector
Upper_confidence_limits	Optional/vector
Lower_confidence_limits	Optional/vector

Back-end platforms: Genstat, SCA

This task is used in a prototype KBFE for time-series forecasting using Box–Jenkins methodology (Lores *et al.*, 1989). Table 2 shows an example entry in the task knowledge base for the SCA implementation of the forecast task. In this table, we have shown the definition of control and aggregation represented both internally (Prolog) and externally (an expert user command language): of course, only the internal representation will be retained in the task knowledge base.

Table 2. An example entry in the task knowledge base.

Task: Forecast
Description: Given a model specification, this task forecasts X time periods ahead from a time series Y
Platform: SCA
Specification:

(*Internal Prolog representation*)

```
forecast (P1 . . . Model_spec. Steps_ahead . . .):–
  ensure_model_specified (Model_spec. Model_name).
  action (sca_generate_forecast (Model_name. Steps_ahead)).
  check_confidence_intervals (P1 . . . Pn).
  action (sca_graph_forecast (P1 . . . Pn)).

ensure_model_specified ([ ], Model_name):–
  action (sca_specify_model (P1 . . ., Model_name, . . . Pn)).
ensure_model_specified ([P1 . . ., Model_name, . . . Pn], Model_name).

check_confidence_intervals (. . ., "CI", . . .):–
  action (sca_confidence_intervals (P1 . . . Pn)).

check_confidence_intervals (. . ., " ", . . .).
```

(*Expert user's definition*)

```
IF model not specified
  ACTION: sca_specify_model (p1 . . . pn)
ENDIF
ACTION: sca_generate_forecast (Model_name, steps_ahead)
IF confidence intervals requested
  ACTION: sca_generate_confidence_intervals (p1 . . . pn)
ENDIF
ACTION: sca_graph_forecast (p1 . . . pn)
```

An action may contain the following data structures:
a name;
- a description;
- implementation platform;
- a set of input/output parameters;
- a set of preconditions;
- an associated back-end input description (template);
- an associated back-end output description (extraction definition); and
- a set of postconditions.

Table 3 shows an example entry in the action knowledge base for an action which forms part of the SCA implementation of the 'Forecast' task described in Tables 1 and 2.

Table 3. An example entry in the action knowledge base.

Action: sca_generate_forecast
Description: Uses SCA to generate a series of forecasts
Preconditions: Model must have been specified in SCA

Input parameters:

Name	Type	Description
Model_name	Obligatory/string	Name of SCA model specification
Steps_ahead	Optional/integer	Number of forecasts required, default is 24
Output_spec	Obligatory/binary vector	Output requirements

Output parameters:

Name	Type
Forecasts	Optional/vector
Standard_error	Optional/vector

Back-end input description (template file):

```
uforecast model «model_name».
IF «steps_ahead» ‹› 24
  nofs are «steps_ahead»
```

Back-end output description (extraction file):

```
IF «output_spec(1) = 'forecast'»
  look under 'Forecast'
  extract column
IF «output_spec(2) = 'standard error'»
  look under 'std_err'
  extract column
```

Postconditions: None

3 FROM SPECIFICATION TO IMPLEMENTATION: BACK-END I/O DESCRIPTIONS

In order to execute and process actions on a given back-end package, some means of generating back-end commands and processing the resulting output must be employed. Currently we are using the concepts of templates and extraction definitions (Lores *et al.*, 1989), although the architecture of the BEM does not preclude the possibility of some other approach — possibly grammar-based — being incorporated in the future.

For each action, the expert user must define a template and an extraction definition using the template generator and extraction definition tool developed at UPC (Lores *et al.*, 1989). The template generator is basically an editor which allows the expert user to superimpose control over raw back-end commands, producing a file which at run time the template engine 'mixes' with the action input parameters to provide the actual back-end input. The extraction definition tool consists of a graphic editor for highlighting relevant or desired information from ASCII output files produced by back-end applications, allowing again the superimposition of control in order to extract information based on the action output parameter specification. It automatically generates an extraction definition file which the extraction engine interprets at run time. Examples of template and extraction definitions can be found in Table 3.

The complete process of implementing a task therefore is as follows. The task manager receives a message from a KBFE component and, assuming no particular back end is specified, makes a decision based on knowledge in the environment knowledge base as to which is the appropriate back end to use. It then interprets the definition of control and action aggregation, making appropriate calls to the action manager. On completion of the task, a message is sent back to the calling component with the appropriate task output. On receiving a request to execute an action from the task manager, the action manager invokes the template engine to mix the action input parameters with the template, executes the back end and finally invokes the extraction engine which interprets the back-end output via the extraction definition and action output parameters.

4 KNOWLEDGE IN THE BACK-END MANAGER

It is clear that the BEM requires a considerable amount of knowledge and that much of that knowledge is similar to that required by the knowledge-based modules. There is, however, a significant distinguishing feature. When a task is given to the BEM, it should be fully specified, so that the knowledge available must be complete in the sense of being sufficient to execute that task. On the other hand, knowledge-based modules will typically be concerned with advising and helping the user to make decisions, so that they would normally operate in conjunction with the user. Thus, the knowledge available to the knowledge-based modules may be incomplete or tentative while the knowledge available to the BEM must be clear and complete.

5 CONCLUSIONS

It may be that problem domain issues and implementation issues may never be completely separable — experience at UPC (Prat *et al.*, 1985,

1989) has shown that a strategy for designing 'problem-oriented' as opposed to 'back-end application-oriented' KBFEs often involves a combination of methodologies both top-down (from the point of view of the end-user's problem) and bottom-up (from the functionality of the available back-end software), leading to their inevitable intertwining. However, this intertwining should occur only at the level of the definition of control and aggregation of actions, and not at the level of strategy definition in the control and aggregation of tasks. The proposed framework for the BEM should leave the front-end Harness and knowledge-based modules as free as possible from implementation issues, although for the presentation layer of the Harness realistically to provide the user with appropriate semantic feedback it may be that direct access to some of the implementation knowledge encoded in the BEM will be necessary.

ACKNOWLEDGEMENTS

This work was partly financed by the EEC through ESPRIT2 (Project 2620) and by the CICYT (Spanish Government) (TIC 880643).

REFERENCES

Edmonds, E. A. and McDaid, E. (1990). An architecture for knowledge-based front-ends. *Knowledge Based Systems*, 3, 4, 221–224.

Green, M. (1985). Report on dialog specification tools. In: *User Interface Management Systems*, G. E. Pfaff (ed.). Berlin: Springer Verlag, 9–20.

Lores, J., Fletcher, P. and Prat, A. (1989). *Progress and experiences in the design of a prototype back-end manager for time series analysis using Genstat and SCA*. Internal ESPRIT report.

Pfaff, G. E. (ed.) (1985). User interface management systems. In: *Proceedings of the Workshop on User Interface Management Systems, Seeheim, 1983*. Berlin: Springer Verlag.

Prat, A., Marti, M. and Catot, J. M. (1985). Incorporating expertise in time series modelling: the STATXPS system. *Statistical Software Newsletter*, 11, August, IASC, 55–62.

Prat, A., Ginebra, J., Catot, J. M. and Lores, J. (1989). Expert system for forecasting. *Proceedings of Development of Statistical Expert Systems. Eurostat News*, 342–347.

6. Practical Issues of Separability

Report on the Interface of the UIMS to the Application

G. Enderle

Reprinted from: *User Interface Management Systems.* Pfaff (editor). Springer Verlag, pp 21–29, 1985.

This is another report from a working group at Seeheim. They did not propose a model, but they provided a fairly comprehensive review of what were the current issues in achieving separation.

Report on the Interface of the UIMS to the Application

G. ENDERLE

SEL AG, Helmuth-Hirth-Strasse 42, 7000 Stuttgart 40, Federal Republic of Germany

1 SCOPE AND GOAL

The goal of the workshop was to find, evaluate and describe models, principles, methods and tasks for the design of user interface management systems (UIMSs). This working group concentrated on aspects of this overall goal that are related to the interface between the application and the UIMS.

One application was given specific attention: computer–aided design (CAD). On the one hand, CAD is an application that relies on computer graphics as a basic component of the whole system. On the other hand, it is an application where a favourable user interface is of special importance. The application is the most relevant part of the interactive system. If we look at the application–UIMS interface from the viewpoint of the application, we can identify certain requirements which a UIMS must fulfil to serve the application in an optimal way. A problem of specific interest at the application–UIMS interface is the division of responsibility for graphical output between the application and the UIMS.

2 PROBLEM AREAS

Three major problem areas related to the application interface of a UIMS were addressed:

the configuration of a UIMS with respect to a specific application;

the responsibility for creating and managing graphical output; and

the services and functions available at the communication interface between the application and the UIMS.

In order to gain a common basis for the discussion of these questions, an

THE SEPARABLE USER INTERFACE
ISBN 0-12-232150-2

overall structure of the interactive system had to be agreed on. In all problem areas, special attention was paid to aspects relevant to CAD.

3 STRUCTURE OF USER INTERFACE MANAGEMENT SYSTEMS

The application–UIMS interface can be situated at different places within the overall system, depending on the structure of the system. A discussion of problems related to an interface can be successful only on the basis of an agreed system structure. However, since it was not the goal of this workshop to select and prescribe a specific system structure, the application–UIMS interface was identified in several UIMS system structures. An attempt was made to address the problem areas in such a way that the principles and solutions stated could be applied to all UIMS structures.

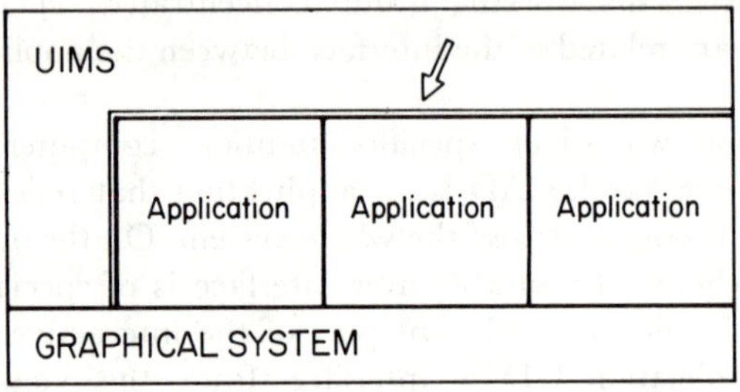

Figure 1. External control.

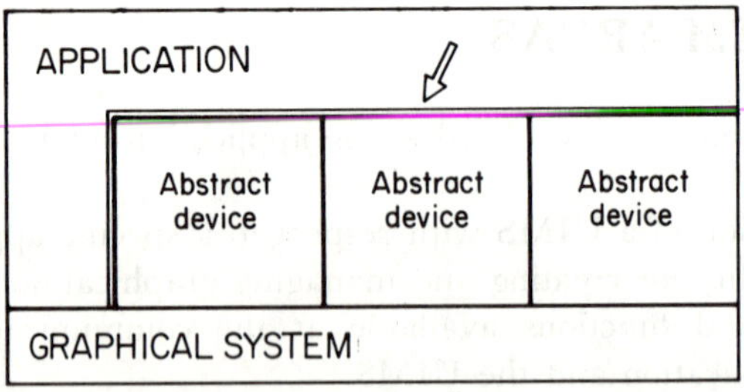

Figure 2. Internal control.

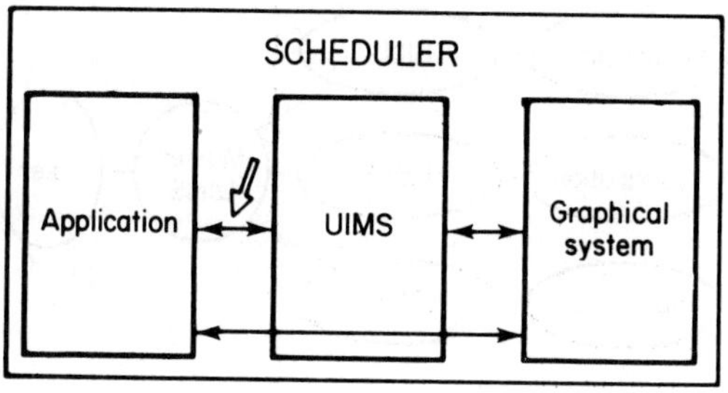

Figure 3. Parallel processes.

Two of the UIMS structures were the result of the Seattle *Workshop on Interactive Techniques*: external control and internal control. Figures 1 and 2 show these structures with the application–UIMS interface. A third structure was identified where the application, the UIMS and the graphics package are on one level, i.e. they are parallel processes that are synchronized by means of multitasking facilities. The processes exchange information between them; one of the interfaces is the application–UIMS interface (Fig. 3).

In the course of describing the parallel system structure, an interesting new question was identified, that deserves more investigation in the future: that of multiple parallel interactive processes. This means that one user, at one workstation, deals with different independent applications. In many cases, such a technique is presented to the user by a number of windows on a screen, where every window is associated with a different application process (see Fig. 4). The user selects the process with which he wants to communicate, for example, by moving the cursor into the corresponding window.

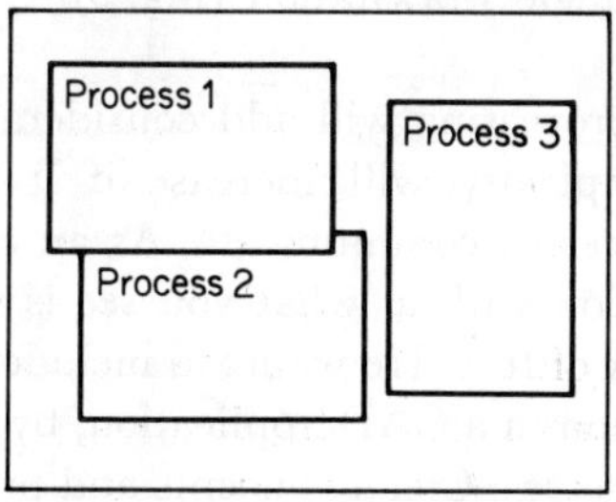

Figure 4. Windows associated with different application processes.

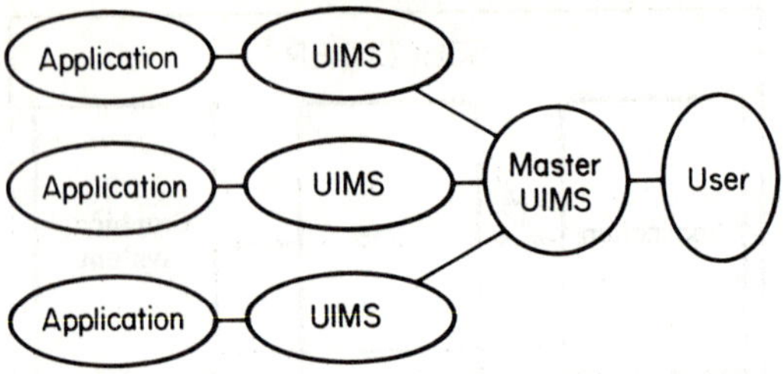

Figure 5. Parallel application processes and UIMSs, one master UIMS.

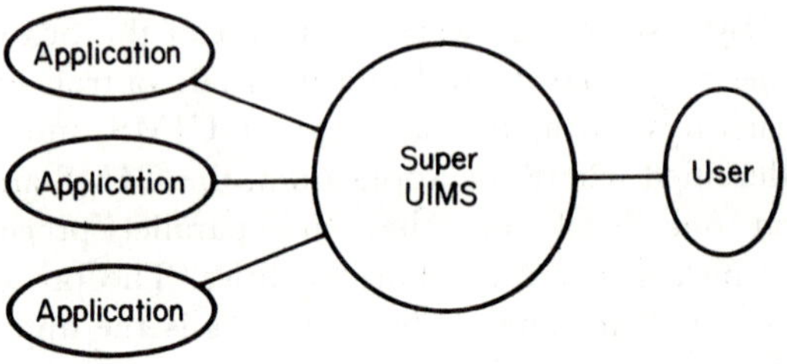

Figure 6. Parallel application processes, one super UIMS.

How does a UIMS handle this type of parallel processing? There are (at least) two obvious possibilities.

(1) Every application has its own UIMS and one interface to this UIMS. In addition, one 'master UIMS' coordinates and manages the overlaying of the parallel processes for one workstation (Fig. 5).

(2) There is one 'super UIMS' that has interfaces to all applications. It handles all the application interfaces as well as the overlaying of the parallel processes for a single workstation (Fig. 6).

This type of parallel processing will add considerable complexity to the interactive system. Complexity will increase if it is required that the different application processes communicate. As an example, suppose that in a typesetting application with a 'what you see is what you get' option, the user identifies a block of text. He wants to include this block of text in a drawing under construction in a CAD application, by dragging it across the boundary of the two processes. Clean concepts and principles are needed to handle this situation and to retain a favourable user interface. There remains considerable work for the future in this area.

4 TWO GRAPHICS MODES

In the course of evaluating the properties and functions of the interface between the application and the UIMS, two modes of graphics output could be identified that are related to the role of graphics for the application within the interactive system.

(1) *Direct graphics*. Direct graphics are direct representations of the application database that is being created and modified by the interactive process. Examples are:

painting systems and film animation, where a graphical representation in many cases is the only result of the interactive process;

CAD systems, where normally one of the results of the design process is a number of drawings, graphical representations of FEM nets or of results; and

business graphics systems, e.g. slide production systems.

(2) *Symbolic graphics*. Symbolic graphics are used to support the interactive process and enhance the user interface. They are not the final result of the application. There are many examples of this category:

simulation systems, which may have as their primary result the record of a sequence of events, actions and reactions that are a mapping of the real-world processes to be simulated;

in a computer chess game, graphics are used to display the state of the game to the user; the result of the game, however, is the sequence of moves.

Of course, certain applications which use primarily direct graphics, may well use symbolic graphics for handling interaction. In the following sections it is seen that support of the two graphics modes gives rise to different properties and UIMS requirements.

5 CONFIGURATION OF A UIMS WITH RESPECT TO A SPECIFIC APPLICATION

One question in this area is whether or not it is possible to design a UIMS as a universal tool that can be used for many types of application. If such a tool can be designed that can be configured and adapted to several kinds of applications, the next question concerns which parts of the UIMS will have to be changed in the configuration process. The following application-oriented components of the dialogue specification have been identified ('dialogue' is the term describing the actual interactive process when the user is communicating with the system; the 'dialogue specification' comprises those parts of the UIMS that define the set of possible dialogues):

menus, screen layouts, tablet layouts;
error messages to be displayed to the user;
help messages to be displayed to the user;
prompts (text prompts, graphics, acoustics);
icons (icons are graphical symbols that are defined at UIMS configuration time; they are used for user communication);
list of task names (e.g. application subroutines to be called by the UIMS, or UIMS subroutines to be called by the application);
list of variable names (defining the address space common to the application and the UIMS);
mechanisms for UIMS–application communication (message passing, global common, subroutine parameter passing);
selection of interaction techniques (the UIMS should offer a number of such techniques that can be selected at configuration time);
constraints on graphical output (e.g. only drawings of a certain scale might be allowed on certain output devices);
constraints on graphical context (e.g. colours assigned by the application have specific meanings, and are not to be changed by the UIMS); and
constraints on graphical input (e.g. locator values are only allowed on a grid).

Besides the dialogue specification, the responsibility for output can change if the application changes (see next section).

6 GRAPHICAL OUTPUT

There are a number of questions when dealing with the generation of graphical output within an interactive system. The first question is which component is responsible for graphical output, the UIMS or the application, and in particular which component is responsible for the mapping of application data structures to the graphical representation. In the opposite direction, who does the mapping of graphical input to the application data structure for picking? If the data have to be passed between the application and the UIMS, should this be done by sharing data structures or by duplicating data structures? The following are suggestions that were agreed on with the aim of keeping application-related functions within the application while grouping general user interface management functions within the UIMS. This should allow the design of a UIMS as a universal tool that can be configured to a specific application without changing the whole structure of the UIMS.

The responsibility for graphical output depends on the type of application. The application is responsible for creating the graphical output for direct graphics. This output is created at run time during the interactive process. The mapping of application data structures to a graphical representation is the task of the application program. For symbolic graphics, the UIMS will generate graphical output. The basic tokens (icons) of this output are designed at configuration time. The mapping of application data structures to a graphical representation is done by the UIMS (e.g. the state of a chess game is mapped to the picture of a chessboard with pieces). For both modes of graphics, management of the output (device control, window management) is done by the UIMS.

For direct graphics, the application data structures often have to be made available to the UIMS so that it can control output generation and picking. How this access is achieved is a software engineering problem that need not be dealt with in this UIMS-related context. Duplication of data structures should be avoided (to avoid consistency problems). For modification of application data as a result of a user request, the UIMS should activate a service of the application for the UIMS. One such service could be to ask the application for permission to change a value, changing the value, and notifying the application that the value has been changed. All data that are related only to the functions of the UIMS are contained in a UIMS data structure that cannot be accessed by the application.

7 PICKING

The responsibility for interpreting a pick input is also dependent on the type of objects being picked. For direct graphics objects, interpreting the pick input is done by the application. The setting of the pick context (the scope of the picking) is done by the UIMS using application data. For symbolic graphics, both the interpretations of the pick input and the setting of the picking context are done by the UIMS.

8 THE COMMUNICATION INTERFACE BETWEEN APPLICATION AND UIMS

The communication interface between the application and the UIMS defines a set of services (tasks performed by one component at the request of the other component) and protocols (syntax for the communication needed to accomplish these services) that allow cooperation between the two processes. Naturally, these protocols differ for different system structures (see section 2). For external control, the interface will always be controlled by the UIMS, for internal control by the application. For parallel processes, the control of the communication interface can be symmetrical; functions can be invoked in either direction. The following is a list of functions that are required irrespective of the system structure:

services of the UIMS for the application and the corresponding protocols;

services of the application for the UIMS and the corresponding protocols;

handling of feedback loops over the application; and

management of areas such as graphics output context (e.g. window management), error handling, help on application errors, undoing, backing out, journalling, checkpointing and restarting.

Table 1 shows the services which have been identified. Services of the UIMS for the application are the most important for internal control structures. Services of the application for the UIMS support external control structures. For parallel processes, both types of services are necessary.

Table 1. Services at the application–UIMS interface.

Services of the UIMS for the application	Services of the application for the UIMS
Give a value matching constraints	Give a value (e.g. for use in help functions)
Switch input sources (e.g. between user and journal)	Give a value to be used instead of user input
Tell the user a value	Perform graphics update
Display some graphics	Set application state variable to a given value
Handle an application error	Grant permission to change application data
Set output context	Give pick support
Set dialogue scope	Give task status
	(Re-) Set task status to a (previously saved) state
Undo something	Undo something

9 CAD/CAM ASPECTS

There are certain characteristics that are specific to CAD and similar application areas. Since one final result of a CAD/CAM application is always a graphical representation (e.g. scaled and dimensioned drawings, representations of 3D objects, of FEM nets and of results of calculations), it uses primarily direct graphics. The graphical representations are so specific to the application that they are part of the application. Also, the contents of the interactive technique library can be very specific to the application: they need redesigning as the application changes. Therefore, they must also be considered part of the application. In the CAD area, many constraints are imposed on the user and the UIMS by the application (e.g. prescribed scalings or conformance to standards). In a CAD application, feedback loops will be executed in more cases with the application involved than in other areas.

10 CONCLUSIONS

It seems that it is possible to design a UIMS as a general tool that can serve a range of different applications and still serve the user and the application in an excellent way. In the configuration phase, the UIMS can be adapted to the needs of the application without redesigning all or major parts of it.

That one universal tool, however, does not yet exist, although in this workshop a number of principles and functions have been identified that can serve as guidelines for setting up such a general UIMS. This working group addressed in particular the problems related to the interface between the application and the UIMS, and the functions and services needed at that interface. Special attention was given to the area of CAD/CAM. This is a very complex application. If the ideas outlined in this report could be demonstrated to work in the context of a CAD/CAM application, this would be good evidence that such a configurable UIMS could serve a wide range of other applications as well.

Application Modelling in a User Interface Management System

J. L. Alty and P. McKell

Reprinted from: *British Computer Society Working Series People & Computers: Designing for Usability.* Harrison & Monk (Editors) Cambridge University Press, pp 319–335, 1986.

In this paper the idea of introducing an 'application expert' into the user interface system is discussed. A simple system was implemented and empirically evaluated, leading to a revised architecture in which the application model, or expert, has a more pro-active role.

Application Modelling in a User Interface Management System

J. L. ALTY AND P. McKELL

Heriot-Watt/Strathclyde MMI Unit, Strathclyde University, Glasgow, UK

1 INTRODUCTION

A set of interactions between a user and a computer application can be considered to be a system involving three major cooperating processors: a human being, an interface processor and a task processor. The interface processor can be further subdivided into three components: an I/O processes, a dynamics processor and a description of the application (Edmonds, 1982). The dynamics processor will contain a specification of how the dynamics of the interactions are to be managed, whilst the description of the application will involve the objects to be manipulated, allowable transactions, possible sequences (or plans) and valid instantiations of the objects involved. Edmonds regards the interface processor as the part of the system which represents the users' model of it. More recently, the user model has been represented as a distinct module in the interface processor (Jerrams-Smith, 1985).

The task–dialogue separation paradigm embodied in the above approach has been developed further by Green (1984), with the description of the application being incorporated into what has become known as the application model (or application expert). Green recognized that a user model would be required but suggested that the design of the application model should be based upon the user's view of the semantics of the application. In other words, the application model contains significant elements of a user model. Little work exists at present on application modelling in human–computer interaction, although approaches adopted in intelligent knowledge-based systems research clearly provide candidate representation formalisms (for example, the rule-based approach (Hayes-Roth *et al.*, 1983), the blackboard model (Erman *et al.*, 1981), and the object-oriented paradigm (Bobrow and Stefik, 1983)).

THE SEPARABLE USER INTERFACE
ISBN 0-12-232150-2

Ball and Hayes (1980) have described a technique for representing task-specific knowledge in user interface design. All task-specific knowledge is contained in a declarative database termed a 'tool description'. This is accessed via a 'user agent' which establishes from the user's point of view what functional capability of the application is required. The tool description contains a specification of:

the actions to be performed;

the parameters required (with defaults, types, etc.); and

a description of the abstract objects manipulated.

This tool description is a passive structure which specifies everything which the user agent needs to know about the task. In terms of our earlier descriptions, the user agent is a form of dynamics processor and the tool description corresponds to a static application model.

Finin *et al.* (1983), in reviewing the limitations of current help systems, noted that 'present approaches to providing help to inexperienced or infrequent users fail because current help systems have no real understanding of who they are trying to help, the topic they are providing information about, or the information they can provide'. 'Understanding who is being helped' is a user model issue, 'the topic they are providing information about' is an application model concern and 'the information to be provided' is the concern of both components. Finin also makes interesting comments about 'satisficing'. A user might be achieving his aims but in an inefficient manner. A sympathetic help system should be able to identify such situations and offer instruction and improve usage of commands.

The WIZARD system (Shrager, 1981; Shrager and Finin, 1982) is an experimental help system which was constructed to recognize situations in which the user might need help when accessing Unix. To do this, it recognizes sequences of invalid commands (plans), considers appropriate instantiations and attempts to give advice in satisficing. WIZARD uses a knowledge base which contains the objects and processes which underly the task domain, the generic and specific tasks provided by the system, and a previous history of user activity. Thus WIZARD contains a form of active application model, although the distinction between it and the user model is rather blurred. Finin has emphasized that help systems must play an active role. We concur with this viewpoint, and regard the application model as an active process going beyond the static description of Ball and Hayes.

Probert (1984) discussed the requirements of intelligent front ends and identified three major aspects: a user model, a dialogue assistant and a system model. This latter module acts as a 'road map' of the application to the user, and is therefore a form of application model. It acts as a gateway to the application.

2 WHAT CONSTITUTES AN APPLICATION MODEL?

In our view, much of the current literature does not distinguish clearly between the user model and the application model. We follow Probert in placing the application model directly on the access path to the application. We see it having two major roles:

as a custodian of input integrity for the application; and

as a source of advice and guidance to the user model.

It should be an active process which analyses user input, passes valid commands to the application or identifies problems in the user input for referral back to the user model for resolution.

The application model's function is to provide an 'expert' view of the application. In this sense, it can be regarded as the lowest level of a user model (the model of a perfect expert). It contains a description in expert terms of the objects and processes which make up the application. This expert view provides a 'bedrock' on which all other front-end processing is based. It is a fixed and definable anchor point above which may be developed other descriptions which will be best placed in the user model. Such higher-level descriptions will be more difficult to specify and will be heavily dependent on the user. The existence of an anchor point is therefore crucial to successful design and realization. Thus, the application model provides a solid foundation on which to build a supportive and adaptable user interface.

Taking the above points into consideration, we propose a modified form of Green's architecture for a user interface management system (UIMS) which separates out explicitly the user model component, thus removing

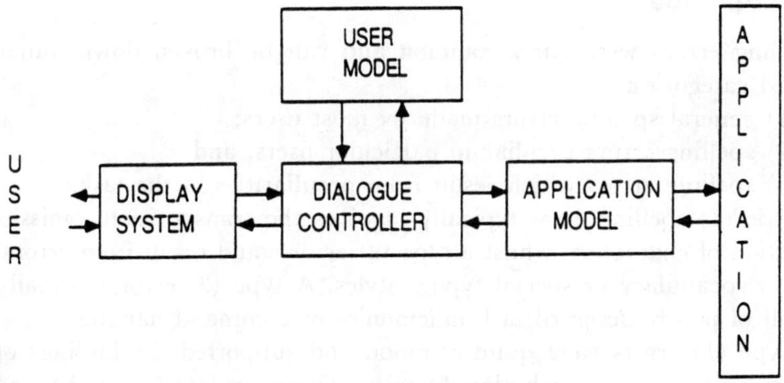

Figure 1. A user interface management system architecture.

the need to incorporate user model information in the application model. A block diagram of our approach is given in Fig. 1.

3 COMPONENTS OF AN APPLICATION MODEL FOR COMMAND-DRIVEN SYSTEMS

We define a command-driven system to be one in which the user input consists of command lines, each command line comprising a command verb followed by a list of arguments (possibly none). Possible user command sequences may be highly structured, in that certain commands can only follow other commands, or any command may be input at any time (as say in Unix). Many applications of this form exist.

In order to identify the various components of such an application model and develop an appropriate architecture, we have carried out a detailed study of the types of errors produced when novice and expert users interact with Unix. We chose Unix for two reasons. Firstly, the Unix system has been studied extensively and a considerable body of knowledge already exists concerning user errors. Secondly, the Unix can be thought of as a very general application; thus any results obtained should be applicable to more restricted domains. Our goal was to find an architecture which can be generally applied to command-driven systems. The errors were collected by logging all user activity on a VAX 11/780 running under Unix. The resulting log files were examined (from a Unix standpoint) in order to determine what application knowledge would be needed to identify the nature of any error. This study revealed a number of modules which will be required in any application model.

3.1 Spelling

Spelling errors were fairly common and can be broken down into three broad categories:

(1) general spelling errors made by most users;
(2) spelling errors peculiar to particular users; and
(3) spelling errors which result from peculiarities in the task.

A type (1) spelling error typically involves the transposition, omission or addition of characters, whilst a type (2) error could result from errors in a user's vocabulary or special typing styles. A type (3) error is usually the result of poorly designed task mnemonics or command naming.

Type (1) errors were quite common and supported the findings of the extensive literature which already exists. Damerau (1964) found that 80% of all spelling errors were accounted for by the following rules:

transposition of two letters;
one letter extra;
one letter missing; and
one letter wrong.

Yannakoudakis and Fawthrop (1983) and Durham *et al.* (1983) have conducted studies which support Damerau's conclusions. However, the work of Durham is more relevant to our work since it involved the use of interactive command systems.

We conclude that the spelling errors characterized by domains (1) and (3) above, should be resolved in the application model, and those in domain (2) above, should be the concern of the user model. We have therefore included a spelling checker module in our application model. It acts on subcomponents of commands.

3.2 Syntax

Syntactic knowledge of an application is concerned with the physical form of the command, the types of the arguments used, and their order. We are not concerned here with detecting whether or not instantiations or the arguments actually exist. Thus the command:

cat fred

would be regarded as syntactically correct even if the file *fred* did not exist. Nor are we concerned with 'invalid' sequences of commands: the command is treated totally in isolation. Syntactic checking should be the responsibility of the application model.

3.3 Instantiation

Instantiation errors are the result of mapping command arguments onto the real world. Typical instantiation errors would include nonexistence of objects (e.g. incorrect filenames) or syntactically correct parameter values which cannot be realized (e.g. PRINT line 30, of a 20-line file). Instantiation errors often result from incorrect spelling. Another form of instantiation error in Unix results from specifying a filename outside the working directory. This was a common error amongst inexperienced users in our log files. In such cases the instantiation module should be able to conclude that the reason for noninstantiation is concerned with violation of the current instantiation context. We expect that errors in instantiation context will be important in other applications.

3.4 Planning

All the previous errors which have been discussed have involved individual commands only. However, an important class of errors observed involve context (or user plans). Unix provides a particularly interesting problem in this respect. Most commands can be declared to the system at any time. However, a sequence of individually entered commands need not make sense. Many other applications do not have such a shallow command structure: once a command is issued, the possible variety of subsequent commands can be very limited. Valid plans may therefore limit the possible command sequences semantically (as in Unix) or physically (as in highly structured command systems).

Hanson *et al.* (1984) analysed command groups in Unix in terms of their modularity. Modularity expresses the property of being able to precede or follow a wide variety of commands. Commands such as *ls* and *cat* are used frequently in a supporting role before and after many commands. They are therefore highly modular. Other commands, such as *cp*, show little modularity and are effectively treated as single units (*cp* is, however, often preceded by *chmod*). Thus, although commands can be input to Unix in any order, there is a highly preferred usage pattern. Commands which provide status information, manage processes and edits are all highly modular.

It is important therefore that any application model has a planning element in it to check and advise users on valid plans. In systems where the command structure is deep such planning information will be crucial; otherwise, the user becomes fixed in an incorrect path. In shallow systems such as Unix it is equally important because of the freedom with which the user can input commands. Without appropriate planning guidance users wander aimlessly around the system and, more seriously, do not develop an appropriate model of the system. Thus any application model will need to have a task plan knowledge base in order to place commands in context and advise users in cases of error.

3.5 Goals

A common error we observed in inexperienced Unix users was a lack of ability in successful goal execution. Users who were obviously confused (i.e. apparently switching between plans) freely admitted that whilst they knew what they wanted to do, they had difficulty in translating these goals into command sequences. Of course, goals can be defined at many levels and much user goal information will be the responsibility of the user model. From an application point of view, however, there will be a clear set of application goals which can be defined. Each of these goals will then be associated with a corresponding set of plans. Although in Unix many of the real-world goals cannot be mapped directly onto a set of Unix goals, a set of generic goals has been suggested. Hanson *et al.* (1984) found from analysis of usage patterns that commands could be clustered into five broad goals:

orientation;
editing;
process control;
social; and
task-specific.

These goal command sets can be subdivided further and associated with sets of application plans. Advice from an application model to the user model at this level would be of immense benefit in improving explanations and advice.

3.6 'Satisficing'

From our observations many inexperienced users achieve their goals but in an inefficient manner. The shallow structure of Unix encourages this approach. 'Satisficing' involves the identification of such inefficient sequences and the provision of advice to the user on how to improve their use of the system. Such an approach has been implemented successfully in the SUSI system (Jerrams-Smith, 1985), and although the possible satisficing situations considered by SUSI are rather limited, the approach works. A satisficing module within the application model would observe user interactions over time and only intervene (infrequently) when sufficient evidence had been collected. We regard the provision of such advice as essential in any application model.

4 A PROPOSED ARCHITECTURE

We have identified a number of modules which we consider should comprise the application model. Although the above modules will exist logically with the application model, they will not necessarily exist in a physical sense. Specifically, the three modules (i.e. SPELLING, SYNTAX and INSTANTIATION) are foreseen as separate physical entities in their own right, whereas the other two modules (i.e. USER GOALS and PLANS) will not exist separately but as different levels within the one physical entity. We intend to handle goals and plans using a modified version of the PRIAM system (Davenport and Weir, 1986).

The spelling checker will use Durham's algorithm to detect errors caused by the aforementioned rules. There are several reasons for basing our approach on that of Durham. His work was concerned with interactive user interfaces and, as Durham pointed out, there are a number of differences between constructing a spelling corrector for an interactive interface and one for use in other domains, such as preparing manuscripts (Yannakoudakis and Fawthrop, 1983).

The application model has two main functions: checking input and answering queries. To check the input it will take into account the number of levels at which a user can make a mistake (i.e. SPELLING, SYNTAX, INSTANTIATION, PLANS and GOALS). To answer queries, it will access its GOALS, PLANS and INSTANTIATION modules to formulate appropriate replies.

A key issue in designing an application model is how the various proposed modules will work together. Our first thoughts were to have a straightforward hierarchical system which would operate in three modes (Fig. 2). The modes shown are bottom-up, top-down and blackboard. The bottom-up mode would be invoked to check the user input for errors. Input would simply pass up through the levels until an error was detected. This would cause the application model to switch to blackboard mode, with all levels cooperating to suggest possible correct interpretations for the error input. Top-down processing would be invoked whenever a query was

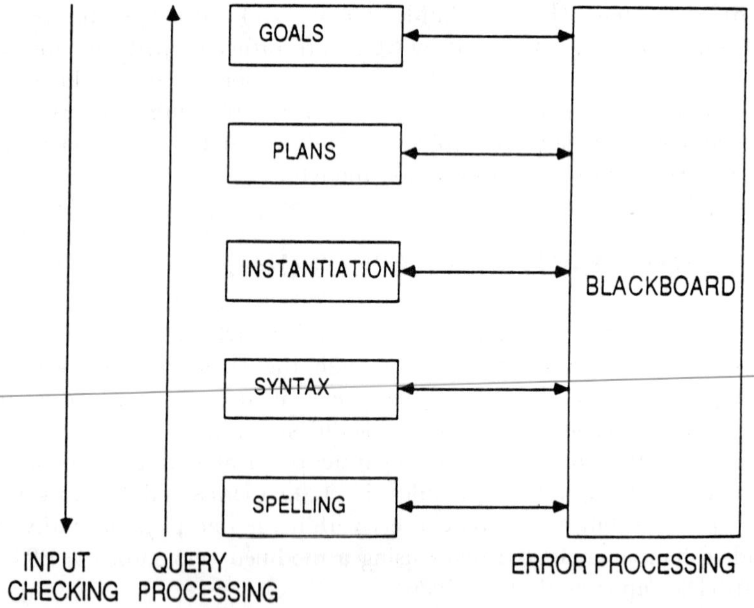

Figure 2. Original architecture proposed.

detected. This top-down process would only involve GOALS, PLANS and INSTANTIATION to check that all the required objects were currently instantiated.

However, an investigation into the power and flexibility, both present and potential, of PRIAM (Davenport and Weir, 1986) caused us to rethink the internal workings of the application model. It became apparent that PRIAM provided a possible solution to the problem of how to represent the knowledge of the application in terms of domain goals, thus allowing the user to interact with the application at a higher level.

PRIAM is a plan recognizer, designed to work in a bottom-up manner, and in which plans are stored as sequences of commands. PRIAM operates by checking its input to see if it initiates any known plans. If so, it reports this and the relevant next command to the user. On subsequent input PRIAM checks that the user is following this plan. If, at any time, the user deviates from it PRIAM will ask him if he wishes to

(1) abandon the current plan;
(2) suspend the current plan; or
(3) reinvoke the current plan, ignoring the last input.

In our case the dialogue will take place with the dialogue controller, which converses with the user model to formulate actual user output. This leads to an architecture in which all input is first examined by the PLANS module, to see if it matches any of the 'next' templates of any of the currently instantiated plans. If this is the case then it establishes that the input is part of a currently instantiated plan.

The next requirement is to show that the objects to which the arguments refer (1) exist and (2) are of the correct type. To ensure that this is so, we call on both the INSTANTIATION and the SYNTAX modules to perform these checks. If the response is positive, the input can be sent to the application. Notice that we have not called upon the SPELLING module during this process. The SPELLING module is called upon only when an error is detected in the input to any of the other modules. Command lines on the Blackboard have additional fields to indicate if a particular module has processed them and to report information discovered about the items during processing. Process fields with no entry will automatically invoke an appropriate module. If any module adds to the information fields it untags the process fields so that other modules can re-examine the command line.

5 STRATEGIES FOR CONTROL

The above scenario describes interactions between the modules when no errors have been detected in the input. When an error is discovered the interaction between modules becomes much more profound. In such cases the modules interact in a blackboard-like manner to detect the error and suggest possible corrections. This statement highlights one of the basic assumptions in the design of our application model, i.e. that it will not try to generate the definitive correction for each and every error. Instead, it will suggest possible alternative corrections and leave it to the user (or perhaps the dialogue controller and the user model) to decide.

It is essential that the application model embodies a sensible control structure for organizing the modules that use the blackboard. The control strategy will, in fact, be based upon that which a real application expert would adopt when faced with an input error. We have taken many of the errors in our Unix user log files and followed them through using a 'hand-worked' strategy to identify the errors and how our defined modules would process them. In defining our strategy we were guided by the work of Davies (1984) on the layering of interaction models. Davies suggested that a set of interaction models should be ordered by some metric. The diagnosis then begins at the lowest level and invokes higher levels only on failure. The individual interaction models are based upon different sets of assumptions about the nature of the error. We also considered it appropriate to adopt a model-based strategy from considerations outlined in Coombs and Alty (1984), in which different models can be inconsistent between themselves.

Our control strategy is as follows. We define four possible models, as shown in Table 1. The models are ordered in ascending likelihood of error occurring (errors in both parts are less likely than errors in one part). The strategy is shown in Fig. 3. We have also included the provision for additional models (application dependent) above Model 4.

On initial user input there is only one candidate command line and we enter Model 1. The command line is analysed for a match using the PLANS, INSTANTIATION and SYNTAX modules. If a match exists, it is assumed that the command is valid and it is sent to the application. In this way, a correct

Table 1. Error models.

Model	Argument OK	Argument error
Command OK	1	3
Command error	2	4

Model 1 represents a correct command line; Model 2 has a command error with a correct argument; Model 3 has a correct command with an argument error; Model 4 has an error in both components.

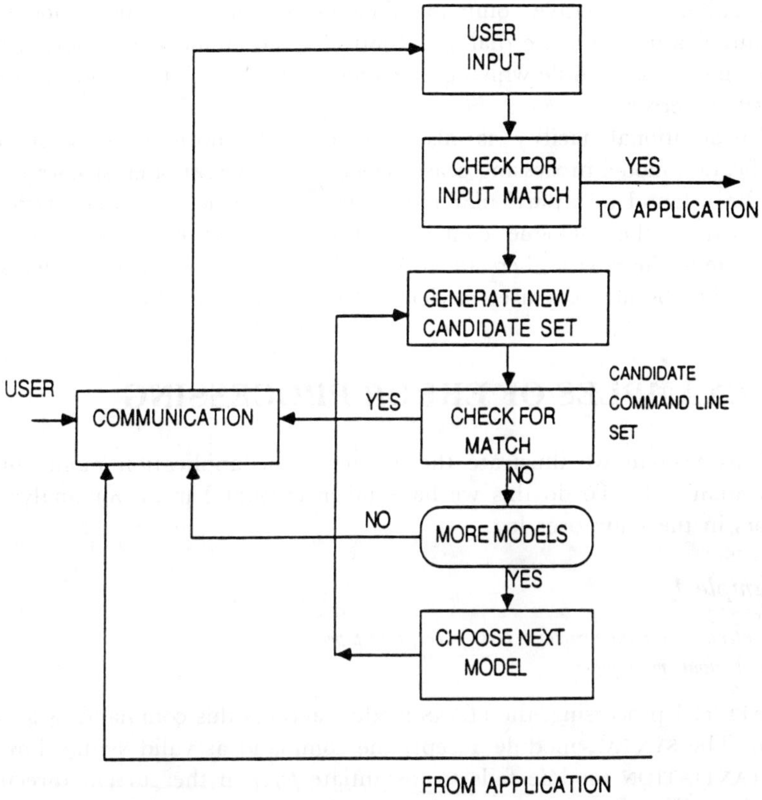

Figure 3. Proposed control structure.

command requires the minimum processing.

If the command does not match, it is passed to the next higher model (provided that all models have not already been used) and the four modules — PLANS, SPELLING, INSTANTIATION and SYNTAX — cooperate using the blackboard to generate a new set of candidate command lines. These then become the input to the next higher model. Processing continues and if no match is found again, the next higher model is used. This process continues until the models are exhausted. At this point, the PLANS component would offer a range of possible commands which could be input as part of the current plan (in Unix this would not be helpful because any command can be input at any time, but in other, more structured command systems such information could be very helpful). It also is possible that higher-level domain-dependent models could be added at this point. If no candidate solutions are found, this fact is reported to the dialogue controller which may submit alternative command lines derived from the user model. In communicating with the dialogue controller the application model uses a communicating module which gathers together all the information deduced about the error.

An additional facility is also provided. In normal circumstances, application model processing ceases when a possible set of error corrections has been found in a particular model. However, when this information is returned to the dialogue controller it can request error processing to continue to the next higher model. Use of this facility is a user model issue or, in the absence of a user model, will be a user decision.

6 EXAMPLES OF ERROR PROCESSING

In this Section we illustrate the action of the application model in its 'guardian' role. To do this we have taken examples from our analysis of errors in the Unix user log.

Example 1

contents of current directory: *text*, *paper*, *conf/piper*
user input: *more piper*

In Model 1 processing, the PLANS module accepts this command as a valid plan. The SYNTAX module accepts the command as valid syntax but the INSTANTIATION module fails to instantiate *piper* in the current directory. However, it succeeds in instantiating it in directory *conf*. The match has succeeded and the dialogue controller is informed, which in turn will (under the guidance of the user model, if it exists) advise the user of this possible interpretation. In addition, it could point out that the user has made a context error. If the dialogue controller requests further error processing, Model 1 processing will fail and Model 2 processing will commence. The SPELLING module will be invoked to try alternative spellings of *more* which are also valid commands. If any alternatives are found the SYNTAX module will check that the current argument (*piper*) is still syntactically correct and the INSTANTIATION module will try to re-instantiate. In fact, in this particular case no alternative would be found and the system would move to Model 3 processing. The SPELLING module would now attempt to produce alternative spellings of *piper*. The INSTANTIATION module would find an existing instantiation and this new command line would again be offered to the dialogue controller. If this was rejected, Model 4 processing would be invoked but no further candidates would be found.

Example 2

contents of current directory: p930a fred jim
user input: cat 930a

The PLANS module examines this input and decides that it is a valid plan. Then the SYNTAX module finds that this is an acceptable syntax, but the INSTANTIATION module cannot find the file *930a*. Thus Model 1 processing fails and Model 2 is invoked. The command is analysed by the SPELLING module and a set of alternatives is produced — *cal*, *ccat* and *at*. These three candidates:

cal 930a
ccat 930a
at 930a

are then placed on the blackboard. The SYNTAX module rejects *cal 930a* because the argument is incorrect (it must be a number), it accepts *ccat 930a* because this contains a valid filename, and it accepts *at 930a* since the argument here is also valid. The INSTANTIATION module now examines the remaining two candidates. It rejects *ccat 930a* because the file does not exist (if a file of that name existed it would have been accepted by the INSTANTIATION module but would then have been rejected by the SYNTAX module if it is assumed that the file was not in compressed format). Finally, the candidate *at 930a* is returned to the user (or dialogue controller). If the dialogue controller requested further processing, Model 3 would be entered and candidates including *cat 930a*, *cat p930a*, etc. (there would be quite a large number here) would be generated. These would then be checked by the INSTANTIATION module which would reject all except *cat p930a*. This would then be returned. If again the user (or dialogue controller) rejected this, Model 4 processing would be entered. The SPELLING module would generate a large number of possibilities for both argument and command name. These would be severely cut down by the SYNTAX and INSTANTIATION modules, and only *cal 930* would be selected and returned.

The second function of the application model is to answer queries from the user or the dialogue controller. To do this, the PLANS module accesses the database of possible plans. In the case of Unix these will be plans arranged under the five generic goals identified by Hanson. The subgoals of these plans will also have plans, and so on. These goals will be the 'expert' real-world goal names.

7 AN INITIAL APPLICATION DOMAIN

Whilst our work on Unix has been valuable in assisting with the specification of an architectural form of application model, we were anxious to investigate the utility of the design in a more highly structured domain. We required a more structured application in order to provide a rigorous test of the planning and goal levels of the model. Furthermore, we wanted to choose a domain in which the users, whilst expert in the domain, were not computing experts as well.

Whilst we were considering possible domains we were approached by an organization who wished to improve the interface to an application program used by petroleum engineers. Interestingly, the suggested application had most of the features we required.

The application is a computer program which performs pressure profile calculations for single-phase (gas, oil, water) or multiphase (gas–liquid) flow on vertical or near-vertical wells. It can handle a variety of phase mixes and provides a range of correlation information. The program is used by petroleum engineers who are not usually computer experts. They are, however, used to accessing computer application packages. The program has been available for about 5 years and has a user base of about 40 engineers. The program is very flexible. Most of the facilities of the program can apparently be used in any order. It is command-driven and several combinations of keywords can have the same effect. Overall, there is no unique way of specifying a problem to the system.

A typical engineer uses this system only about twice per annum so that experience of using the program is limited. By the time a new run is required most users have forgotten how to use it. Petroleum engineers are busy people. They do not wish to spend a great deal of time with user manuals, nor do they find it worthwhile to attend training courses because of the long intervals between usage. We are now developing an application model for this application written in OPS83 on a SUN workstation. OPS83 is efficient and should provide the minimum degradation to the response time.

REFERENCES

Ball, E. and Hayes, P. (1980). Representation of task specific knowledge in a gracefully interacting user interface. *Proceedings of AAAI*, 116–120.

Bobrow, D. S. and Stefik, M. (1983). *The Loops Manual.* Xerox Corporation.

Coombs, M. J. and Alty, J. L. (1984). Expert systems: an alternative paradigm. In: *Developments in Expert Systems.* M. J. Coombs (ed.). London: Academic Press, 135–157.

Damerau, J. F. (1964). A technique for computer detection and correction of spelling errors. *Communications of the ACM*, 7, 3, 171–176.
Davenport, C. and Weir, G. (1986). *PRIAM: a plan recogniser for intelligent assistance and monitoring*. AMU8602/01.
Davies, R. (1984). Reasoning from first principles in electronic trouble shooting. In: *Developments in Expert Systems*. M. J. Coombs (ed.). London: Academic Press, 1–21.
Durham, I. *et al.* (1983). Spelling correction in user interfaces. *Communications of the ACM*, 26, 10, 764–773.
Edmonds, E. (1982). The man–computer interface: a note on concepts and design. *International Journal of Man–Machine Studies*, 16, 231–236.
Erman, D. *et al.* (1981). The Hearsay-11 speech-understanding system: integrating knowledge to resolve uncertainty. In: *Readings in Artificial Intelligence*. B. L. Webber (ed.). Troga, 349–389.
Finin, D. *et al.* (1983). Providing help and advice in task oriented systems. In: *IJCAI-83*, 176–178.
Green, M. (1984). *Report on dialogue specification tools*. Draft IFIP Working Party Report.
Hanson, S. J. *et al.* (1984). Interface design and multivariate analysis of Unix command use. *ACM Transactions on Office Information Systems*, 2, 1, 42–57.
Hayes-Roth, F. *et al.* (1983). *Building Expert Systems*. Addison-Wesley.
Jerrams-Smith, J. (1985). SUSI — a smart user system interface. In: *Proceedings of Conference BCS Human Computer Interaction Group 1985*. P. Johnston and S. Cook (eds). Cambridge: Cambridge University Press, 211–220.
Probert, D. (1984). Intelligent front-ends — opportunities. In: *Edited Highlights from the Joint Alvey MMI/IKBS Workshop on Applications Driven Research (1984)*. Available from the Alvey Directorate, Millbank Tower, London.
Shrager, J. (1981). *Invoking a beginner's aid processor by recognising JCL goals*. Computer and Information Science, University of Pennsylvania, Report MS-CIS-81-7.
Shrager, J. and Finin, T. (1982). An expert system that volunteers advice. *Proceedings of AAA–82*.
Yannakoudakis, E. J. and Fawthrop, D. (1983). The rules of spelling errors. *Information Processing and Management*, 19, 2, 87–99.

Implementation of a Program's Designer Model

Pedro Szekely

Reprinted from: *Separating the User Interface from the Functionality of Application Programs*. PhD thesis CMU–CS–88–101, Carnegie-Mellon University, pp 108–127, 1988.

Szekely's PhD was specifically concerned with user interface separability and in this section the core of his argument is presented. A number of separability implementation techniques are compared and characterized.

Implementation of a Program's Designer Model

P. SZEKELY

1 INTRODUCTION

An implementation of a program is a specification of its designer's model that can be executed by the computer. This paper discusses implementation techniques that can be used to partition the implementation of a program into a functionality and a user interface module. The techniques discussed do not require the implementation to be written in any specific programming language. This paper is about programming techniques, and the results are valid for any programming language that can support the techniques.

All implementation techniques discussed here specify the functionality of a program with an *application interface*, which is a declaration of a set of types, variables and procedure headers. The user interface is implemented as a program module that makes use of the facilities provided by the application interface. The implementation techniques discussed differ in the way in which they encode the program's functionality in the application interface, and in the way in which the user interface module makes use of the facilities provided by the application interface.

Note that the user interface module is just like any other program that makes use of the facilities provided by an application interface. Strictly speaking, programs do not need a user interface because users can use the functionality by writing a program that calls the appropriate routines in the application interface. The user interface is just a program that allows users to exercise those facilities more conveniently, by manipulating the input and output devices rather than by writing programs.

The paper compares the implementation techniques in terms of their ability to implement a wide variety of programs and a wide variety of user interfaces (generality), and in terms of their ability to hide the implementation of user interface design decisions from the implementation of the program's functionality (modularity). Even though modularity is the

THE SEPARABLE USER INTERFACE
ISBN 0-12-232150-2

primary interest of this research, generality must be considered also because, as will be seen, many techniques trade-off modularity for generality. Other criteria for evaluating the quality of implementation techniques are not discussed in detail. Run-time efficiency is discussed only informally, pointing out potential bottlenecks. Issues such as ease of programming, or whether a technique can be used to implement the user interface for existing programs, are not considered as important as generality and modularity, and are ignored.

2 THE PRESENTER/FUNCTIONALITY BOUNDARY

Presenters need two kinds of knowledge about their models in order to present them, i.e. contents knowledge and changes knowledge. Both kinds of knowledge must be supplied by the application interface, and the many techniques that can do it are discussed below. A general discussion of how presenters themselves should be implemented is beyond the scope of this thesis.

2.1 Contents knowledge

The techniques for supplying contents knowledge to the implementation of presenters can be divided into two classes.

(1) *External.* Presenters of the external type access contents knowledge by calling routines provided by the application interface. In this arrangement, concepts and presenters are implemented as separate types, and thus their implementations are hidden from each other. Concept types must export access routines so that the presenter types can access all the contents knowledge they need.

(2) *Internal.* Presenters of the internal type access contents knowledge by accessing directly the implementation of the concept types. In this arrangement, both a concept and its presenters are implemented as a single type. There is no need for the implementation of presenters to access the contents knowledge through the application interface, so there is no need for the application interface to supply the relevant routines.

The rest of this section is organized as follows. Section 2.1.1 contains examples of how the external and internal techniques could be used to implement the user interface for a chess program, and Sections 2.1.2 and 2.1.3 discuss the advantages and disadvantages of each technique.

2.1.1 Examples

This section uses a chess program to illustrate the use of external and internal techniques to encode contents knowledge in an application interface. Also, the section shows pseudocode fragments of the implementation of presenters to illustrate the way in which the application interface is used. Table 1 shows the fragments of an application interface that encode the contents knowledge for a chess program. The external technique encodes the contents knowledge as routines for the types *Chess*, *Piece* and *Location*. The internal technique encodes the contents knowledge in the data structures that implement these types.

The example assumes that the data structures implementing a type are private, meaning that they are accessible to the routines *implementing* the type operations, but not the routines *using* the type. Hence, in the internal technique, the contents knowledge is not part of the information exported by the application interface but, rather, is part of the information hidden by the application interface.

Table 2 shows fragments of an implementation of presenters using the external and the internal techniques. With the external technique, the chess presentation is implemented by a type, called here *Chess-Presenter*. *Chess-*

Table 1. The contents knowledge for a chess program.

External	Internal
type *Chess*	**type** *Chess*
public	**public**
routine *move-piece(chess, piece, location)*	**routine** *move-piece(chess, piece, location)*
...	...
routine *live-pieces(chess, colour)*	**private**
...	*board-array* An 8 × 8 array holding the live chess pieces
private	
...	
type *Piece*	**type** *Piece* **private**
routine *colour(piece)*	*colour* The colour of the piece
routine *kind(piece)*	*kind* The kind of piece
routine *location(piece)*	*location* The location of this piece
...	*next* A pointer to another piece
	...
type *Location*	**type** *Location* **private**
routine *row(location)*	*row*
routine *column(location)*	*column*
...	

Table 2. Using the contents knowledge in a chess program.

External	Internal
type *Chess-Presenter* **public** **routine** *display*(*chess-presenter*) **private** Reference to the object being presented *model* Size of a board cell (in pixels) *cell-size* ...	**type** *Chess* **public** **routine** *display*(*chess-presenter*) **private** ... *cell-size* ...
routine *display*(*chess-presenter*) **is** *draw-board*( ) *draw-live-pieces*(*live-pieces*(*chess*, *white*)) *draw-live-pieces*(*live-pieces*(*chess*, *black*))	**routine** *display*(*chess*) **is** *draw-board*( ) *draw-live-pieces*(*chess*)

routine draw-live-pieces(*enum*) **is**
for each *piece* = *next*(*enum*) **do**
draw-piece(*piece*)
	routine *draw-live-pieces*(*chess*) **is**
	for *i* = 1 **to** 8 **do**
	for *j* = 1 **to** 8 **do**
	let *piece* = *board* [*i*, *j*] **in**
	if *piece* ≠ *nil*
	then *draw-piece*(*piece*, *i*, *j*)

routine *draw-piece*(*piece*) **is** **let** *loc* = *location*(*piece*) *x* = (*row* (*loc*) − 1) * *cell-size* *y* = (*column* (*loc*) − 1) * *cell-size* *icon* = *look-up-icon*(*colour*(*piece*), *kind*(*piece*)) **in** *draw-icon*(*icon*, *x*, *y*)	**routine** *draw-piece*(*piece*, *row*, *column*) **is** **let** *x* = (*row* − 1) * *cell-size* *y* = (*column* − 1) * *cell-size* *icon* = *look-up-icon*(*piece*. *colour*, *piece*. *kind*) **in** *draw-icon*(*icon*, *x*, *y*)

Presenter exports a routine called *display* that produces the presentation. The routines in terms of which *display* is implemented, *draw-live-pieces* and *draw-piece*, are private to the *Chess-Presenter* type. With the internal technique, it is the type *Chess* that exports the *display* routine. The other routines are also defined as part of type *Chess*, but they are not exported.

The two implementations are very similar. The difference is that the external implementation uses the routines provided by the application interface to access the information to display, while the internal implementation accesses the data structures implementing the types directly. It is clear from the example that the external implementation is more modular than the internal one. A thorough discussion of the benefits of each technique is given in the next sections.

Both techniques for accessing contents knowledge have been used in systems for constructing user interfaces. The following are some examples of systems that use external techniques.

Smalltalk. In Smalltalk, concepts are implemented as classes, and presenters are also implemented by classes called views. The views access the information to be displayed by sending messages to the concept being viewed.

MacApp. MacApp is similar to Smalltalk in that concepts and views are implemented as separate classes. The difference is that the implementation of types is not hidden, and views can, in addition to using the routines in the application interface, access the type implementation directly. The ability to access the implementation of types allows MacApp views to use both the external and the internal techniques.

The following are some examples of systems that use internal techniques.

Traditional programming techniques. The traditional way to implement presenters is for the application interface to export one or more display routines that can be called to display instances of the types exported by the application interface. These display routines are implemented as part of the concept types.

Descartes. In Descartes, presentation is viewed as a type operation, and thus implemented as part of the type, not as a separate type.

2.1.2 Generality

Internal implementations are more general than external ones because they do not restrict in any way the access to a concept's contents knowledge. External implementations are not as general because the application interface may not provide enough routines to access all the contents knowledge needed to construct a particular presentation. Types are defined to provide the routines that define the abstraction embodied by the type, and there is the danger that those routines are not powerful enough to construct every imaginable presentation.

For instance, typical application interfaces for the type *Stack* provide routines *push*, *pop* and *is_empty*, which are not appropriate to access all the entries in a stack. To present a stack it is necessary to access all the stack entries without popping them. The *Stack* type can be extended to provide a routine called, say, *iterator* which returns a function that returns the next stack entry each time it is called. This iterator can be used to access all the stack entries without revealing the implementation of the stack.

The requirement of extending types with routines to access contents knowledge is *not* a great disadvantage of external implementations. Presenters must access the contents information anyway, and it is better if they use a modular method to do it than one that depends on the implementation of the type.

Run-time overhead is not a good argument against external representations either. All clients of a type pay the same overhead when interacting with objects via the type routines. If the overhead is too large for presentation purposes then it is probably too large for the other uses of the object, and the given implementation of the type would be useless anyway. Besides, compiler optimizations such as in-line expansion of procedure calls can eliminate the procedure call overhead.

2.1.3 Modularity

From the point of view of modularity, external implementations are better than internal ones. External implementations enjoy all the usual benefits of modular implementations of programs. In the particular case of implementing presentations, these benefits result in external implementations having the following properties that internal ones do not have, or have to a lesser degree.

(1) No changes to the implementation of a presenter type are needed when the implementation of a concept type is changed, provided that the application interface is not changed. The routines *draw-live-pieces* in Table 2 illustrate this point. Suppose the implementation of type *Chess* is changed, and rather than representing the chess board as an array, it is represented as a linked list containing the pieces on the board. The external implementation of *draw-live-pieces* is not affected. However, the internal implementation has to be rewritten. The **for** loop has to be changed to a **while** loop that traverses the linked list. In addition, if the application interface is changed, the portions of presenter types that need to be changed can be found easily. In a strongly typed language, the statements that need to be changed are flagged as errors by the compiler.

(2) No changes to the implementation of concept types are needed when the implementation of a presenter type is changed. In addition, new presenter types can be defined for an existing concept type without having to change the implementation of the concept type, and without worrying about interactions with existing presenter types. Table 2 again illustrates this point. The external implementation stores the presentation state in an instance of type *Chess-Presenter*, while the internal implementation stores the presentation state together with the game state in an instance of type *Chess*. In the external implementation, all changes to the presentation are encapsulated in type *Chess-Presenter*. No changes to type *Chess* are required. Thus, a user interface designer/programmer can experiment with different presentations of a concept without having to change the implementation of the concepts.

(3) The application interface makes it possible to use a presenter type with many concept types, not just one. If a presenter type is implemented using the external technique, it uses certain routines of the application interface to access the contents knowledge. That presenter type can be used to present any concept type whose application interface provides at least those routines. It does not matter whether the implementation of the concept types is different. However, if a presenter type is implemented using the internal technique, it cannot present concept types whose implementations are different, because it depends on one particular implementation.

Consider the concept of a connected graph. Not only are there small variations in the behaviour of different classes of graphs (e.g. different orders in which the nodes can be traversed), each one requiring a different implementation, but there are many ways to implement a graph. A graph can be implemented as an adjacency matrix, as a pair of sets, one of nodes and one of arcs, as a table of nodes in which each node points to the list of nodes it is adjacent to, and so on. If a presenter type for graphs is implemented using the external technique, it can be used to present all the variations of graphs just mentioned. However, if the graph presenter is implemented using the internal technique, a different implementation of the graph presenter is needed for each graph implementation, or at least for the implementations that differ substantially from each other.

(4) Different programming languages can be used for the implementations of the concept types and the presentation types. The application interface provides a clean boundary where program segments written in different languages can meet. For instance, the concepts types can be implemented in Pascal or C, and the presenter types, or part of them, can be implemented in Lisp.

(5) External implementations provide better support for sharing code among presentation types. The presentation types can be organized in an inheritance hierarchy such as Smalltalk's and MacApp's view hierarchy, the Symbolics window system flavour hierarchy, or Scofield's editor heirarchy. The inheritance allows presenter types to share common behaviour.

Table 3 shows portions of the Smalltalk *Object* and *View* hierarchies. The *Object* hierarchy describes the Smalltalk system concepts, and the *View* hierarchy describes the Smalltalk presenters. Note that the two hierarchies do not share behaviour except for the fact that *View* is a subclass of *Object.* If Smalltalk presentations were implemented using an internal technique, then the two hierarchies would have to be collapsed into one because an object and its views would be defined in the same class. However, collapsing the two hierarchies is very awkward because the two hierarchies do not share any behaviour.

Table 3. The Smalltalk *Object* and *View* hierarchies.

Object hierarchy	*View* hierarchy
Object	*View*
Magnitude	DisplayTextView
Character	FormMenuView
Date	FormView
Time	FormHolderView
Number	ListView
Float	BrowserListView
Fraction	ClassListView
Integer	MessageCategoryListView
...	...
Collection	StandardSystemView
SequenceableCollection	BrowserView
LinkedList	DebuggerView
ArrayedCollection	...
Array	StringHolderView
Bitmap	BrowserCodeView
String	FileView
...	FillInTheBlankView
Set	...
Dictionary	
...	
View	

(6) When a presenter is implemented using the external technique, the state of the presenter is completely separate from the state of the concept being presented. This makes it easier to partition the implementation of a program so that the functionality and the user interface execute as separate processes, perhaps in different machines.

(7) Presentation types can be implemented in isolation, i.e. without being associated with any other type. The implementation of such presenters can specify a set of routines that they will call to access the contents knowledge they need. Such isolated presentation types can be customized to present a large number of unrelated concept types by matching the routines mentioned above with routines from the concept type's application interface.

(8) Presentation types can have identical programming interfaces. For instance, all presenter types could provide routines called *display* and *erase*. This makes it easier to construct programs that manipulate presenters in a generic way. For instance, a structured presenter can display all of its subpresenters by calling the *display* routine on each of them. The structured

presenter does not need to know anything about its subpresenters except that the *display* routine is defined for each of them. If presenters are implemented using the internal technique they cannot have identical application interfaces: the display routines of each presenter must have different names, making it harder to construct programs that manipulate presenters in a generic way as illustrated above.

2.2 Changes knowledge

The techniques for supplying changes knowledge to the implementation of presenters can be divided into two classes.

(1) *Announcements.* The routines in the application interface communicate changes knowledge to the implementation of presenters by calling a routine to inform presenters about a change. The techniques based on announcements can be further classified into two categories.

Direct. A direct announcement is a call to the particular presenter routine that will update the presentation to reflect the change.

Indirect. Indirect announcements are *not* directed to any particular presenter. Indirect announcements are essentially broadcasts about changes that occur in concepts, and any presenters interested in them can receive them. Each presenter that receives an indirect announcement can then update its presentation as appropriate.

(2) *Recognition.* The routines in the application interface need not do anything to communicate changes to presenters. The presentations must monitor the behaviour of their models and recognize when a change of interest to them occurs. The monitoring can be done by monitoring the state of values, or by monitoring the routines that modify the values.

Active values. An active value is a piece of program state with an associated routine so that if the state is changed, the routine is invoked automatically. Active values can be used to communicate changes knowledge by making the relevant portions of the state of a model active, and associating with this a routine that communicates the change to the appropriate presenters.

Daemons. A daemon is a routine that can be associated with another routine so that if the second routine is invoked, then the first routine is also invoked. There are two kinds of daemons: a *before* daemon, which is called before the monitored routine is called, and an *after* daemon, which is called after the monitored routine exists. Daemons can be used to communicate changes knowledge by installing them on the routines that make changes of interest to presentations. In that way, when the monitored routines are called, the *before* daemons can inform presenters about changes that are about to occur, and the *after* daemons can inform presenters about changes that have just occurred.

The main difference between active values and daemons is that active values recognize changes to the state of an object irrespective of the routine that makes the change. Daemons only recognize the changes done by the routines which have daemons associated with them. Even though daemons and active values use a routine that essentially announces the changes to the presenter, this routine is invoked automatically, without explicit intervention of the routines that make the change.

The rest of the section is organized as follows. Section 2.2.1 contains examples of how announcement and recognition techniques could be used to implement the user interface for a chess program, and Sections 2.2.2 and 2.2.3 discuss the advantages and disadvantages of each technique.

2.2.1 Examples

This section shows how the change 'a chess piece has been moved' can be implemented using the techniques discussed above. The presenters of the chess program use this change to update the screen each time a chess piece is moved. Consider the implementation of the chess program's *move* operation. *Move* has to take care of captures and castling, so that a call to *move* can actually result in several pieces being moved. Suppose then that *move* is implemented in terms of a lower-level routine called *set-location* that is used to change the location of a single chess piece. The job of *set-location* is to update the *location* component of the *Piece* record, and perform certain book-keeping. The implementation shown below supposes that each piece is represented by a record. The location of a piece is stored in a component of the record called *location*. The value *nil* indicates that the piece is not on the board. In addition, all the pieces on the board are collected in a list called *live-list* and all the pieces not on the board are on a list called *captured-list*:

```
routine set-location(chess, piece, new-location) is
  if piece.location = nil
    The piece is being moved back into the board
    then remove-from-captured-list(chess, piece)
         add-to-live-list(chess-piece)
  piece.location = new-location
  if new-location = nil
    The piece was captured
    then add-to-captured-list(chess, piece)
         remove-from-live-list(chess, piece)
```

The rest of this section shows how to implement the 'chess piece moved' change based on the implementation of *set-location* described above.

Table 4 illustrates how announcements can be used to communicate the

Table 4. Communicating changes knowledge by announcements.

Indirect announcement	Direct announcement
routine *set-location(chess, piece,*	**routine** *set-location(chess, piece,*
new-location) **is**	*new-location)* **is**
let *old-location = piece.location* **in**	**if** *piece.location = nil*
if *piece.location = nil*	**then** *remove-from-captured-list(chess,*
	piece)
then *remove-from-captured-list (*	*add-to-live-list(chess, piece)*
chess, piece)	
add-to-live-list(chess, piece)	**else** *erase (piece)*
piece.location = new-location	*piece.location = new-location*
if *new-location = nil*	**if** *new-location = nil*
then *add-to-captured-list(chess, piece)*	**then** *add-to-captured-list(chess, piece)*
remove-from-live-list(chess, piece)	*remove-from-live-list(chess, piece)*
announce (chess, piece-change, piece,	**else** *draw-piece(piece)*
old-location)	
registry:	
...	
(chess54, piece-change)	
→ *update-display(chess-presenter73)*	
...	

'chess piece moved' change. The programs in both sides of the table are identical to the one described above, except for the underlined portions, which perform the announcements. Indirect announcements are implemented by calling the *announce* routine, with parameters that describe the nature of the change. *Chess* is the object that suffered the change, the value *piece-moved* is a constant that identifies the nature of the change, *piece* is the piece that was moved, and *old-location* is the location where the piece was stored before it was moved. Note that there are no calls to any display routines when indirect announcements are used.

The bottom part of the table shows how announcements are linked to presenters. The association between objects and presenters that are interested in changes to those objects is recorded in a table. The table registers objects and change identifiers with routines to be called when the corresponding object suffers the change indicated by the change identifier. For instance, the table shown specifies that if *announce* is called with parameters *chess54* and *piece-change* the routine *update-display* is called with parameter *presenter73*. Thus, if the value of variable *chess* is *chess54*, then the effect of the call to *announce* is to inform *presenter73* of the change.*

* All excess parameters to *announce* are passed to the registered routine. In the example given above, the values of *piece* and *old-location* would be passed to *update-display*.

The table could contain multiple entries for *chess54*, each one pointing to a different presenter. In this way multiple views of a concept can be implemented without the code implementing the concept knowing it.

Direct announcements are illustrated in the right-hand side of Table 4. Changes to pieces are announced by calling directly the display routines that update the display in the appropriate way. The exact meaning of the procedures used in the example is not important. Note that they have to be called from appropriate places in the code of *set-location*, thus entangling the implementation of a concept with the implementation of the concept's presentation.

Table 5 shows how the recognition-based techniques can recognize the 'chess piece moved' change. The left-hand side shows how a daemon for the *set-location* routine can be used to recognize the changes done by *set-location*. The daemon first records the old location of the affected chess piece, then calls the *set-location* routine, and finally announces the changes done by the *set-location* routine. There is no need to modify the implementation of *set-location* to announce the changes. Note that the daemon could call the routine that updates the display directly instead of using the *announce* routine.

The main difference between an active value and a daemon is that the daemon associates a routine with a routine, while the active value associates a routine with a value. A value is made active by associating with it a routine that is called automatically when the value is used in the right-hand side of an assignment statement. In Loops this is done by embedding the value in a specially tagged data structure which contains essentially the value and the routine to be called. The assignment statement recognizes these special data structures and calls the routine.

Whereas daemons are typically defined at compile time, active values can be installed and removed at run time. In addition, active values can be used to recognize changes in selected objects, whereas daemons will be triggered each time the daemoned routine is called, irrespective of whether it is called on an object of interest to the presentation or not.

Table 5. Using recognition to communicate changes.

Daemons	Active Values
daemon *set-location*(*chess*, *piece*, *new-loc*) **is** **let** *old-loc* = *location*(*piece*) **in** *set-location*(*chess*, *piece*, *new-loc*) *announce*(*chess*, *piece-change*, *piece*, *old-loc*)	**trigger** *set-value*(*new-value*) **is** **let** *old-value* = *value* **in** *set-value*(*new-value*) announce(*chess*, *piece-change*, *piece*, *old-value*)

The right-hand side of Table 5 shows the routine that must be associated with the *location* component of the *piece* record in order to trigger the *piece-change* announcement. When the value of the *location* component is about to be set, the trigger is called automatically. This trigger, in addition to setting the value of the variable, executes code that communicates the change.

Both techniques for communicating changes knowledge have been used in systems for constructing user interfaces. The following are some examples of systems that use indirect announcements.

Balsa. In the Balsa system, the announcements are called *interesting events.* When a routine in the application interface performs a change that is of interest to presenters, it calls a routine called *interesting-event* with a parameter that describes the nature of the change. A registry mechanism similar to the one described above is used.

Smalltalk. In Smalltalk, when a method performs a change that is of interest to presenters, it sends the changed object a message called *changed* with a parameter that describes the nature of the change. A registry mechanism is used to register with each object the views that are interested in changes to the object. When the object receives the *changed* message, a message called *update* is sent to each of the views registered with the object; the object that describes the nature of the change is passed to the views as a parameter of the *update* message.

The following are examples of systems that use direct announcements.

Traditional programming techniques. In traditional programming techniques, when a routine makes a change that must be presented it executes directly a sequence of statements that update the presentation to reflect the change.

Built-in output facilities of programming languages. Statements such as **printf** in C, **format** in Lisp and **writeln** in Pascal are also examples of direct announcements. These statements update directly the presentation of concepts to reflect changes in the concepts.

The following are examples of systems that use active values.

Peridot. Peridot uses active values to connect the application and the user interface. The active values can be changed by either the application or the user interface, and the other will be notified to make the necessary updates.

Descartes. In Descartes, the data structures corresponding to concepts being presented are made active. Whenever a value is assigned to those data structures, the Descartes run-time system calls a routine that announces the changes.

Loops. In the Loops language, a value is made active by making it an instance of a special class, and supplying a routine that will be called when the value is changed. Thus, when a presented value is made active a routine is supplied that updates the values presentation when the value is changed.

A technique similar to daemons is used in MacApp. Operations are invoked from objects called *commands*, which are part of the user interface. The *command* object announces the changes done by the corresponding operation by calling a routine specifying the portions of the display that need to be updated. Strictly speaking, this technique is not based on daemons, but the effect is the same. Announcements are made by calling routines after the execution of a routine in the application interface.*

2.2.2 Generality

Techniques based on announcements are more general than techniques based on recognition. Any change can be announced by calling an announcement routine from the routine that makes the change.

Recognition techniques based on active values have the following shortcomings:

(1) Implementation techniques based on active values can only recognize changes in data structures, and so are unable to recognize changes to program state that are not represented explicitly in terms of data structures. For instance, active-value-based techniques cannot typically recognize invocation and termination of routines.

Suppose that a command is presented by an icon that is highlighted when the routine it invokes starts executing, and is unhighlighted when the routine terminates its execution (e.g. the menu bar item in Macintosh interfaces). Such an interface can be implemented conveniently with daemons, but not with active values.

(2) With active values it is difficult to recognize changes at the right level of abstraction. The problem is that a single change at the conceptual level might be implemented by many changes to data structures. Active values can recognize each of the individual changes, but they cannot recognize how a pattern of individual changes constitutes a single change at the conceptual level.

Consider a sort program with a graphical interface that continuously presents the sequence of elements being sorted. Each time two elements in the sequence are swapped, an animation shows the two elements moving to their new place in the sequence. To implement such an interface the presenter of the sequence expects to be informed about the change 'elements i and j were swapped'.

Suppose the sequence is implemented with an array. One could try to implement the interface with active values by making each entry in the

* Of course, these 'daemons' are not invoked if the operation is not called from a *command* object.

array an active value. In that way, each time an array entry is modified the presenter is informed about it. Such an implementation is sufficient to keep the presentation of the array up to date, but it is not adequate to inform the presenter about the 'elements *i* and *j* were swapped' change. This change is defined by two orchestrated changes to the array, which cannot be identified as a single change by active values. However, if the sequence provides a routine called *swap* to swap to elements, the 'elements *i* and *j* were swapped' change can be identified easily by a daemon for the *swap* routine.

Recognition techniques based on daemons have the following shortcomings.

(1) Changes that occur during the execution of a routine cannot be recognized. From the point of view of a daemon, a routine is atomic (except if it calls another routine that can also have daemons attached to it). Thus, daemons do not provide adequate support for the implementation of progress reports.

(2) Daemons cannot recognize detailed descriptions of changes. With daemons it is possible to recognize that a routine was invoked and that it terminated, but it might not be possible to recognize what it did. For simple routines, the parameters with which the routine is called, and the result values, may provide enough information about the change that the routine performed, but that is not always the case.

(3) When a daemon is attached to a routine it will be executed every time the routine is called, irrespective of its parameters. This makes it difficult to use daemons to recognize changes on some instances of a type, but not on others.

Suppose a program uses two instances of a type, only one of which is presented to the user. If daemons are used to recognize changes, they will recognize changes to both instances, even though only changes to the presented instance are useful. Recognizing changes in the instance that is not presented is not an error, but it wastes resources because there is no presenter interested in those changes.

Another drawback of daemons is that they are typically defined at compile time, so it is hard at run time to turn them on and off selectively. This drawback becomes apparent when an object can have several different presentations, each of which must be informed about different kinds of changes. Since the daemons are defined at compile time, they will recognize the changes needed by all potential presentations, irrespective of whether only one or few of them are in use at any given moment.

Active values do not have these drawbacks. An active value can be installed at run time in any particular object, to recognize any particular change.

2.2.3 Modularity

Recognition-based techniques are more modular than announcement-based techniques because their implementation does not require adding any code to the implementation of the functionality of a program. Announcement-based techniques have the following disadvantages with respect to recognition-based techniques.

(1) It is necessary to find the appropriate places in the functionality implementation from where the announcements should be made. This can lead to the common error of some routine changing a displayed object, but forgetting to call the relevant update routine.

(2) Changing the implementation of the functionality requires making sure that the proper change announcements are still made. This can lead to the same error mentioned above.

(3) Changing the implementation of presentations, or defining new presentations, requires changing the implementation of the functionality to insert the code that produces the appropriate announcements.

(4) If the functionality code is sprinkled with calls to procedures to make announcements, the same code cannot be used in contexts where the announcements are not necessary, or in contexts where different kinds of announcements are necessary.

However, indirect announcements are more modular than direct ones. At least the implementation of the functionality routines is not interspersed with calls to particular update routines.

A Case Study of User Interface Management System Development and Application

Jerry M. Manheimer, Rodney C. Burnett and Jo Ann Wallers

Reprinted from: *Proceedings of CHI'89*, pp 127–132, 1989.

This paper demonstrates practically that separability can work. One of the important practicalities that was identified was the need for both 'tightly' and 'loosely' coupled relationships. This need, at least in part, was foreshadowed in the Seeheim model although the details of the requirements were not clear at that time.

A Case Study of User Interface Management System Development and Application

J. M. MANHEIMER, R. C. BURNETT AND J. A. WALLERS

Lockheed Austin Division, 6800 Burleson Road, Austin, TX 78744–1016, USA

1 INTRODUCTION

The user interface is often one of the most problematic components of a software system. The design issues are frequently complex, and the implementation and subsequent modification of a user interface can be error-prone and expensive. These problems with user interfaces have motivated the development of user interface management system (UIMS) packages. The overall purpose of a UIMS is to allow the efficient development of high-quality user interfaces.

To accomplish this goal, a UIMS separates the user interface from the application components of a computer program. The separation between the user interface and applications enables a UIMS to support the independent specification and management of the interface through high-level tools and facilities. Tools for user interface specification, such as screen builders and dialogue editors, can reduce the amount of time required for interface development and prototyping. Facilities for interface management can simplify applications by freeing them from dialogue management tasks.

Although the potential benefits of UIMS technology have induced the development of several UIMS packages (e.g. Hayes and Szekely, 1983; Schulert *et al.*, 1985), some commercially available, many developers question the overall utility of the UIMS approach (Rosenberg *et al.*, 1988). Some UIMS critics argue that because a UIMS package is based on an abstraction of contemporary user interfaces, it will become obsolete as advances in user interface technology occur. Others contend that the

THE SEPARABLE USER INTERFACE
ISBN 0–12–232150–2

separation between the user interface and applications is contrived. In most systems, the user interface and applications are linked in numerous and sometimes subtle ways: thus, separation can impair rather than facilitate interface development.

It is apparent that there is a conflict between the potential benefits of UIMS technology and the concerns of developers over its utility. Concerns that stem from deficiencies in older UIMS packages will be eliminated by advances in UIMS technology. However, doubts about the overall validity of the UIMS approach can be mitigated only by the successful application of UIMS packages in a variety of development efforts. In this paper, a UIMS approach that has been implemented and employed successfully in several applications is presented. The UIMS — the Lockheed user Interface System (LUIS) — is written in the C programming language and currently runs on several graphics workstations (e.g. SUN, Apollo, Silicon Graphics and MacIntosh II computers). The UIMS approach embodied in LUIS and applications of the package are discussed in the following sections of this paper. Where possible, application experience is used to address key issues in the UIMS technology area.

2 LUIS OVERVIEW

LUIS was developed to support user interface prototyping and management development tasks. In the former task, developers who may not be programmers require a tool that will allow them to prototype and evaluate interface designs. In the latter task, programmers require a tool that will allow them to implement user interfaces efficiently for operational systems.

2.1 The LUIS user interface model

The LUIS user interface model is based on an object-oriented approach that decomposes a user interface into a set of basic objects. A goal in developing the model was to provide a level of detail that would not sacrifice flexibility at the expense of ease of use, or vice versa. In other words, the objects in the model should be high-level enough to be grasped easily by users, yet low-level enough to subserve a broad range of user interface styles.

In the LUIS interface model, four object classes are provided: *structural*, *user input*, *display* and *functional*. Sample objects from the first three classes are depicted in Fig. 1. Structural objects divide a user interface into meaningful segments by grouping related objects. The *panel* structural object supports high-level segmentation by dividing a user interface into

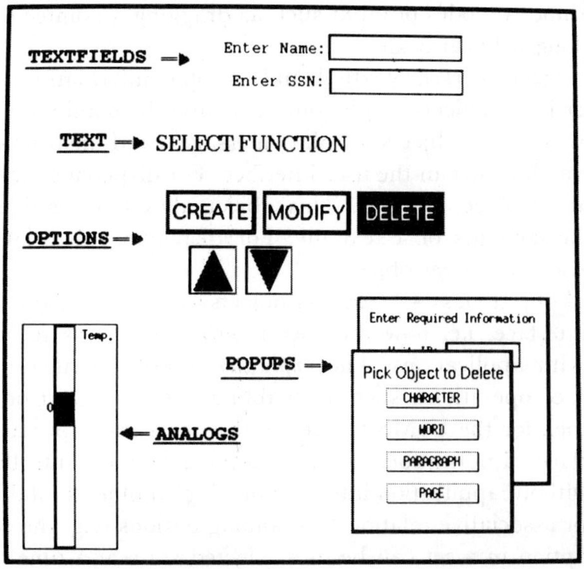

Figure 1. Sample LUIS objects.

broad functional areas. A *pop-up* is a structural object included within a panel that implements a lower-level segment in the user interface. Panels and pop-ups are roughly analogous to screens and windows but are meant to provide structure to a user interface rather than emulate a windowing system such as X-Windows. A user interface built with LUIS can run within a window or occupy the whole display; the segmentation of the user interface that is designated with LUIS structural objects is an abstract notion that is independent of the environment hosting the package.

User input objects are provided to allow input from the end user, i.e. the user of the software system employing the UIMS. LUIS provides four input objects: *option*, *textfield*, *text-editor* and *analogue*. *Option* objects are the components of menus. They are picked by the end user to select from a discrete set of alternatives. For cases in which the number of alternatives cannot be enumerated readily, *textfields* are provided. These objects allow character-string input from the end user by supporting single-line text editing. *Textfields* are used typically as the building blocks of form-based user interfaces. They are useful when great structure and little flexibility are required for text entry. In the inverse case, in which little structure but great flexibility is required (e.g. filling out a note pad), the *text-editor* object is used. This object is a full-screen text editor that allows the end user to enter text in an unrestricted format. The fourth input object type, *analogue*, allow continuous modes of input such as dragging a pointer to a particular position along a linear scale.

Display objects present textual and graphic information to end users. Unlike user input objects, *display* objects cannot be manipulated directly by the end user. *Text* objects display messages and instructions that are relatively small in size in the user interface. For displaying large amounts of text, a *text-file* object is used. This object allows the end user to scroll through the contents of a text file. For displaying pictorial information, LUIS provides an *image* object.

The final object class — *functional* objects — specifies the management of the user interface, i.e. how the user interface responds to events and its interface with applications. The *implication* object specifies a sequence of user interface operations, such as enabling another object or changing an object's label, for the UIMS to carry out when various events occur in the user interface. Implications provide a vehicle for controlling the user interface without application intervention. *Logical* objects establish mutually exclusive or associative relationships among options (e.g. the condition that only one option in a set can be in a selected state at a time). *State* objects are used to specify expressions that are evaluated during interface execution. States allow developers to test if certain patterns of events have occurred in the user interface. *Action* objects are used to define calls from the user interface to applications. Through actions, developers specify the information that needs to be sent from the user interface to the application and how to interpret messages that are sent back.

2.2 User interface specification

A user interface based on the LUIS interface model can be specified with a textual command language or an interactive interface editor. The command language tool is based on the LUIS interface definition language. This language provides a set of statements for declaring user interface objects and defining their attributes. Developers using this specification method insert language statements in an 'author file' and then invoke the language parser which builds a binary representation of the user interface. The LUIS interface editor is an alternative specification tool that allows developers to define and manipulate objects interactively through menus and mouse operations. The editor, shown in Fig. 2, can be invoked when a user interface is executing to allow on-line modifications of the interface that can be tested promptly when the editor is exited. The editor produces an author file that corresponds to the user interface after the editing session, thereby allowing the command language and editor tools to be used interchangeably. A third specification tool, the LUIS graphics editor, supports the

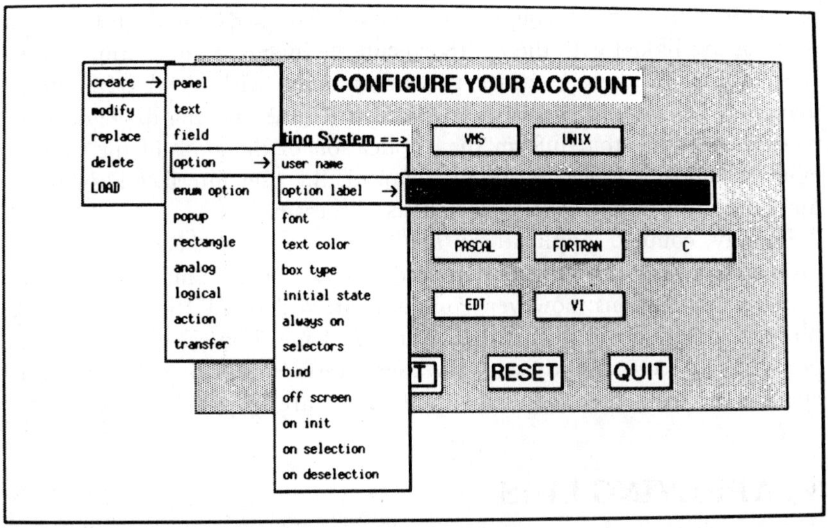

Figure 2. The LUIS Interface Editor menus shown over an account configuration user interface.

interactive creation of special graphics objects that may be required in user interfaces. Images, icons and analogue objects are developed with this editor and imported into the user interface with either the command language or interface editor tools.

2.3 System-level architecture

The system-level architecture of a UIMS specifies the nature of the interaction between the user interface and the application components of a software system. The architecture determines how easily the UIMS can be integrated with applications and its applicability in real-time systems.

Figure 3 depicts the LUIS system-level architecture. In this architecture, the interface manager runs in conjunction with a set of applications. The main responsibility of the interface manager is to implement the specified user interface. It does this by accessing the binary representation of the interface and carrying out its meanings as events occur in the user interface. The applications carry out system functions that may be initiated from the user interface but are not directly involved in its operation. LUIS assumes that applications need information about the state of the user interface and, in turn, may need to alter the state of the user interface.

Applications can be interfaced with LUIS through two alternative types of architecture: tightly coupled and loosely coupled. The tightly coupled routines are linked with the LUIS executable image. A subroutine interface is available for these routines to communicate with the LUIS interface manager, i.e. to send messages to manipulate the ongoing dialogue and to receive messages that inform the application of the state of the dialogue. When a tightly coupled routine is invoked, the user interface is suspended until the application has completed its processing.

Loosely coupled applications are programs that execute in external processes. These applications send and receive the same messages as tightly coupled applications: however, communication with LUIS is accomplished through an interprocess communication package. Loosely coupled applications execute concurrently with the user interface, allowing the end user to operate the user interface while applications are in progress.

3 APPLYING LUIS

LUIS has been used in several applications throughout Lockheed. In some instances, LUIS has been used solely for rapid prototyping. In other projects, LUIS has been employed as the UIMS in fully operational systems. Several of these systems were based on distributed architectures in which the UIMS runs in one process and a set of applications execute concurrently in distinct processes.

The users of LUIS have been, for the most part, either human factors engineers or software developers. The two user groups correspond to the two functions of a UIMS: prototyping and evaluating interface designs, versus managing the user interface in operational systems. The two groups have generated different but sometimes overlapping requirements for the

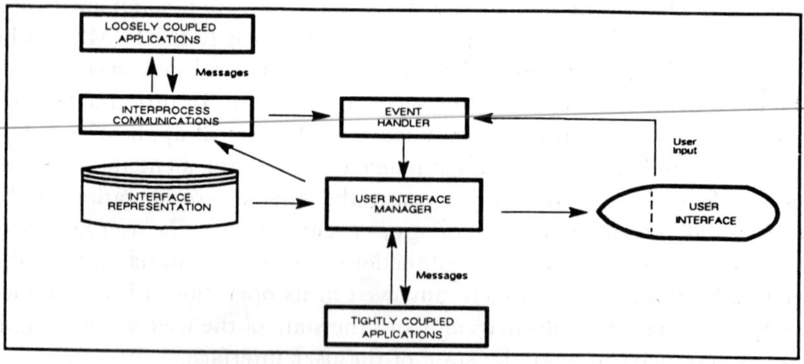

Figure 3. LUIS system-level architecture.

package. The prototypers tend to argue for a greater variety of user interface styles and higher-level specification tools for the UIMS, whereas software developers typically stress improved UIMS performance and more direct mechanisms for applications to manipulate the user interface. In the following Sections, we discuss our experience applying LUIS in relation to several issues in the UIMS area.

3.1 Declarative versus procedural user interface models

The LUIS interface model is predominately declarative in nature. Developers build a major portion of a user interface by declaring objects and assigning values to object attributes. This enables developers to focus on defining the contents of a user interface without concern for the procedural aspects of its implementation. Accordingly, a declarative model is readily learned by nonprogrammers and lends itself to menu-based interface specification.

Although declarative features are desirable, we have found that they limit the scope of the interface model. Declarative methods can become unwieldy when used to specify a user interface that can change dynamically on the basis of complex conditions. Accordingly, we have found that the use of both procedural and declarative components solves many of the problems evident in older, purely declarative UIMSs. Most of the LUIS functional objects are carriers of procedural information. For example, *implication* objects are analogous to sequences of subroutine calls, and *state* objects are derived from the **if–then–else** programming construct. The capability to sequence interface operations and define expressions increases UIMS flexibility and allows the UIMS to carry out *some* help and error-checking operations without application intervention.

Although procedural components add power to an interface model, some argue that procedural specification can make the UIMS unusable by nonprogrammers. Our experiences do not support this contention. We have found that high-level procedural components that are based on fairly simply programming constructs and embedded in a declarative context can be understood and used by nonprogrammers. Obviously, this does not eliminate the need for programmers in integrating applications with the UIMS. However, through both declarative and procedural specification, a nonprogrammer can develop a quasifunctional user interface that allows the testing of many aspects of a dialogue prior to application integration.

3.2 Separation of the user interface from applications

In applying LUIS, we have found that applications often need to intervene extensively in the operation of the user interface. Consequently, many of the enhancements that we have made to LUIS over the years extend the UIMS–application interface. We have increased the informational content of messages sent to applications from LUIS as well as the range of user interface operations that applications can initiate. In general, our experiences do not support the Seeheim model of UIMS design (Green, 1985), which assumes a high degree of separation between the user interface and applications.

Although the separation between the user interface and application is problematic, we do not feel that it invalidates the UIMS approach as some would argue. Rather, it underscores the need for a robust UIMS–applications interface that can support efficient and comprehensive application intervention. We believe, following others (e.g. Hayes *et al.*, 1985), that a robust UIMS–applications interface can be realized through a client–server model of dialogue control. Accordingly, the UIMS functions as the dialogue server for client applications, allowing applications to define and invoke actions on the user interface that are carried out by the UIMS. Through a robust client–server model, the UIMS can support intervention yet still hide most of the details of dialogue presentation and management from applications.

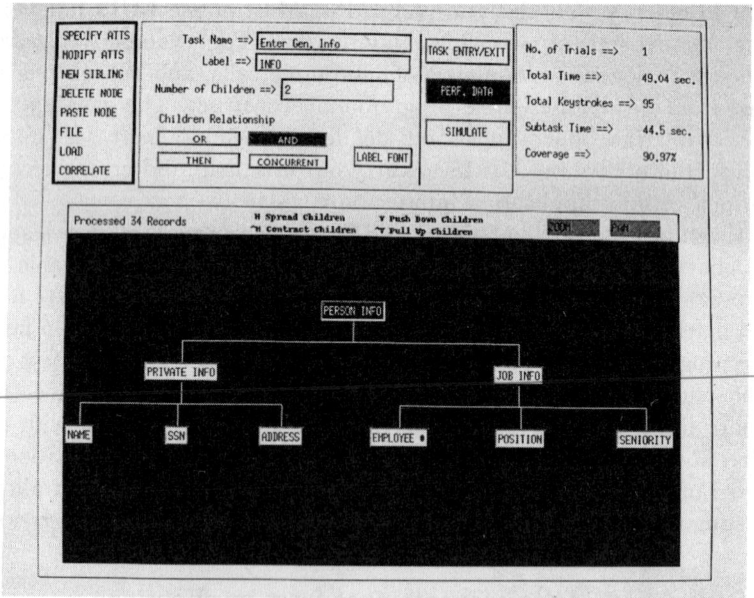

Figure 4. A task-modelling editor allows the association of performance data with user tasks.

The applications that have been integrated with LUIS have varied with respect to the separability dimension. In most cases, applications have required a manageable number of interactions with the user interface, thereby supporting separation. In other cases, applications have required very extensive control over the user interface, making separation difficult to achieve. In these cases, a shared-control model of UIMS–application integration was applied in which tightly coupled applications are initially called from the UIMS but maintain control until a terminating event, and perform time-critical user interface operations directly by bypassing the UIMS. Even in these systems the UIMS was useful, because there were several components of the user interface that could be specified and managed independently.

3.3 UIMS flexibility

The high-level nature of a UIMS inherently reduces its flexibility and therefore the likelihood that it can be used to implement particular interaction techniques. In fact, a UIMS is considered to be dangerous by some critics because it forces developers to implement only those user interfaces that are available through the package.

Thus, a major problem confronting UIMS development teams is how to provide UIMS users with adequate flexibility without compromising efficiency. Providing many objects in a UIMS docs not guarantee flexibility, because a user interface is more than a set of objects. Rather, a user interface can be viewed as a set of interrelated structures whose components are basic interface objects, such as options and text-fields. Structures differ not just in terms of their components but also in terms of the relationships among components. Therefore, a truly flexible UIMS provides the means to create structures from objects and the means to specify different relationships among the created structures, as well as among the objects within a structure.

Nevertheless, if a UIMS embodies a reasonable trade-off between efficiency and flexibility, it can facilitate the prototyping and iterative improvement of a fairly large variety of user interface designs. The UIMS then allows developers to fine-tune a design through the empirical testing of functional prototypes, which is quite useful in a field that currently lacks proven *a priori* evaluation methods. Through prototyping, the UIMS-generated interface may attain higher levels of usability than the 'optimal' interface that is outside the scope of the UIMS.

3.4 User interface evaluation

Given that a UIMS's support for prototyping compensates, in part, for limitations in flexibility, we believe that the prototyping *and* evaluation facilities provided by a UIMS should be as powerful as possible. Often these facilities are directed only towards the rapid development of prototypes and offer no support for prototype evaluation. We feel that this is due to the tendency of many developers to treat prototyping as an end in itself, rather than as only the first step toward the rigorous evaluation of a design.

In our development of LUIS, we have built facilities to help developers evaluate prototypes. The first facility developed was a response logging capability (e.g. Buxton *et al.*, 1983) in which LUIS records and time-stamps all end-user responses that occur during interface execution and writes these data to a file for examination. However, we quickly discovered that interpretation of these data was problematic. In large interfaces, voluminous amounts are logged and written due to the fact that the recorded responses are fairly low-level. Consequently, it is difficult to summarize such large quantities of data to assess where a prototype requires improvement.

It became apparent that there was a need to map the performance data to a high-level semantic structure such as a model of the user's tasks, so that performance data (e.g. number of keystrokes and response latencies) could be summarized for each task. Thus, a task modelling editor (Fig. 4) was built that allows developers to build hierarchical task structures, map LUIS objects into the components of the structure, and summarize performance data for each component. We are in the process of evaluating this tool to assess its effect on the user interface evaluation process.

4 CONCLUSIONS

We have found that an object-oriented UIMS that provides robust mechanisms for applications to control the user interface can be very useful in many development projects. We have also discovered that a flexible UIMS can be used successfully by nonprogrammers as well as programmers through the careful division of the dialogue into procedural and declarative components. In general, our experiences have given us confidence that the UIMS approach is valid, and that the judicious employment of a UIMS can improve user interfaces in many applications.

REFERENCES

Buxton, W., Lamb, M. R., Sherman, D. and Smith, K. C. (1983). Towards a comprehensive user interface management system. *Computer Graphics*, 17, 335–42.

Green, M. (1985). Report on dialogue specification tools. In: *User Interface Management Systems*. G. Pfaff (ed.). Berlin: Springer Verlag, 9–20.

Hayes, P. J. and Szekely, P. A. (1983). Graceful interaction through the COUSIN command interface. *International Journal of Man–Machine Studies*, 19, 3, 285–305.

Hayes, P. J., Szekely, P. A. and Lerner, R. A. (1985). Design alternatives for user interface management systems based on experience with COUSIN. In: *Proceedings of the Conference on Human Factors in Computer Systems, San Francisco, CA, April 1985*, 169–175.

Lowgren, J. (1988). History, state and future of user interface management systems. *SIGCHI Bulletin*, 20, 1, 32–44.

Rosenberg, J., Hill, R., Miller, J., Schulert, A. and Schewmake, D. (1988). UIMSs: threat or menace? In: *Proceedings of the CHI'88 Conference on Human Factors in Computing Systems, Washington, DC, May 1988*, 197–200.

Schulert, A. J., Rogers, G. T. and Hamilton, J. A. (1985). ADM — a dialog manager. In: *Proceedings of the Conference on Human Factors in Computer Systems, San Francisco, CA, April 1985*, 177–183.

7. Looking Backwards (and Forwards)

The Separable User Interface: a Conversation

William M. Newman and Ernest A. Edmonds

Transcript of a conversation held at EuroPARC, Cambridge, U.K. 18th April 1991

The Separable User Interface: a Conversation

EDMONDS: *I would like to discuss your early work, where we are now in terms of user interfaces and something about the future. Can we begin with your memory of the research that led to the Reaction Handler.*

NEWMAN: The work was done as part of my PhD project, at Imperial College, concerned with graphics applications. Looking back, it always strikes me how little I knew at the time. It was a bit presumptuous, really, as I had built only one interactive application at that time: an application for architectural design. It was concerned with architectural layout and it was the sum total of my experience of what it meant to design interactive applications.

Was that application innovative, a research topic in itself?

Yes; and various lessons came out of it. The main one was that writing such programs was hard.

Was that why you invented the Reaction Handler?

The way that the Reaction Handler came about was very much a technology driven idea. I had been playing with ring structures. They do not seem to be mentioned much today, but you recall them: ring structures that had two way pointers — sideways and up and down. I became quite fascinated with them and built a package to facilitate implementing them. It then occurred to me that I might be able to use them to represent the dialogue. Well, I then thought about which aspects of the dialogue I was going to represent.

So I think I have told you the reason why I did it: the rest of the reasons followed. They were retro-fitted. It seemed, however, that there were an enormous number of reasons for doing it that way.

I will turn my question round the other way. Having done it, what did you find the main benefit was? For example, was it in the speed of implementation?

THE SEPARABLE USER INTERFACE
ISBN 0-12-232150-2

That was the other rather embarrassing aspect of it, that having had this idea I spent the rest of my PhD on building the interpreter that would allow me to program the Reaction Handler and, of course, in writing up. It was only towards the end that I realised that it would be important to test this idea in some way. So I implemented a few demonstrations, using the network language of the Reaction Handler, and employing logical devices. In terms of testing or validating the claims that I was making, I think that is about as far as it went. I went off to Harvard and spent another six months building a graphical interface to the network language which was more of a step forward, in some respects, than these demonstration programs.

I think it was another ten years before such graphical tools became an accepted idea?

The graphical version was not very widely promoted in truth. It was published in a book of papers, preprints of CG68 at Brunel University, and dropped out of sight.

My impression was that all the ideas you had then were rather difficult for the commercial world to absorb.

Yes, in fact I then shifted direction slightly. I went to America in 1968 and did the work on the graphical language and then moved fairly directly into computer graphics — display procedures. I always tended to be rather influenced by the people around me. My direction was where the interests of my colleagues seemed to lie. At Utah the people were enormously interested in graphics systems and image synthesis.

Comparative early work in the user interface was done, in fact, by people working in computer graphics. However, you moved in the other direction.

Yes, as far as the Reaction Handler was concerned that really was where it languished, as far as I was concerned. For a period, until about 1975, I was developing various systems derived from the display procedure idea. The advantage of that from my point of view was that I think it pushed me on.

When you first presented the Reaction Handler idea, did you get much response or interest in it?

When I gave the paper at AFIPS in the spring of 1968 there was absolute dead silence. I do not think, then, very many people were even thinking about user interfaces, let alone about specifying them graphically with a light pen. It wasn't as if it took the industry by storm. However, the Reaction Handler attracted interest from a few people. Tom Sancha, for example, wrote a system in the same vein.

One thing that particularly interests me is the relationship between the Reaction Handler, in effect the user interface, and the procedural, or application, code. In your system, the user interface was in control in that it called the application code. That was quite a radical proposal at the time. Even today, I often meet software people who find that a difficult concept to accept.

Well, yes, you are quite right and I must observe that I don't do things that way myself at the moment, but I think that is partly because of modern technology. It seems to be assumed that the user interface description is embedded in the program. At least, that is the way it seems to be in my recent experience of building applications. The software tools that we use most often assume that the application code is in control. Of course, I work mainly on prototyping new¨pplication ideas, and when you are building something that is innovative you are less likely to find user interface tools a complete solution. Your priorities are different. A formal user interface language may not be a good solution for research-oriented work, where one is always wanting to circumvent standard methods.

The reason I entered this game, was to help a research project of mine to deliver the goods, and that worked. However, my early system was not very useful to the software 'man in the street' and I suspect that as we developed it for others to use we made the ways of getting round it, as it were, more obscure.

I suspect that the man in the street hasn't really thought very hard about user interface structures. In any case, the Reaction Handler concept has not yet found its way into regular computing.

The concept of the Light Handle, however, is there.

The concept of widgets, you mean?

Yes, widgets are now an everyday concept. That is very important.

Something else I would like to raise is that by using an explicit representation of the dialogue we make it available for explicit design decisions. There are two different aspects — and it depends on what you want to understand about the design. Representing the dialogue helps with the design of the interchanges between the user and the machine. However, the exchanges between the user interface and the application code are also important but have received much less attention. If we had a better form of representation there, in effect a cleaner split, then I would have thought the designer would be in a better position to make clear choices relating to, shall we say, functional aspects of the design.

I agree with you, it is in some respects a problem unless the technology is simply going to fit into the available representations. You were at the Alvey 'User Interface Design' workshop at Cosener's House in 1985. I am sure that you remember Mark Cutter's discussion of his design of the MacDraw user interface. He discussed the implementation of the MOVE command. Although the model that the user was supposed to hold was very simple, implementing it involved all manner of very precise checks on how far the mouse had moved before letting up, because if you didn't move it very far you might just leave it where it was, etc. It could not be described at the level of syntax, it wasn't even syntax. It wouldn't fit a state diagram representation. But maybe we have moved on and maybe we can represent that sort of thing. But the point is, that we couldn't then.

Maybe the lesson is a general rule that for the user interface in application development, well structured, standardised approaches are desirable but less so when one is being innovative. Current graphics standards are very useful because all sorts of things get done more or less for free, but if you are doing something innovative you may have to step round them.

It's back to the question of, who is your clientele? I think in product development there is an enormous incentive, obviously, just to make sure that the customer likes the product and innovation might be very important. Whereas when developing applications in-house, which I suspect is really by far the biggest clientele for this kind of thing, you have a situation where the user population is smaller. You just want to get something in the hands of your users so you can observe what is good and bad about it. Then it turns out to be something that can benefit significantly from the sort of approach we are talking about.

Another issue is the influence of these ideas on design method. It could be in that area that most lessons have been learnt.

Those lessons ought to get through and I think that may have happened up to a point. But in relation to design methods, I think of Jonathan Grudin who showed how hard it is to do anything iterative with end-users in real product development situations. User interface design is in some ways disadvantaged because it isn't really recognised, although it needs to be a central concern of the development team. It's a skill that gets picked up by programmers and later dropped.

The concept of the user interface, the Reaction Handler, has an importance in the architecture of systems. Using that model, looking at it like that, could be thought of as influencing the approach to design as much as the technological issues.

One way of interpreting that point is in terms of how user interfaces become recognised in application development. You don't have to follow the rather risky approach of building the internal software first and hoping you can add the user interface later — you can design and test the user interface at the outset. I think that that is a fairly important fact. Thus, a user interface tool may play a role in the initial prototype and that is something that became very clear when the graphical version of the Reaction Handler was built: you could define and test a new interface in a matter of minutes.

There are two issues now that were not important 20 years ago that perhaps matter considerably today. IO devices were not very interesting for quite a while, but now they are interesting again. It has almost gone back to the early days, when we were just starting to get interactive systems and the exciting points were to do with devices. Look, for example, at EUROPARC's prototype NoTime recording device that I am using now. Do you have any feeling about that?

Yes, this is certainly interesting. We seem first to have reached a plateau where Xerox Alto standards became universal for a while: everybody had WIMPs. We are beginning to move off that plateau. I think the reasons are two-fold really: one is that the Alto and the Macintosh represent a very demanding kind of user interface. They assume that the user's whole working activity is bound up in the thing that is going on on the screen — enabling them to get even more done by focusing even more attention on it. But now there are beginning to be so many things around you involving computers and you really can't assume that people approach these devices as if they were highly interactive systems. It's actually turning out that we are interacting a lot of the time with low-intensity devices, such as the electronic badge that I am wearing, and I think we have got to rethink the devices that we want to use. At the same time new technologies are suddenly beginning to make new interaction styles possible because of the amount of computing power available.

The other modern thing that we have to recognise is the major change that we are experiencing in communications and the distribution of computing power.

An element of that in what the new user interface must deal with, because of distribution, is that many things can start to happen in parallel. When I come in in the morning, I am starting a process that simply tracks where I am today for the benefit of others in the laboratory. I am aware, if I think of my environment in these terms, that there are going to be other on-going processes that I interact with. The concept of an environment that simply moves from one state to another isn't going to fit. Many applications aren't like that. If they have to be described in states, they may not map onto the user's situation well. Suppose the user sees the system in terms of objects and actions: modelling that in terms of states is not going to help you — it is not going to help you to simulate usability. So that is why I think that user interfaces will continue to present a design challenge.

The point that you are making is particularly important. The issue is of the representation helping the designer in the sense that he or she can use it to make decisions. Alternatively, we can consider the representation as being one intended to help the user understand the system. It is often assumed that they should be the same representation, but is that the case?

I don't really have the answer, but perhaps it is the users' model that the designer should start with? Users form a variety of models of the system depending on their level of experience and familiarity, on the task being performed, and on the style of interface. They may switch from a state model to an object-based model to a mapping model. The designer can't really work with all of these representations, but has to choose a single one that appears best suited to the design problem. In choosing a representation, what the designer is trying to do is to optimise various aspects of 'usability' by any means available.

What do you think the main issues are for the future?

One impression that comes across most clearly is that it is really hard to bring psychological results into user interface design. The question quite a lot of people are trying to answer is, 'is it worth it to try or, should we be looking at other sources, such as social science?'. What I have learned from working here is, now that we are getting systems that are highly distributed, we see many unexpected effects because of group behaviour. We're learning to look to social scientists to help us understand these effects.

We are working in a field that is still relatively new and where, for reasons that we talked about earlier, methodology tends not to take hold. I find it interesting to compare it with other forms of design. The things that I find common to most areas of established design disciplines, are, first of all, designers tend to go through an apprenticeship where they learn quite a bit about the implementation side, because they are going to design things that will be implemented. Clearly the same is true in architecture or almost any design area. On that basis, it doesn't make very much sense to ask a psychologist to implement a design. The other thing you notice in design is that people tend to be quite knowledgeable about other designs that have been built and that have worked, why they worked and why some didn't work. I don't think this gets about in user interface circles at all. For those reasons user interface design is very difficult and I think anybody who might be able to help is brought in, including, of course, the psychologist.

Just to go back to the organisation of design, it seems to me that the concept of the Reaction Handler could be quite significant in that context.

Yes, in two ways. Separability gives the designer a technical advantage, in that the user interface can be designed more easily and implemented more quickly. It also offers a management advantage. Many companies, Xerox included, have separate teams working on the user interface and on the software. It's a way of dividing up the problem that seems to work – most of the time. Once in a while, however, we encounter problems when the existing software architectures fall short of supporting the use of new technologies, and there isn't a clean way of separating the user interface. This is happening a lot now with multimedia technologies. What this says to me is that the boundary between user interface and supporting hardware/software is constantly changing as technology advances. We're always encountering new problems. The basic validity of separability doesn't change, but we face a constant challenge in maintaining the ability to achieve it.

Bibliography

AHO, A. V. and ULLMAN, J. D. (1977) *Principles of Compiler Design.* Reading, MA: Addison-Wesley.

ALLEN, J. R. (1973). The cybernetic centaur: advances in computer-assisted instruction. *Computers and Humanities*, 373–387.

ALTY, J. L. and MCKELL, P. (1986). Application modelling in a user interface management system. *In: People and Computers: Designing for Usability.* M. D. Harrison & A. F. Monk, (eds), Cambridge.

ANDERSON, R. H. and SIBLEY, W. L. (1972). *A new approach to programming man–machine interfaces.* Report No. 876. Advanced Research Projects Agency, Santa Monica.

ANSON, E. (1980). The semantics of graphical input. In: *Methodology of Interaction.* R. Guedj *et al.* (eds). Amsterdam: North-Holland.

ANSON, E. (1982). The device model of interaction. *Computer Graphics*, 107–114.

ARBIB, M. A. (1969) *Theories of Abstract Automata.* New Jersey. Prentice-Hall.

BALL, E. and HAYES, P. (1980). Representation of task specific knowledge in a gracefully interacting user interface. *Proceedings of AAAI*, 116–120.

BARTEE *et al. Theory and Design of Digital Machines.* McGraw-Hill.

BASS, L., LITTLE, R., PELLEGRINO, R., REED, S., SEACORD, R., SHEPPARD, S. & SZCZUR, M. R. (1991). The Arch Model: Seeheim Revisited. Paper presented for *User Interface Developers' Workshop at CHI '91*, 2–26.

BELL & MATHER, Operational control of Ptarmigan Communication System. *IEE Conference Publication No. 139.* Institute of Electronic Engineers.

BLACK, J. L. (1977). A general purpose dialogue processor. *Proceedings of the National Computer Conference*, 397–408.

BOBROW, D. S. and STEFIK, M. (1983). *The Loops Manual.* Xerox Corporation.

BOLT, R. A. (1984). *The human interface.* Lifetime Learning Publications.

BORUFKA, H. G., KUHLMANN, H. W. & TEN HAGEN, P. J. (1982). Dialogue Cells: A Method for Defining Interactions. *IEEE Computer Graphics and Applications.* 25–33.

BRACHMAN, R. (1985). I lied about the trees. *AI Magazine*, 80–93.

BURGESS, C. J. (1972). Compile-time error diagnostics in syntax-directed computers. *Computer J.*, **15,** 302–307.

BUXTON, W. & MYERS, B. A. (1986). A study in two-handed input. In: *Proceedings CHI '86 Conference on Human Factors in Computing Systems (Boston, April 13–17, 1986).* New York: Association for Computing Machinery.

BUXTON, W., LAMB, M. R., SHERMAN, D. & SMITH, K. C. (1983). Towards a comprehensive user interface management system. *Computer Graphics*, **17,** 35–42.

BUXTON, W., LAMB, M. R., SHERMAN, D. & SMITH, K. C. (1983). Towards a comprehensive user interface management system. *SIGGRAPH '83.*

CARBONELL, J. R. (1970). AI in CAI: An artificial-intelligence approach to computer-assisted instruction. *IEEE Transactions on Man-Machine Systems*, 190–202.

CHEATHAM, T. E. & SATTLEY, K. (1964). *Syntax-directed compiling.*

COCKTON, G. (1987). A new model for separable interactive systems. In: *Proceedings of Interact '87.* Bullinger and Shackel (eds). Amsterdam: Elsevier.

CONWAY, M. E. (1963). Design of a separate transition-diagram compiler. *Communications of the ACM*, **6,** 396–408.

COOMBS, M. J. & ALTY, J. L. (1984). Expert systems: an alternative paradigm. In:

Developments in Expert Systems. M. J. Coombs (ed.). London: Academic Press.

CORBATO, F. J. and VYSSOTSKY, V. A. (1965). Introduction and overview of the MULTICS system. *Proceedings of the Fall Joint Computer Conference*.

COTTON, I. W. (1971). Languages for graphic attention-handling. In: *Advanced Computer Graphics*. R. D. Parslo and R. E. Green (eds). New York: Plenum Press.

COUTAZ, J. (1987). PAC, an object oriented model for dialog design in Human-Computer Interaction — INTERACT '87. H. J. Bullinger and B. Shackel (Editors). *Elsevier Science*, 431–436.

DAMERAU, J. F. (1964). A technique for computer detection and correction of spelling erros. *Communications of the ACM*, **7,** 171–176.

DANCE, J. R., GRANOR, T. E., HILL, R. D., HUDSON, S. E., MEADS, J., MYERS, B. A. & SCHULERT, A. (1987). The run time structure of UIMS-supported applications. *Computer Graphics*, **21,** 2.

DATE, C. J. (1981). *An Introduction to Database Systems*. Reading. MA: Addison-Wesley.

DAVENPORT, C. & WEIR, G. (1986). *PRIAM: a plan recogniser for intelligent assistance and monitoring*. AMU8602/01.

DAVIES, R. (1984). Reasoning from first principles in electronic trouble shooting. In: *Developments in Expert Systems*. M. J. Coombs (ed.). London: Academic Press.

DAVIS, M. R. & ELLIS, T. O. (1964). The RAND tablet: a man–machine graphical communication device. *Proceedings of the Fall Joint Computer Conference*. 325–331.

DENERT, E. (1975). *PLAN2D — a concept and syntax of a two-dimensional programming language* (in German). Dissertation. Technical University of Berlin, Cybernetics Faculty.

DENERT, E. (1975). A method for the design and implementation of an interactive software system using PLAN2D editors and ADAGE graphics systems (in German). Technical University of Berlin, Cybernetics Faculty, Pub. No. 75–23.

DENERT, E. (1977). Specification and design of dialogue systems with state diagrams. In: *Proceedings of the International Computing Symposium, Liège*. Elsevier, North Holland.

DERKSEN, J. (1983). *Een ontwerp van programmeergereedschap voor dialoogsystemen debaseerd op dialoogoellen (Tools for dialogue systems based on dialogue cells)*. TNO-IBBC Rapport Nr. B1–83–62/68.0.0004.

DOWSEY, M. W. (1974). Easy author-entry systems: a review and a prototype. *International Journal of Man–Machine Studies*, 401–419.

DURHAM, I. *et al.* (1983). Spelling correction in user interfaces. *Communications of the ACM*, **26,** 764–773.

EDMONDS, E. A. (1974). A process for the development of software for non-technical users as an adaptive system. *General Systems*, **19,** 215–217.

EDMONDS, E. A. (1978). Adaptable man/machine interfaces for complex dialogues. In: *Proceedings of the European Computing Congress*, London.

EDMONDS, E. A. (1981). Adaptive man–computer interfaces. In: *Computer Skills and the User Interface*. M. J. Coombs and J. L. Alty (eds). London: Academic Press.

EDMONDS, E. A. (1982). The man–computer interface: a note on concepts and design. *International Journal of Man–Machine Studies*, **16,** 231–236.

EDMONDS, E. A. (1990). The emergence of the separable user interface. *ICL Technical Journal*, **7,** 54–65.

EDMONDS, E. A. & GUEST, S. P. (1977). An interactive tutorial system for teaching programming. In: *IERE Proceedings 36 — Computer Systems and Technology*, IERE, London.

EDMONDS, E. A. & GUEST, S. P. (1978). SYNICS — *a FORTRAN subroutine package for translation,* Report No. 6, Man–Computer Interaction Research Group, Leicester Polytechnic.

EDMONDS, E. A. & GUEST, S. P. (1979). *A man–computer dialogue system*. Report No. 27, Man–Computer Interaction Research Group, Leicester Polytechnic.

EDMONDS, E. A. & MCDAID, E. (1990). An architecture for knowledge-based front-ends. *Knowledge-Based Systems* **3(4),** 221–224.

ENDERLE, G. (1985). Report on the interface of the UIMS to the application. In: G. E. Pfaff (ed.), *User Interface Management Systems*, Springer Verlag.

ENGLISH, W. K., ENGELBART, D. C. & BERMAN, M. I., (1967). Display selection techniques for text manipulation. *IEEE Transactions*, HFE–8, 5–17.

ERMAN, D. *et al.* (1981). The Hearsay-11 speech-understanding system: integrating knowledge to resolve uncertainty. In: *Readings in Artificial Intelligence.* B. L. Webber (ed.). Troga.

FEINGOLD, S. L. (1967). PLANIT — a flexible language designed for computer–human interaction. *AFIPS Conference Proceedings*, **31,** 545.

FILLAT, A. I. & KRANING, I. A. (1970). *Generalized organization of large data-bases: a set-theoretic approach to relations.* MIT, Cambridge, MA. Tech. Rep. MAC-TR-70.

FININ, D. *et al.* (1983). Providing help and advice in task oriented systems. In: *IJCAI-83.*

FITTER, M. J. & GREEN, T. R. G. (1981). When do diagrams make good computer langauges? In: *Computing Skills and the User Interface.* M. J. Coombs and J. L. Alty (eds). London: Academic Press.

FLORENTIN, J. J. (1977). Automatic generation of interactor programs. In: *Proceedings of the International Conference on Displays for Man–machine Systems, Lancaster.* IEE Pub. No. 150. Institute of Electronic Engineers.

FOLEY, J. & VAN DAM, A. (1982). *Fundamentals of Interactive Computer Graphics.* Reading, MA: Addison-Wesley.

FOLEY, J. D. & WALLACE, V. and CHAN, P. (1984). The human factors of computer graphics interaction techiques. *IEEE Computer Graphics and Applications*, **4,** 13–48.

FOSTER, J. M. & ELCOCK, E. W. (1969). ABSYSI: an incremental compiler for assertions: an introduction. *Machine Intelligence*, **4,** 423.

FOSTER, J. M. (1970). *Automatic Syntactic Analysis.* London: Macdonald.

FOXLEY, E. & KING, P. (1968). A meta-semantic language for use with a top-down syntax analyser. *Proceedings of the IFIP Conference*, 366–372.

FRYE, C. H. (1968). CAI languages: capabilities and appalications. *Datamation*, 34–37.

GAINES, B. R. & FACEY, Pl. V. (1977). BASYS — a language for programming interaction. *IERE Proc. 36, Computer Systems and Technology.*

GARRET, M. T. & FOLEY, J. D. (1982). Graphics programming using a database system with dependency declarations. *ACM Transactions on Graphics*, **1,** 109.

GOLDBERG, A. & ROBSON, D. (1983). *Smalltalk-80: The Language and its Implementation.* Reading. MA: Addison-Wesley.

GRAHAM, R. M. (1968). Protection in an information processing utility. *CACM.*

GRANOR, T. E. (1968). *A user interface management system generator.* Graphics Lab. 12, Computer Science Dept., University of Pennsylvania. Technical Report MS–CIS–86–42.

GRAPHICS STANDARDS PLANNING COMMITTEE (1979). Status report of the Graphics Standards Planning Committee. *Computer Graphics*, **13**.

GRAY, J. C. (1967). *Compound data structures for computer aided design: a survey.*

GRAY, P. D., KILGOUR, A. C. & WOOD, C. A. (1988). Dynamic reconfigurability for fast prototyping of user interfaces. *Software Engineering Journal*, November 1988, 257–262.

GREEN, M. (1981). A methodology for the specification of graphical user interface. *Computer Graphics*, **15,** 99–109.

GREEN, M. (1981). A methodology for the specification of graphical user interfaces. *SIGGRAPH '81.*

GREEN, M. (1984). Design notations and user interface management system.

GREEN, M. (1984). *Report on dialogue specification tools.* Draft IFIP Working Party Report.

GREEN, M. (1985). Report on dialogue specification tools. In: *User Interface Management Systems.* G. E. Pfaff (ed.). Springer Verlag, Berlin.

GREEN, M. (1985). The University of Alberta user interface management system. Proceedings of SIGGRAPH '85. *Computer Graphics*, **19,** 205–213.

GREEN, M. (1986). A survey of three dialogue models. *ACM Transactions on Graphics*, **5,** 244–275.

GUEST, S. P. (1982). The use of software tools for dialogue design. *International Journal of Man–Machine Studies*, **16,** 263–285.

HALL, P. A. V. (1977). *Man-computer dialogues for many levels of competence.* Internal Report, Scicon, London.

HANSON, S. J. *et al.* (1984). Interface design and multivariate analysis of Unix command use. *ACM Transactions on Office Information Systems.* **2,** 42–57.

HAYES, P. J. & SZEKELY, P. A. (1983). Graceful interaction through the COUSIN command interface. *International Journal of Man–Machine Studies,* **19,** 285–305.

HAYES, P. J., SZEKELY, P. A. & LERNER, R. A. (1985). Design alternatives for user interface management systems based on experience with COUSIN. In: *Proceedings of the Conference on Human Factors in Computer Systems, San Francisco, CA, April 1985.*

HAYES-ROTH, F. *et al.* (1983). *Building Expert Systems.* Addison-Wesley.

HEISTAND, R. E. (1964). An executive system implemented as a finite state machine. *CACM,* **7,** 669–677.

HEKMANPOUR, S. and INCE, D. C. (1987). Evolutionary prototyping and the human–computer interface. In: *Proceedings of INTERACT 87.* H. J. Bullinger and B. Shackel (eds). Amsterdam: North Holland.

HILL, R. D. (1986). Supporting concurrency, communication, and synchronization in human–computer interaction — the Sassafras UIMS. *ACM Transactions on Graphics,* **5,** 3.

HILL, R. D. (1987). Event-response systems — a technique for specifying multi-threaded dialogues. *Proceedings SIGCHI+GI'87: Human Factors in Computing Systems, Toronto, Ontario, Canada, April 5–9, 1987.*

HILL, R. D. (1987). Supporting concurrency, communication and synchronization in human–computer interaction — the Sassafras UIMS. *ACM Transactions on Graphics.*

HOMER, E. D. (1966). An algorithm for selecting and sequencing statements as a basis for a problem-oriented programming system. In: *Proceedings of the 21st ACM National Conference,* New York, NY, 1966.

HOPGOOD, F. R. A. & DUCE, D. A. (1980). A production system approach to interactive program design. In: *Methodology of Interaction.* R. A. Guedj, P. J. W. ten Hagen, F. R. A. Hopgood, H. A. Tucker and D. A. Duce (eds). Amsterdam: North-Holland.

HUDSON, S. E. (1986). *A user interface management system which supports direct manipulation.* Ph.D. Thesis, University of Colorado, Boulder, CO.

HURLEY, W. (1989). *A generative taxonomy of application domains.* Doctoral Dissertation, George Washington University, Washington, DC.

HURLEY, W. D. & SIBERT, J. L. (1989). Modelling User Interace — Application Interactions. *IEEE Software,* January, 71–77.

HUTCHINS, E. L., HOLLAN, J. D. & NORMAN, D. A. (1986). Direct manipulation interfaces. In: *User Centered System Design.* D. A. Norman and S. W. Draper (eds). Hillsdale, NJ: Erlbaum Associates.

IBM (1969). *COURSEWRITER III Student Text.* Form No. GC20–1706. White Plains, NY: IBM Corporation.

INNOCENT, P. R. (1982). Towards self-adaptive interface systems. *International Journal of Man–Machine Studies,* **16,** 287–299.

JACOB, R. J. K. (1983). Using formal specifications in the design of a human-computer interface. *Communications of the ACM.*

JACOB, R. J. K. (1986). A specification language for direct manipulation user interfaces. *ACM Transactions on Graphics,* **5,** 283–317.

JAMES, E. B. (1975). *Adaptive analysis: a model for perception.* Report No. 74/45, Dept. of Computing and Control, Imperial College, London.

JENSEN, K. & WIRTH, N. (1975). *PASCAL User Manual and Report. Lecture Notes in Computer Science 18* (2nd edn). New York: Springer Verlag.

JERRAMS-SMITH, J. (1985). SUSI — a smart user system interface. In: *Proceedings of Conference BCS Human Computer Interaction Group 1985.* P. Johnston and S. Cook (eds). Cambridge: Cambridge University Press.

JOHNSON, C. I. (1968). Principles of interactive systems. *IBM Systems Journal,* **7,** 147.

KASIK, D. J. (1982). A user interface management system. *SIGGRAPH '82.*

KRAMMER, G. (1980). On computer problem-solving interaction. In: *Methodology of Interaction.* R. A. Guedj, P. J. W. ten Hagen, F. R. A. Hopgood, H. A. Tucker and D. A. Duce (eds). Amsterdam: North-Holland.

LAFUENTE, J. M. (1977). *The specification of data-directed interactive user-computer dialogues,* Ph.D. Thesis, Cornell University, Ithaca, NY.

LAFUENTE, J. M. & GRIES, D. (1978). Language facilities for programming user-computer dialogues. *IBM Journal of Research and Development*, **22,** 145–158.

LANTZ, K. A. *et al.* (1987). Reference models, window systems, and concurrency. *Computer Graphics*, **21**.

LECHNER, R. J. & STALLINGS, W. W. (1973). A minisystem programming language. In: *Proceedings of the ACM National Conference, 1973.* 174–182.

LIPSCOMB, J., PIQUE, M., BROOKS, F. P. & WRIGHT, W. V. (1981). The GRIP-75 man–machine interface [videotape]. *SIGGRAPH Video Review 4.* New York: Association for Computing Machinery.

LOCK, K. (1965). Structuring programs for multiprogram time-sharing on-line applications. *Proceedings of the 1965 Fall Joint Computer Conference.*

LORES, J., FLETCHER, P. & PRAT, A. (1989). *Progress and experiences in the design of a prototype back-end manager for time series analysis using Genstat and SCA.* Internal ESPRIT report.

LOSBICHLER B. & MÜHLBACHER, J. (1974). Entwicklung eines Mensch-Machine-Kommunikationsystems durch top-down Entwurf. *Angewandte Informatik*, **16,** 453–463.

LÖWGREN, J. (1988). History, state and future of user interface management systems. *SIGCHI Bulletin*, **20,** 32–44.

MAGUIRE, M. (1981). *A study of the problems of man–computer dialogues for naive users.* Ph.D. thesis. Leicester Polytechnic.

MAHER, P. K. C. & BELL, H. V. (1977). The man–machine interface — a new approach. *Proceedings of the International Conference on Displays for Man/Machine Systems*, IEE Pub. No. 150. Institute of Electronic Engineers, London.

MANHEIMER, J. M., BURNETT, R. C. & WALLERS, J. A. (1989). A case study of user interface management system development and application. In: *Proceedings CHI '89*, ACM Press, New York.

MARTIN, J. M. (1973). *Design of Man–Computer Dialogues.* Englewood Cliffs, NJ: Prentice-Hall.

MCCORMACK, J. & ASENTE, P. (1988). An overview of the X toolkit. In: *Proceedings of the ACM SIGGraph Symposium User-Interface Software.* New York: ACM.

MORAN, T. (1980). A framework for studying human–computer interaction. In: *Methodology of Interaction.* R. A. Guedij, P. J. W. ten Hagen, F. R. A. Hopgood, H. A. Tucker and D. A. Duce (eds). Amsterdam, North-Holland.

MORAN, T. (1981). The command language grammar, a representation for the user interface of interactive computer systems. *International Journal of Man–Machine Studies*, **15,** 3–50.

MYERS, B. A. (1987). Creating dynamic interaction techniques by demonstration. *Proceedings of CHI + GI '87.*

MYERS, B. A. (1988). *Tools for creating user interfaces: an introduction and survey.* Carnegie-Mellon University, Pittsburg, PA, CMU-CS-88-107.

MYERS, B. A. & BUXTON, W. (1986). Creating highly interactive and graphical user interfaces by demonstration. Proceedings of SIGGRAPH '86. *Computer Graphics*, **20,** 249–258.

NEWMAN, W. M. (1967). *Definition languages for use with the Reaction Handler.* Imperial College. London. Computer Technology Group, Report 67/9.

NEWMAN, W. M. (1967). *The ASP-7 ring structure processor.* Imperial College, London. Computer Technology Group, Report 67/8.

NEWMAN, W. M. (1968). A graphical technique for numerical input. *Computer Journal*, **11,** 63–64.

NEWMAN, W. M. (1968). A system for interactive graphical programming. In: *Spring Joint Computer Conference.* AFIPS Press, 47–54.

NEWMAN, I. A. (1978). Personalised user interfaces to computer systems. *Proceedings of the European Computing Congress, London.* Online, London.

OLSEN, D. R. (1984). Push-down automata for user interface management. *ACM Transactions on Graphics*, 3, 3.

OLSEN, D. R. (1985). Presentational, syntactic and semantic components of interactive dialogue specifications. In: *User Interface Management Systems.* G. E. Pfaff (ed.) Springer Verlag, Berlin.

OLSEN, Jr. D. R. (1990). Propositional production systems for dialog description. *Proceedings of CHI '90.* 57–63.

OLSEN, D. R. Jr. & DEMPSEY, E. P. (1983). SYNGRAPH: a graphical user interface generator. SIGGRAPH '83 Conference Proceedings. *Computer Graphics*, **17,** 43–50.

PARNAS, D. L. (1969). More on simulation languages and design methodology for computer systems. *Proceedings of the Spring Joint Computer Conference.*

PARNAS, D. L. (1969). On the use of transition diagrams in the design of a computer interface for an interactive computer system. *Proceedings of the National ACM Conference.* ACM Publications, New York. 379–385.

PARNAS, D. L. & DARRINGER, J. A. (1967). SODAS and a methodology for system design. *Proceedings of the Fall Joint Computer Conference.*

PFAFF, G. E. (ed.) (1985). User interface management systems. In: *Proceedings of the Workshop on User Interface Management Systems, Seeheim, 1983.* Berlin: Springer Verlag.

PHILLIPS, C. S. E. (1967). Networks for real-time programming. *Computer Journal*, **10,** 46.

PRAT, A., MARTI, M. & CATOT, J. M. (1985). Incorporating expertise in time series modelling:
the STATXPS system. *Statistical Software Newsletter*, **11,** 55–62.

PRAT, A., GINEBRA, J., CATOT, J. M. & LORES, J. (1989). Expert system for forecasting. *Proceedings of Development of Statistical Expert Systems. Eurostat News*, 342–347.

PRAT, A., LORES, J., FLETCHER, P. & CATOT, J. M. (1990). Back-end manager: an interface between a knowledge-based front end and its application subsystem. *Knowledge-Based Systems.* **3(4),** 225–229.

PROBERT, D. (1984). Intelligent front-ends — opportunities. In: *Edited Highlights from the Joint Alvey MMI/IKBS Workshop on Applications Driven Research (1984).* Available from the Alvey Directorate, Millbank Tower, London.

RHYNE, J. *et al.* (1987). Tools and methodology for user interface development. *Computer Graphics*, 78–87.

ROBERTS, L. G. (1964). *Graphical Communication and Control Languages.* Information System Sciences, Spartan Books.

ROOS, D. (1966). *ICES System Design.* Cambridge, MA: MIT Press.

ROSE, G. A. (1965). Light-pen facilities for direct view storage tubes. *IEEE Transactions*, EC-**14,** 637–639.

ROSENBERG, J. (1988). UIMSs: threat or menace? In: *Proceedings of CHI, 1988 (Washington, May 15–19).* New York: ACM.

ROSENBERG, J., HILL, R., MILLER, J., SCHULERT, A. & SCHEWMAKE, D. (1988). UIMSs: threat or menace? In: *Proceedings of the CHI'88 Conference on Human Factors in Computing Systems, Washington, DC, May 1988.*

ROSENBERG, V. (1973). A technique for monitoring user behaviour at the computer terminal interface. *Journal of the American Society of Information Science*, **24,** 71.

ROSENTHAL, D. S. H. (1983). Managing graphical resources. *Computer Graphics.*

ROSENTHAL, D. S. H., MICHENER, J. C., PFAFF, G., KESSENER, R. & SABIN, M. (1982). The detailed semantics of graphics input devices. *SIGGRAPH '82.*

ROSS, D. T. The AED approach to generalized computer-aided design. *Proceedings of the ACM 20th Anniversary Conference.*

ROSS, D. T. *AEDJR: an experimental language processor.* MIT Electronic Systems Laboratory. Memorandum 211.

SCHMUCKER, K. J. (1986). MacApp: an application framework. *Byte*, 189–192.

SCHULERT, A. J., ROGERS, G. T. & HAMILTON, J. A. (1985). ADM — a dialog manager. In: *Proceedings CHI '85 Human Factors in Computing Systems (San Francisco, April 14–18, 1985).* New York: Association for Computing Machinery.

SHNEIDERMAN, B. (1983). Direct manipulation: a step beyond programming languages. *IEEE Computer*, **16**, 57–69.

SHNEIDERMAN, B. (1987). *Designing the User Interface.* Addison-Wesley.

SHRAGER, J. (1981). *Invoking a beginner's aid processor by recognising JCL goals.* Computer and Information Science, University of Pennsylvania, Report MS-CIS-81-7.

SHRAGER, J. & FININ, T. (1982). An expert system that volunteers advice. *Proceedings of AAA.*

SIBERT, J., BELLIARDI, R. & KAMRAN, A. (1985). Some thoughts on the interface between user interface management systems and application software. In: *User Interface Management Systems.* G. E. Pfaff (ed.). Springer Verlag, Berlin.

SIBERT, J. L., HURLEY. W. D. & BLESER, T. W. (1986). An object-oriented user interface management system. Proceedings of SIGGRAPH '86. *Computer Graphics*, **20,** 259–268.

SIMONSEN, R. & RENSHAW, K. (1974). CAI — boon or boondoggle? *Datamation*, 90–102.

SISSON, N. (1986). Dialogue management reference model. *SIGCHI Bulletin*, **18,** 34–35.

STACK, T. R. & WALKER, S. T. (1971). AIDS — advanced interactive display system. *AFIPS Conference Proceedings*, **38,** 113.

STALLING, W. (1974). Some aspects of an interactive dialogue-generation facility. In: *Proceedings of the International Conference on Systems, Man and Cybernetics*, IEEE Service Center, New Jersey, USA.

STRUBBE, H. J. (1985). Report on role, model, structure and construction of a UIMS. In: *User Interface Management System.* G. E. Pfaff (ed.). Springer Verlag.

SUTHERLAND, I. E. (1965). *SKETCHPAD: a man–machine graphical communication system.* MIT Lincoln Laboratory, Lexington, MA. Technical Report TR–296.

SUTHERLAND, I. E. (1966). Computer graphics: ten unsolved problems. *Datamation*, **12,** 22–27.

SUTHERLAND, W. R. *On-line graphical specification of computer procedures.* MIT Lincoln Laboratory. Lexington. MA. Technical Report 405.

SUTTON, J. & SPRAGUE, R. (1978). *A study of display generation and management in interactive business applications.* IBM San Jose Research Laboratory, San Jose, CA. Technical Report RJ2392 (31804).

SZEKELY, P. (1988). *Separating the user interface from the functionality of application programs.* PhD Thesis, CMU–CS–88–101. Carnegie-Mellon University.

TANNER, P. P., MACKAY, S. A., STEWART, D. A. & WEIN, M. (1986). A multitasking switchboard approach to user interface management. Proceedings of SIGGRAPH '86. *Computer Graphics*, **20,** 241–248.

TEN HAGEN, P. J. W. (1980). A conceptual basis for graphical input and interaction. In: *Methodology of Interaction.* R. A. Guedj, P. J. W. ten Hagen, F. R. A. Hopgood, H. A. Tucker and D. A. Duce (eds). Amsterdam: North-Holland.

TESLER, L. G. & ENEA, H. J. (1968). A language design for concurrent processes. *AFIPS Conference Proceedings*, **32,** 403.

THEBERGE, H. & BEAVERSTOCK, E. (1974). Narrowing the generation gap between virtual machines and minicomputers. In: *Proceedings of the National Computer Conference.* 285–287.

VAN DEN BOS, J. (1980). High-level graphics input tools and their semantics. In: *Methodology of Interaction.* R. A. Guedj *et al.* (eds). Amsterdam: North-Holland.

WILKES, M. V. (1972). Associative tabular data structures. *International Journal of Computing and Information Science*, 225–233.

WIRTH, N. (1971). The programming language PASCAL. *Acta Informatica*, **1,** 35.

WOOD, C. A. & GRAY, P. D. (1990). *User interface–application communication in the Chimera UIMS.* Glasgow University, Department of Computing Science Research, Report CSC/90/R1.

YANNAKOUDAKIS, E. J. & FAWTHROP, D. (1983). The rules of spelling errors. *Information Processing and Management*, **19,** 87–99.

ZINN, K. L. (1968). Programming conversational use of computers for instruction. In: *Proceedings of the ACM National Conference, 1968.* 85–92.

ZURCHER, F. W. & RANDELL, B. (1968). Multi-level modeling — a methodology for computer system design. *Proceedings of the IFIP Conference.*

Index

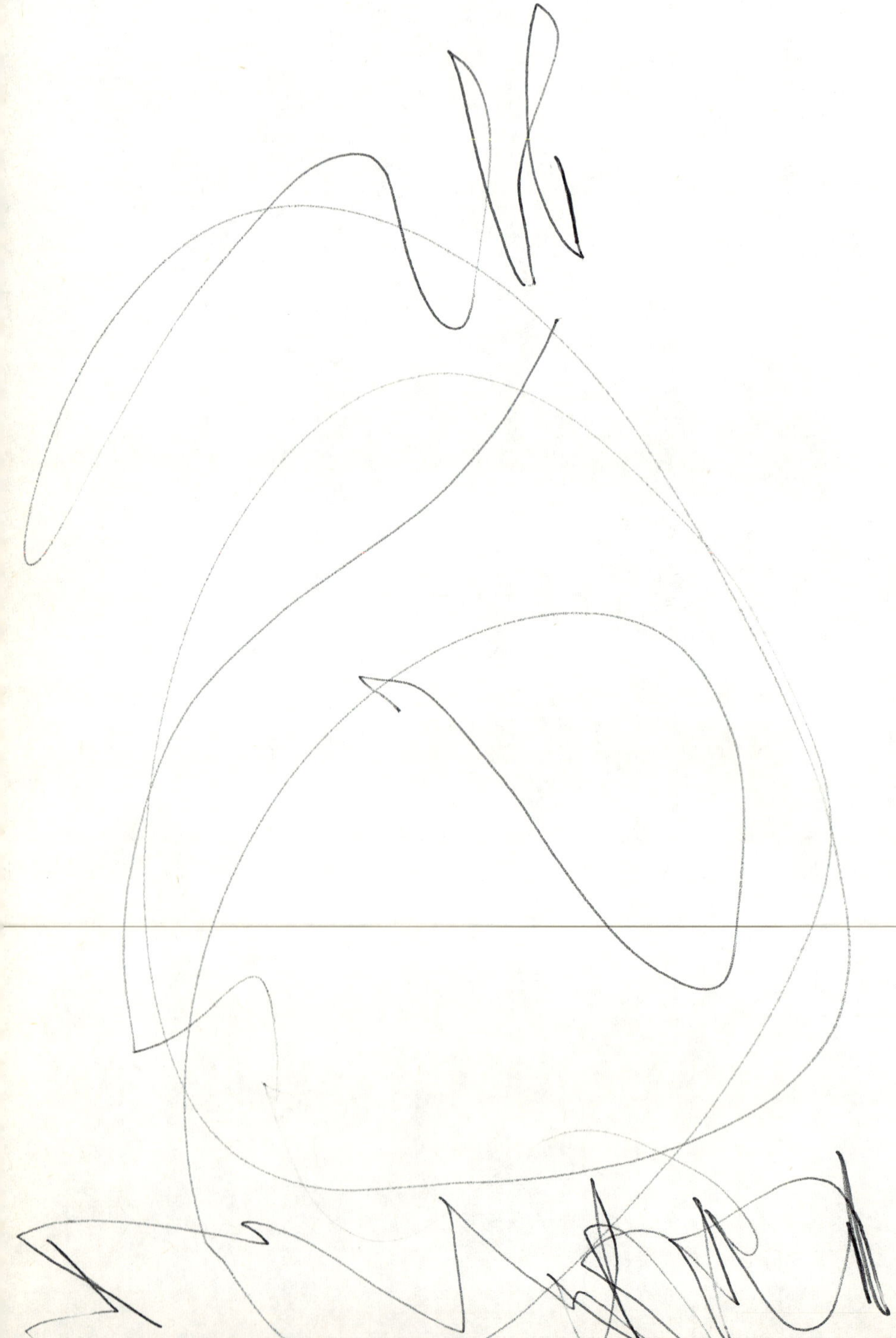